A GLIMPSE INTO THE VULNERABLE LIFE OF A SUPERSTAR

Elvis' FBI file, reprinted here for the first time, reveals the bizarre turbulence in which he lived and died. It not ony tells of Elvis' love–hate relationship with the FBI, but of his growing isolation, his drug abuse, a waning career, and fear for his life. All the intrigue surrounding Elvis didn't stop when he died. It followed him to the grave and continues to this day. This is the sensational book that adds a new chapter to a sensational life.

ELVIS

TOP SECRET

ELVIS

TOP SECRET

THE UNTOLD STORY OF ELVIS PRESLEY'S SECRET FBI FILES

by

Earl Greenwood

&

Kathleen Tracy

A SIGNET BOOK

While all the events in this book are true, some names have been changed.

SIGNET
Published by the Penguin Group
Penguin Books USA Inc., 375 Hudson Street,
New York, New York 10014, U.S.A.
Penguin Books Ltd, 27 Wrights Lane,
London W8 5TZ, England
Penguin Books Australia Ltd, Ringwood,
Victoria, Australia
Penguin Books Canada Ltd, 10 Alcorn Avenue,
Toronto, Ontario, Canada M4V 3B2
Penguin Books (N.Z.) Ltd, 182–190 Wairau Road,
Auckland 10, New Zealand

Penguin Books Ltd, Registered Offices:
Harmondsworth, Middlesex, England

First published by Signet, an imprint of New American Library, a division of Penguin Books USA Inc.

First Printing, December, 1991
10 9 8 7 6 5 4 3 2 1

Printed in the United States of America

A very special dedication to my mother, Nora Greenwood, who passed away last year. Her support, love and dedication will be missed by many people. To my good friends, Timothy D. Perez, his son, Timmy, his parents, Mr. & Mrs. Robert Perez, and his sister, Diane Hernandez, who are strong Elvis fans and never stopped supporting me on the publishing of this book. To Todd McDurmont for his valuable time and assistance. To the following Elvis fan clubs and dedicated Elvis fans for their loyal support and assistance for which I will always be grateful: The Elvis Special Fan Club, King of Our Hearts Fan Club, Maria Columbus, Robin Rosaaen, Susan Ragan, and Irene Maleti.

Contents

VERY SPECIAL GRATITUDE TO
THE FEDERAL BUREAU OF INVESTIGATION
FOR THEIR ASSISTANCE.

Introduction

When the Freedom of Information Act was passed, one of the more startling discoveries was the FBI's private collection of surveillance files on private American citizens. Under orders from the Bureau's late director, J. Edgar Hoover, our nation's police force kept dossiers on a variety of people believed to be dangerous, subversive, or merely individualistic and different.

Among the celebrities targeted for observation was Elvis Presley. Hoover seemed to have a special obsession with the fluid moves and suggestive dance style of the young singer, whom he frequently called a danger to the morals, values, and very soul of America's youth. The FBI began keeping a dossier on Elvis in 1956. Reporters and law-enforcement officials across the country were encouraged to report to the Bureau Presley's on-stage activities, which were all meticulously recorded and filed. From the time Elvis first burst upon the national scene in 1956 until his death twenty-one years later, the FBI systematically kept tabs on Elvis.

But the files themselves only hint at the full story of Elvis and his double-edged relationship with the FBI. While the terror and paranoia he felt for his safety forced Elvis to depend on the Bureau for protection, his innate southern mistrust of authority always nagged at the back of his brain. His dependency might have ignited his fascination with the Bureau, but it was never an easy union.

It's no small irony that at the same time secret files were being compiled on Elvis, the FBI was working to protect him from enemies both real and imagined. Time after time, Elvis was forced to call upon the Bureau to protect him. Throughout his career, Elvis and his family were the targets of numerous death threats. The singer endured violence-tinged hate mail and countless attempts at blackmail and slander. In the beginning he was more apt to dismiss the threats, but as he got older, he agonized over his safety to the point where he was afraid to leave his home. Toward the end of his life, Elvis was in constant contact with the FBI, begging them to protect him from an assortment of dangers, both real and imagined. He reported every "mysterious" phone call and suspicious person he spotted in front of Graceland.

Elvis' prison of fame made for strange bedfellows and unlikely alliances beyond the FBI—his fears even became the foundation for his curious friendship with Howard Hughes. Presley met Hughes in Las Vegas and they eventually became secret late-night phone companions. They would commiserate until dawn on the pitfalls of fame, and they discovered they shared similar fears and suspicions. Hughes found Presley's simplicity appealing and Elvis looked up to the reclusive millionaire as a mentor—he hoped Hughes could teach him how to enjoy his success and take better control of his life. But Hughes's deepening instability and bleak outlook ultimately served only to make Elvis's anxiety that much worse.

In the early seventies, Elvis became increasingly convinced somebody within his inner circle was plotting to kill him. He turned to the FBI in desperation, believing they were the only ones who could protect him. But by the middle of the decade, the FBI unofficially dismissed Elvis's personal calls as the rantings of a whacked-out drug abuser. When he sensed their disbelief, Elvis abruptly concluded that the FBI had been bought off and was in on the plot. If Hughes had convinced him of anything, it was that everybody has a price. But in the end, when he felt jeopardized and threatened by nearly everyone around him, Elvis came full circle and sought to join the FBI as a special agent.

The Elvis FBI file is 663 pages and, according to the Bureau's public information clerk, it is the most frequently requested celebrity file. Here for the first time, the files are reprinted. Whenever possible, censored names and places have been identified, along with an explanation of the circumstances surrounding a particular file or group of files.

Taken alone, the file gives a glimpse into the vulnerable life of a superstar and the times in which he lived and died. Together with Chapters 1–6 and the epilogue, they not only tell the story of Elvis's love–hate relationship with the FBI, but also of his growing isolation caused by drugs, his waning career, and his fear for his life.

After all this time, I know it's hard to imagine there's any new ground to cover with Elvis. But most of what's been written about him has only skimmed the surface of his lifelong fascination with law enforcement. And while his last years of drug abuse have been well chronicled, his secret friendship with Howard Hughes hasn't. I think these are important pieces of the complex puzzle that was Elvis that warrant time and attention.

The intrigue that surrounded Elvis didn't stop when he died. It has followed him into the grave and it continues to this day. In recent years, I've uncovered information that indicates that Elvis's long-held belief that he was the target of a conspiracy might not have been just drug-induced paranoid ramblings. There is evidence that certain death threats were manufactured "in house," an attempt by Colonel Tom Parker and others to further control Elvis via the leverage of fear—instead of forcing Elvis to get off drugs, they conspired to let him literally drug himself to death. Only now are people starting to come forward with information that bears out the belief Elvis was the victim of a death plot. If nothing else, details of what happened inside Graceland in the hours following Elvis's death will show how wealth and fame made Elvis little more than a commodity to those around him. That was ultimately something from which nobody, not even the FBI, could save him.

CHAPTER ONE

Southern Justice

The heat shimmered off the flat, sand-covered horizon, creating a mirage of water pools. From his hotel room, Elvis peeked through the curtains and squinted painfully at the harsh glare of unrelenting sunlight. God, he hated the desert—and he hated Las Vegas. Nothing good had ever really happened to him here. He ached to be back at Graceland in his own bed, walking the grounds with his dogs, chatting with friendly fans standing faithfully at the front gate. But the British Invasion and the Woodstock generation had made Elvis passé before his time and this forsaken gambling resort was a necessary professional oasis for him. Here, polyester-clad audiences reaffirmed nightly that he was still the King. But not everyone adored him, especially not the youth who were once the wind beneath his wings. Elvis spent hours every day in front of the television, amazed at the new crop of "superstars"—everyone from Diana Ross to Jesus Christ himself. The young people had changed so much it grieved Elvis. Hostility replaced innocence. Teenagers occasionally heckled him, mocking his black, lacquered hair and his penchant for sequined jumpsuits. He pretended not to hear but the laughing rang in his ears late into the night, often drowning out the applause in the sold-out showrooms. Only a variety of pills dulled the noise. But they barely took the edge off the fear.

It used to be if you didn't like a performer, you turned off the television or didn't buy his albums. Now, they wanted to kill you. Elvis had lived through other death threats—so many he lost count. But this one, the one haunting his every waking moment, was different. They tried to hide the danger from Elvis, but he knew. He saw the concern in everyone's eyes. This one was for real. And it was in Las Vegas, where nothing good ever happened to him.

Elvis closed the curtain and turned to face the empty room. The girl from last night had already left, leaving a hint of perfume in the stale air. He heard voices outside the door and felt both relief and despair. The round-the-clock security instituted since the threat's seriousness was determined gave him a certain measure of hope, but he despised being a prisoner. Who would have ever thought a Presley would be seeking out the help of the law?

Like the poor everywhere, Elvis grew up with a healthy distrust and resentment of authority in general and police in particular. His earliest encounter with Mississippi law enforcement left an indelible scar when his father Vernon was arrested and sent to jail for forging a check. Considering he was only a toddler, it's doubtful Elvis remembered the incident. But over the years, Vernon's imprisonment became such a part of family lore that as an adult Elvis would claim to have the image of Vernon being led away burned into his mind's eye and would give detailed accounts of the arrest and its aftermath.

"I 'member the sheriff walkin' up and daddy got all pale. But when the sheriff told daddy to come on, he just stood up and followed him out the door.

"Mama was wringin' her hands and askin' what was goin' on. Daddy didn' say a word, just stood there, his head hangin' down like a whipped dog.

"The sheriff told mama daddy had forged a check from the lumber company where he worked but had done such a bad job, they caught it first thing.

" 'Ain't even smart 'nuff not to get hisself caught.'

"Mama's face went white as daddy's but she didn' say a word. She jus' stared at daddy, who couldn't look her in the eye. All he could do is say he was sorry.

"The whole time, even though he was actin' tough on the outside, you could tell the sheriff was grinnin' inside. Real mean-spirited, like he was gettin' a real kick out of draggin' daddy off to jail. He said to mama in a cold voice, " 'You and your little one better say goodbye now 'cause you ain't gonna see Vernon for a long time. We gotta teach him a lesson.'

"It wasn't so much what he said, it was how he said it. He thought we were nothin' more than trash."

Whether or not Elvis truly remembered his father's early run-in with the law isn't important. What is important is how that event helped shape Elvis's attitudes toward authority—attitudes that, based on the poor's collective experience, would not have been that positive to begin with. Some sharecroppers considered lawmen the devil's kin. My family shared the same regional distrust of lawmen, but we weren't obsessed with them the way some others were. Then again, nobody in my family had ever been to jail, either. Neither had the Presley's, until after Vernon's arrest. That was their first experience and it wasn't pleasant, as generations of itinerant workers before them had learned. They developed an "us against them" mentality, whose credo was never trust anyone wearing a badge.

"Oh, some of 'em might act nice enough, but they're just waitin' for the chance to get you. That's jus' the way they are."

As if deputies had an inborn mental disorder. To many, it's probably exactly how it seemed. Southern justice has a reputation for being especially harsh and subjective. The impoverished sharecropping families were often the innocent victims of local sheriffs who seemed to relish exerting their power over the indigent transients who struggled to make ends meet doing the backbreaking labor that helped well-off farm owners become even more wealthy.

Considered the lowest of the social-strata low, sharecroppers were often regarded as a dangerous and untrustworthy lot. American gypsies of the soil. For the most part, policing duties were handled by just one or two sheriffs, who were also sometimes called constables. There wasn't a need for any more than that. Most of their work hours were spent gossiping with the local businessmen. They seldom encountered a dangerous situation—unless an exceptionally heavy drunk they had to carry to jail threatened to throw out their backs. On the rare occasions a crime was committed it usually involved theft—acts of desperation by people struggling to get by. Naturally, it was assumed one of the sharecroppers was involved. Because of their meager and despairing existence, that assumption was often correct, which fed a vicious cycle of harassment and human suffering.

The sharecroppers were duly respectful of the sheriff to his face and subtly rebellious behind his back. They countered the wariness and unease they felt in the company of authority by incorporating it into daily life. Parents would scare their children into obeying them with dire warnings.

"If you don' clear the wood out back, I'll get the sheriff to come and take you away."

"I'm gonna have my daddy call the po-lice on you" was a familiar childhood taunt.

Disputes often led to threats that one side would turn in the other, but in reality, while the sharecroppers might not necessarily like or trust one another, they trusted authority even less. The chances of a sharecropper calling the sheriff on someone were about as likely as them picking cotton in white gloves. Besides, the odds of the sheriff paying much attention to a sharecropper's complaints were just as slim. They were the bottom of the barrel and treated that way.

Vernon's arrest made him a marked man with the local sheriff. From the time Vernon was released from prison until the Presleys left Tupelo, Mississippi for Memphis, the sheriff kept an especially watchful eye on the family. It was a given that if you got into trouble once, you'd get into trouble again—it was just a matter of time. The irony was that overall, Vernon was a likable man. Easygoing and quick with a joke, it was hard to hold much against him. Even the sheriff was occasionally seen sharing a laugh and drink with Vernon. But that didn't mean he trusted Vernon.

Growing up feeling watched for any wrong move had an effect on Elvis. In the presence of any authority figure—the sheriff, a teacher, or a landowner—Elvis was deferential to the point of being passive. Even when he was a national star, Elvis was known for his polite behavior and southern manners. The depth of his frustration against people in positions of power and authority over him didn't translate into an overt disrespect. But deep inside turmoil brewed—a schizophrenic paradox that mirrored the inner conflicts that would ultimately define Elvis. The older he got, the more his inability to stand up to authority ate at him. As a thirty- and forty-year-old man, he would have tantrums behind the backs of his father and Colonel Parker, his manager, but still be unable to confront them in person. As a child, the angers and resentments were just beginning to build.

Because of Vernon's record, Gladys was obsessed with making sure Elvis didn't follow in his father's footsteps. She lectured him endlessly on the importance of staying out of trouble, using every ploy to make sure the message sank in.

Once when he was just five or six, Elvis had a temper tantrum after getting spanked for sassing back to Gladys—the first and last time it ever happened. He was so angry and ashamed he got wild and threw some things around their shack. Gladys made him feel like he was on the road to a life of crime.

"What's gonna become of you and that temper? How're you ever gonna make somethin' of yourself if you act so wild? It's just gonna lead to no good. Don' you go breakin' my heart and wind up like your daddy. Locked away with people calling you no good. Thanks to your daddy, the sheriff's got his eye on us and you better never forget it."

Despite the lectures and his own natural wariness against what they represented, Elvis was not in any way afraid of the local deputies. In fact, he harbored an infatuation with the sheriff's power. The thought of having a lawman's autonomy and power fueled his imagination. To a young boy often choked by powerlessness and poverty, being above the law and free from the authority of others was an overwhelmingly sweet fantasy.

But it was a fantasy that would be considered unrealistic by sharecropper standards. America might be the land of opportunity elsewhere, but not in the rural South during the Depression. "Poor white trash" seldom rose above their heritage. The most they dared hope was to simply put enough food on the table or somehow save enough money to move someplace that offered factory work. By and large, dreams and ambitions were limited—nor were they encouraged by most parents. That is one thing that set Gladys apart. She always believed Elvis would make something of himself, which is why she was so intent on keeping him on the straight and narrow.

As a young boy, Elvis set his sights on being a gas station attendant. At that point, he hadn't even dared to dream about being a singer; imagining himself in such an important position would have been considered downright arrogant. So he aimed at a more reasonable and less lofty goal. Besides being a step above sharecropping, Elvis believed owning a gas station would give him the kind of freedom he yearned for.

"In the field, you always got to answer to the man," Elvis said, referring to the local landowner. "But with your own fillin' station, you ain't got to answer to nobody. Well, daddy says you always got to answer to your wife, but that ain't the same.

"Wouldn' it be great to jus' work what hours you want and spend the day working on cars or just sitting by the front door watchin' everyone goin' by? I jus' don' want to always have someone tellin' me what I can and can't do."

While the Presleys never completely shrugged

off the stigma of Vernon's arrest, it became a familiar burden that lost some of its sting as the years went by. Not because it necessarily hurt any less, but because Elvis learned to bury it inside better. But the facade fell apart when Elvis was thirteen.

Like a recurring nightmare, once again the Presleys' world was changed forever by the sheriff's knock on the door.

Vernon had long since stopped sharecropping, citing a chronic bad back and numbness in his feet when he stood for too long. Gladys resented her husband shirking his duty but had no choice but to assume responsibility for keeping food on her family's table. Still, she constantly nagged at him and occasionally it spurred Vernon into token action. On this occasion, Gladys might have preferred Vernon to have been a little less ambitious.

It was a hot day, so humid the dust would stick to you like a second skin. For the second time in his life, Elvis watched his father being taken away by the local sheriff—this time for moonshining. Gladys was beside herself and cried tears that burned with shame. Her despair fed Elvis's fear and caused him to withdraw. He stood in the corner, shoulders hunched, chin buried into his chest. In a pathetic irony, he was the mirror image of Vernon, who stood out in front of their shack with the same defeated, helpless posture. Elvis couldn't meet the eyes of the other sharecroppers who stood nearby watching, far enough away so the sheriff wouldn't get the wrong impression. When trouble called, nobody was going to lend support or encouragement. It was hard enough scraping by without the law taking a special interest in you.

With Elvis in reluctant tow, Gladys followed Vernon to the local jail. The resolve she showed during her husband's first arrest crumbled completely this time around. While moonshining wasn't that uncommon a crime in the rural South, Vernon was a two-time loser. There was no telling how long they might send him away, considering his previous record.

Later, Elvis remembered that muggy afternoon in the jail.

"Mama jus, couldn' stop crying. She didn' know what was gonna become of us if they sent Vernon away. Even though she constantly complained about him, in her own way she couldn' live without him, I guess. I didn' understand how she could feel two different ways about him at the same time.

"When they first took Daddy away, I felt like dyin'. Mama begged them not to put handcuffs on, but the sheriff just laughed at her. I wanted to hit him and make him stop but that would have made mama that much worse. Everybody was starin' and whisperin' t'each other. Out of the corner of my eye I could see a couple of 'em kind of laughin' at us.

"The jail was worse. It was so hot you could barely breathe. A couple times, mama had to grab on to me. She was so upset I was sure she was gonna pass out on me.

"The sheriff kept sayin' terrible things to mama

and once he even spit at her feet, like we were lower than dirt."

Gladys begged the sheriff to give Vernon a break but it was too hot and he was in too foul a mood to be swayed by her tears. If anything, it seemed to spur him on.

"You people are a disgrace to the rest of the farmin' folk 'round here. 'Specially ol' Vernon here. Lazy as the day is long, ain't ya? All the Presleys are a worthless lot. Always have been. And I 'spect always will be," he said, nodding towards Elvis.

The sheriff sat down at his desk and looked from Gladys to Elvis to Vernon.

"Worthless. Not worth a second thought. Certainly not worth my time. I tell you what. I'm tired of havin' to keep my eye on the likes of you. I think it'd be better for everyone if you jus' pick up stakes and go be a thorn in some other sheriff's side. Get your things together and don' never even think of comin' back. 'Cause if you do, I'll put you back in jail for longer than you can imagine."

On principle, the sheriff kept Vernon overnight, just so he'd remember how unpleasant jail could be. The sheriff's compromise was a backhanded act of kindness, but all Elvis heard were the insults. What stayed in his memory was the awesome threat and power presented by the sheriff's badge and position. It carried the power to change lives with a snap of the fingers. People like the Presleys knew they had no recourse, no higher court of appeal. The local sheriff was the ultimate authority. All they could do was meekly comply.

But their defeated acceptance masked deep shame and anger. The rage Elvis felt was fueled by a sense of powerlessness. He couldn't come to the defense of his family in either word or action. Elvis knew better than to let any of his emotions out. It could only put his family in further jeopardy. Besides, he had been conditioned to keep his feelings bottled up—they were pent-up furies that would finally explode in a flurry of self-destruction later in his adult life.

Vernon moved his family to Memphis in what was supposed to be a fresh start. In many ways, it was. Their housing arrangements were better and there were more opportunities in "the big city." Plus, the Presleys were anonymous—they had left their reputations behind them on the road from Tupelo. But some things couldn't be discarded so easily.

The shame and humiliation of being run out of town had a profound effect on Elvis. He began to show a more volatile side to his personality that hadn't been as apparent in Tupelo. Behind closed doors or out of earshot, he would work himself into a violent tirade against being told what to do by anyone. Except for Gladys. He never allowed those frustrations to slip out, his guilt even stronger than his anger. She was the one authority figure in his life who humbled him. From the time he was a small boy, he felt responsible for his mother. Nor was she shy about letting him know the sacrifices she made for him, always couched in declarations of love—making for a gut-wrenching conflict that Elvis never resolved.

But Elvis was a mass of unexplained behavior. Knowing his resentment at being told what to do, it seemed he passed up every opportunity to free himself. Even when he was the country's biggest star, in the perfect position to call his own shots, Elvis surrounded himself with people who would ultimately direct his actions. He would usually listen, too, although he resented them and hated himself for it. For Elvis, old habits were hard to break.

Memphis was both a blessing and a curse to Elvis. He enjoyed its size and his family's opportunity to lose their notorious reputation. He was more comfortable and didn't feel his every move was under scrutiny. Still, as much as he might wish to forget the past, he would never completely purge it. Periodically things came back to haunt him and to rekindle the memories of his family's shame. For example, when a police car passed by, Elvis's attention would be momentarily riveted, his body subconsciously assuming a momentary defensive posture before relaxing. The funny part was, Elvis never seemed to be conscious of his reaction. It was just instinctual.

Ironically, the very things that made Memphis a haven for the Presleys also presented Elvis with a new set of struggles to wrestle with. He often felt lost and insignificant among all the people in the city. He desperately wanted to find a way to make his mark, especially among his peers at Humes High. If Elvis had been aggressively rebellious, school would have been a living hell—he was already considered a bit of a country bumpkin and any nasty behavior would have made him a complete outcast. So, ever mindful of his upbringing to be polite at all costs, Elvis's teenage defiance took a more stylish turn. Years before it would become the rage, Elvis sported long, dyed black hair lacquered into a swooping front pompadour. He wore clothes of questionable fashion sense and developed an individual style that loudly hinted at his internal unrest.

In class, Elvis was a model, if mediocre, student. He seldom gave his teachers a reason to notice him, much less to confront him. Except for his wardrobe, he ambled through high school virtually unnoticed. The only run-in he had was in his sophomore year with the football coach. Elvis was anxious to join the team and was devastated when the coach told him he couldn't even try out unless he cut his hair. Elvis could only stammer out a feeble protest.

"I'm sorry, son, rules are rules."

The coach was firm but not cruel. In fact, he even came to Elvis's defense when some boy overheard the exchange and threatened to cut Elvis's hair for him. But as Elvis played the incident over and over in his brain, the coach's words became taunts. Yet another person in a position of power was affecting his life. And once again, there was nothing he could do about it except brood.

Elvis found most of his classes a struggle and got little enjoyment from them. But school wasn't a total bust. Elvis found a surprising outlet—Humes

High School's ROTC. It wasn't by choice that Elvis took ROTC—at the time it was a required two-year course for all boys. Nor did it make Elvis want to run out and immediately join the Army. But as time went on, Elvis found himself looking forward to ROTC. It might seem out of character, considering his unconventional style and resistance to following commands. But part of Elvis enjoyed the pageantry and precision of the ROTC. Also, the uniforms looked official and carried the tacit weight of authority. Being a part of such a group meant Elvis was on the inside looking out for once.

On another level, the ROTC probably appealed to young men who were outcasts in various ways. The physically gifted joined the football or basketball teams, the intellectually superior students had their math and science clubs, and the popular kids with good looks or personality were elected to student council. But the students looking for a sense of belonging and command found the ROTC most rewarding. In their military uniforms, class distinctions evened out and it was one rule for all. The thought of being in command of people thrilled Elvis, and it helped make his time in ROTC a welcome distraction from the drudgery of regular classes—a pleasant daydream, the way some people imagine winning the lottery.

Elvis never forgot the unique sense of belonging ROTC gave him. One of the first things he did after becoming famous was to buy Humes ROTC brand-new uniforms. On the few occasions he reminisced about high school, the afternoons of drilling to barked cadence were a memory he always called to mind.

Like teenagers everywhere, Elvis wanted independence. Unlike the majority of his peers, though, he had carried the responsibility of helping support his family since early youth, which tied him to them in ways he couldn't sever. More than once, he held down two part-time jobs while in school. So it seemed particularly ludicrous to him having to answer to his parents like some kid.

"Hell, they act like I don't got a lick o' sense. Every single time I go out the door they gotta tell me to stay outa trouble. What am I gonna do, rob a bank?"

It particularly grated him that Gladys insisted he treat his father with the utmost respect. Elvis considered Vernon a lazy no-count who had never made good by Gladys. If Vernon dared say anything, Elvis's jaw would tighten in response. Elvis would simply say "Yessir," but as soon as Vernon turned away, the boy would shoot his father an icy stare that oozed contempt.

Granted, no teenager likes being told what to do. For that matter, not many adults do, either. But with Elvis, it was an issue with a capital "I"—a private demon that just tore at him in irrational and unhealthy ways. Any assertion of independence was followed by an even greater flood of guilt. It was a case of two steps forward, two steps back. Nor did he learn to cope any better as he got older. If anything, the opposite was true. By the time he graduated from high school, he was the head of his household. Both his parents depended on him to help keep food on the table and a roof over their heads. There was no way to fully live his life without letting his parents down. He didn't care so much about Vernon, but he would just as soon cut off his hand than disappoint Gladys. Which is why he was never so happy and so proud as when he began making a meager but steady living as a regional performer.

In the first year Elvis began performing at Memphis clubs and in various venues in Tennessee, Mississippi, and Louisiana he got to know the local authorities in a way he would have preferred to avoid.

In Beale Street's honky-tonks, policemen patrol the streets looking for brawls to break up and drunks to haul off. Because Beale Street was in a predominantly black neighborhood, instances of harassment were commonplace. It would infuriate Elvis but he knew better than to get involved.

"It'd only mean they'd start hittin' on you, too. I jus' wanna be left alone to sing."

Elvis would have laughed at the thought his singing and his stage antics would be the very thing that would get him into trouble. As his local reputation grew, Elvis developed a following of young girls who would gather around the makeshift stages at fairs and follow his every move with adoring eyes. After doing a set at a bar, Elvis would find many women waiting anxiously to meet him. Since he often played the same places, his reputation preceded him—justifiably so in some cases.

His very look, his singing style, his suggestive way of singing made him notorious. His unconventional personality rubbed a lot of people the wrong way. Many saw him as a bad influence and a danger. And some local sheriffs saw it as their duty to try and save their townsfolk from his seduction. Long before Elvis's dancing became a national scandal, Elvis was confronted by local deputies determined to make him censor his act.

Elvis would listen politely and try to reason with them.

"Yessir, I hear you, but all I'm doin' is singin."

"Don't gimme that. You get up there and stir these girls up—it's indecent and I jus' won't have it. We got community standards we got to upkeep."

Back and forth they'd go—and the sheriff usually got the final say. Several times Elvis was informed he could sing, but he better not move around on stage if he knew what was good for him. The last thing Elvis wanted was to land in some one-room jail. Besides everything else it would mean, it would kill Gladys. All Elvis wanted was to sing, and getting arrested would keep that from happening. So he had no choice but to comply. After one run-in, he walked back to the car, seething with resentment.

"Goddam them to hell. Who'd he think he was, tellin' me how to sing and act on stage. I jus' do what I do. I don' think about it. It jus' comes out that way."

The more his regional fame grew, the more he was confronted by small-town sheriffs and parents' groups. It got to the point where Elvis was almost as famous for his stage presence as he was for his voice. But it was a notoriety Elvis hated and resented. Once again, he felt watched and targeted, which churned up familiar but unwelcome emotions.

"I'm so sick and tired of bein' harassed every time I turn around. Figures they got nothin' better to do. I ain't never yet met a sheriff who knew how to do much else besides sit on their fat asses and pester innocent people. Must make 'em feel like real big shots. Makes me sick. What gives them the right to tell me how to sing?

"I can't wait 'til I'm famous enough to tell 'em all to go to hell. When you're someone important, everybody treats you better. If I can jus' do a little better, I won' have to put up with this anymore."

By 1956, Elvis got his wish and bolted to national stardom. In the blink of an eye he was a household name and nothing would ever be the same. But Elvis would quickly learn that fame had a downside that brought a new set of problems to replace old ones. Fan adoration could fester into dangerous obsession and thousands of hysterical admirers could easily turn into a lethal mob. The passion he could elicit from his fans was matched only by the hatred he stirred up in his detractors. Instead of being his ticket to unlimited freedom, his astounding popularity constrained him in ways he had never anticipated. True, he could pay to privately rent a roller-skating rink, but he couldn't go unnoticed to the movies or for a hamburger anymore without being stopped or followed by fans. And Elvis learned early that fan love could turn lethal.

It never occurred to Elvis he would need personal protection until the first time he felt genuine fear at the hands of his fans. He had moved his family into a house on Audubon Drive shortly after signing with RCA. It was a nice house on a quiet residential street—with a knee-high fence that couldn't even keep a poodle out. One day a relatively small group of fans pinned Elvis against his car and began to crush him in their frenzy to touch him. His father and uncle had to come out and drag him inside to safety. That was the day the reality of how much life had changed sank in.

The constant parade of cars driving by hoping to catch a glimpse of Elvis also created traffic problems and rising neighborhood resentments. Elvis finally conceded he needed help and that's when he hired Red West. At first Red's job was simple crowd control, but the position eventually grew into that of a personal bodyguard.

It must seem pretentious self-indulgence when a celebrity is surrounded by a phalanx of bodyguards, but it wasn't out of sheer ego that Elvis seldom went anywhere alone. He genuinely worried about his safety. Even going to get gasoline could turn into a three-ring circus.

Shortly after his first national record went number one in the nation, Elvis drove to the local gas station to fill up his prized white Lincoln Continental. By the time he pulled up to the pump, a caravan of cars pulled right in behind him. Within minutes, the place was filled with fans saying hello to Elvis, asking for autographs, or just watching, happy to be close. The attendant freaked out and asked Elvis to leave. Elvis was exasperated but understood the guy's position.

"I will as soon as I can get my car out," he said politely.

Elvis got in his car and motioned for the cars behind him to back up. But he was pinned in and the process was taking time—too much time for the attendant's liking. Elvis tried joking his way out.

"I can't very well run these people over. They don' mean no harm, they're just a little too excited."

The attendant was not amused and ordered him to leave. His tone set Elvis off.

"How? Fly?"

Other words followed and the crowd got very quiet as they watched. A collective rumble rose from them when the attendant made the mistake of throwing a punch at Elvis. Elvis swung back and the only thing that prevented a knock-down brawl was that several of Elvis's fans dragged the attendant off.

In retrospect, we all laughed about it, especially after the judge dismissed the gas jockey's lawsuit, but what couldn't be laughed off was the fact Elvis was now a special person in need of special care. With each passing day, the rules for daily life were changing. Elvis's every move was watched and reported. At first, he was so overwhelmed by the exhilaration of wealth and fame that it was easy to ignore the restrictions. But as the newness wore off and the daily reality sank in, Elvis became more affected by his limitations. Money and fame offered a special type of imprisonment, especially for someone like Elvis, who didn't have the capabilities to deal with such issues. He had been a victim of his poverty and would be a victim of his wealth as well.

But that would come into clearer focus later. In the beginning, the biggest threat Elvis faced was reaction to his ground-breaking success. Elvis was a harbinger for the winds of change already blowing away the repression and conservatism of the fifties. He was as much a symbol as a performer. His impact on music, culture, and America's youth as a whole set the stage for his first direct encounters with the FBI, in what would prove to be a long and volatile relationship.

CHAPTER TWO

Early Fame and Controversy

Elvis woke up with a startled gasp and quickly looked around the darkened room for an unseen intruder. When the confusion of abrupt waking passed, he sank back down into his chair and tried to focus on the screen across the room. He took a few deep breaths, trying to steady his pounding heart. He had to hold it together. Elvis would not and could not let his boys see him so jumpy. He was still the King and needed to act accordingly. Besides, Elvis knew there were vultures circling overhead, waiting for the first signs of weakness. He saw the whispering and side glances—they were just waiting for him to crack so they could rob him blind. So much cash and jewelry had already turned up missing—that's why he had taken to sleeping with his doors locked. It was bad enough he had to worry about somebody wanting to murder him without some of those around him wanting to strip him clean. It tripled his anxiety and pushed his paranoia to the breaking point.

Elvis knew it might be getting dark out because the news was on. With the heavy-duty blackout curtains always pulled, it was always nighttime in Elvis's suite.

He liked it better that way—the darkness wrapped him like a security blanket, making him feel less vulnerable. Pretty soon he should eat—his show was only hours away now. They tried to talk him out of performing, saying it was too dangerous. Someone even said foolhardy. But how could he not go on? He simply would not disappoint all the people who had come just to see him. Elvis's whole professional life had been a homage to his fans. They had stood by him when critics and authorities tried to censor him early in his career and continued to cheer him through changing entertainment tastes and music styles. Without his fans and the love he felt from them, he might as well be dead anyway. Threat or no threat, he wasn't going to let them down now.

The only thing faster than Elvis's meteoric rise to the top of the national music charts was the moral right's targeting of him as a danger to America's delicate youth. In April of 1956, a local police officer wrote a letter to FBI Director J. Edgar Hoover to alert him to trouble brewing (A1). He enclosed a column, written by Memphis journalist Robert Johnson, devoted to Elvis, his stunning and sudden popularity, and the controversy his overt sexuality had ignited.

In the column, Johnson reprinted a letter from a distraught mother:

> I wonder what it is going to take before people wake up to what exactly he is doing. All the men and women in my civic clubs are up in arms about it.

Another young man wrote:

> I am a high school senior and have never considered myself a goody-goody. I do all the things most boys my age do. I'll tell you and everybody that I think what he [Elvis] does on television and wherever he sings is a pretty rotten thing. I don't want my mother or sisters to see such things . . . I sure as heck don't like it.

The author of the letter to the FBI wanted Hoover to use his influence to help pass censorship laws preventing Elvis from continuing his personal performances. Not untypically, he believed his request was divinely sanctioned.

> The fine work that our Churches and some of our schools are attempting to do is offset by the freedom exercised in this country of licentiousness. The Apostle Peter warned in his 1st letter about our not using the new liberty for a cloak of maliciousness, but as servants of God.

Hoover answered the letter the day after he got it. On the surface, it seemed to be a standard reply, thanking the writer for sharing his concerns but explaining the FBI had no authority over passing laws. In fact, Hoover had taken the letter very much to heart—and made it the first entry in a secret file he ordered his Bureau to open on Elvis. For years, Hoover had kept dossiers of a variety of citizens he held personally suspect. Back then, people didn't harbor the same mistrust of government they do today. It would have never occurred to anyone, not even Parker, that the FBI was spying on Elvis. It wouldn't be until after the powerful director's death that his questionable, and in some cases possibly illegal, tactics were uncovered. But in the fifties, he was in total command.

The young singer was upsetting the applecart of strict conservatism and McCarthyist control that defined the 1950s. He was a rabble-rouser who incited passions Hoover devoutly believed were best squashed. Elvis Presley was a danger needing control.

Nobody was more surprised at Elvis's huge following than Elvis himself. He would sit backstage after a performance and shake his head in wonder at the people chanting his name out in front.

"All I ever wanted was jus' to sing a little and not be hit with bottles 'cause of it. Hell, where were they all when I wanted a date in high school?" he joked.

But his humor was often tinged with a hard edge of nervousness. On stage, Elvis was in a world of his own and felt in perfect control of his audience. He was a conductor leading a human symphony. Once the music stopped, it became another matter. Without the protection of music, he felt naked and vulnerable. Elvis had never been comfortable around strangers—much less a mob of strangers that could literally crush him.

At the very beginning, he was thrilled to death that anyone liked him. As an amateur singer, he had been heckled off many a stage, so being accepted meant the world to him. When he made a small name for himself as a local performer, he would sign autographs and shake hands for hours out of a deep sense of appreciation. He never, never lost the belief that he was indebted to his fans for allowing him to be a performer. It was one of the things that made him so special.

Even so, Elvis didn't dwell on crowd danger and tried to take it in stride as much as possible—there were too many good things to enjoy and think about. But it was one aspect of success he hadn't counted on.

His joy at reaching the top of the charts was tempered by a number of other factors, too. In the early days of his career, Elvis would read every paper he could get his hands on. Everything happened so fast, it was hard for him to fully absorb the reality of his fame. Reading about it in the paper was proof he wasn't dreaming. After so many years of struggling through life unnoticed—or worse, ridiculed—he couldn't get enough validation. But he learned too soon that not everything written about him was positive.

Nor had he anticipated the hostility he encountered everywhere he went. The crazed adoration of his fans spawned an equally intense counter-reaction of outrage against his overt sexuality. We tried to protect Elvis from it as much as possible because it hurt him so badly. He would read a review calling him names, or an editorial accusing him of being a terrible influence who should be locked up, and his body would sag under the weight of the words. He would close the paper and look up with a pained expression.

"What'd I do to make these people hate me so much? I'm jus' singin', that's all. They act like I'm some kinda criminal."

Nor was everything written even remotely accurate. Like many popular singers before him, Elvis would pick up a paper and read that he had developed throat cancer or, even more disturbing, that he was dead. As rumor of his untimely passing hit various parts of the country, schools reported sharp declines in attendance as distraught students stayed home in premature mourning.

The "Elvis is dead" rumor grew more elaborate over the weeks it circulated. One version said Elvis had been killed by an outraged parent but that the greedy record company was keeping news of his death secret. They had hired an Elvis look-alike and sound-alike to take over, still using the name Elvis.

This is why when the "Elvis is alive" craze sprang up a few years ago, those who knew Elvis weren't that surprised. Rumor and innuendo followed Elvis his entire professional life; it was only a matter of time before someone would do it to him in death. I can only imagine Elvis looking down and getting a good laugh out of it all.

His family wasn't immune from the rampant barrage of stories. I once walked in to find Elvis reading an article in front of a bemused Gladys. Somebody had sent him a newspaper clipping from somewhere in the South that claimed Elvis had shot his mother as a young boy. The reporter went on to demand that Memphis authorities look into the matter immediately. Gladys was horrified that somebody would accuse her son of attempted matricide—or that she had raised a son with such questionable manners.

Reports like these made Elvis laugh in amazement.

"Damn, and I thought the hecklers over on Beale were tough. Well, we oughta tell 'em wishin' I was dead ain't gonna make it so. Still, how can papers report things that ain't true? I thought they were s'posed to check things out first."

"Elvis," Vernon told him, "the only thing papers care about is sellin' papers."

As time went on, his interest in reading about himself dissipated to the point that he didn't even want to see a paper. Out of necessity, Elvis learned to take all reports, both good and bad, with a grain of salt. So did his family. Less amusing to Elvis were the potshots he felt some established performers were taking at him after he burst on the national entertainment scene. His moods swung between anger and deep, confused hurt. And resentment. When stars the magnitude of Steve Allen and Sid Caesar ridiculed him and made him the butt of their jokes, Elvis saw it as a blatant sign of disrespect—a slap in the face. It was bad enough for newspapermen to give you a hard time, but when a fellow performer joined in, it was doubly insulting.

"They think they're better, that I'm some stupid

hillbilly who don't deserve to get anywhere. They'd just as soon me go back to drivin' a truck."

I'd try to calm him down. "It's just jealousy, Elvis. They don't know what to make of you. It happens to every star. I'd see it more as a compliment."

"How can I when I hear them makin' fun of the way I sing—and the way we talk, even. If they don't like my singin' that's one thing. But I feel like they're attacking *me*. They don' even know me. Or mama or any of us."

His own deeply etched insecurities made him particularly vulnerable to criticism of any kind. Typically, Elvis magnified the criticism and minimized the compliments. And some pretty important people came to his defense in the papers. In his column, Robert Johnson quoted Sammy Kaye.

"Some years ago when the teenagers began to Lindy Hop there were persons who called them lunatics and delinquents. I have no doubt the same reception greeted those who first danced the Fox Trot."

King of Swing Benny Goodman agreed, remembering how he was accused of corrupting the youth of his day, too. The message was clear, but Elvis still took the criticisms as a personal assault. In all fairness, it should be pointed out that on occasion Elvis was just as guilty of putting down other celebrities—especially in front of his growing entourage, who egged him on. The only difference was, Elvis kept his comments confined to the privacy of his own house, so in his mind that made it OK.

Jerry Lee Lewis, Pat Boone, and later, Robert Goulet took the brunt of his barbs. Even so, he would have never dreamed of going on the record bad-mouthing another performer.

Many writers initially compared the Elvis sensation to the one caused by Frank Sinatra and his bobby-sox brigade. Elvis would read the analogies and snort.

"I ain't nothin' like Sinatra. Why do they always have t'compare me with anybody? Why can' I jus' be who I am? It's like nobody except the people who come hear me sing wants to accept me for me."

Bravado aside, Elvis was flattered by the comparison, but it also put him in what he felt was a tough position. Sinatra was one of the biggest, most established stars in the nation and Elvis was just starting out. In his mind, the axe was always about to fall and everything would come tumbling down. He perceived the comparisons as expectations to match and surpass Sinatra's success and longevity—an added pressure he resented mightily.

On the flipside, later in his career, when he would hear some hot new singer referred to as "the new Elvis," the agitation would catapult him out of his chair.

"How can they be talkin' about a new Elvis when the original ain't gone anywhere? It's like they can't wait t'get rid of me. When you start out, they say you won't last and when you do, they try and get you to quit. Bastards. They get you comin' and goin'."

Most of those who came to hear him sing simply wanted to get to Elvis, period. A police escort to and from his dressing room and to his car after performances became commonplace. The irony was not lost on Elvis.

"These guys look like they'd just as soon drag me off to jail and throw away the key. Ain't one of 'em yet asked me for an autograph, even though you know they got a wife or daughter's dyin' for 'em to."

Naturally, to their face, Elvis was the picture of politeness. For the most part, in dressing rooms and when talking to the press, Elvis was fairly subdued, his manners on automatic pilot. Also, Elvis was naturally shy and talking to even one person he didn't know well was an effort. Self-conscious about his accent and speaking skills, he covered his nervousness with light humor and just a touch of occasional bravado. Sometimes he was poignantly honest, as he was to a La Crosse, Wisconsin reporter.

"I'm always by myself just before I go on. I'm never really assured. In Las Vegas awhile ago it was really bad. There were a lot of movie stars there and that made it even worse."

While the reporter treated Elvis fairly in his article, others were outraged. Shortly after his May 1956 appearance in La Crosse, Hoover received a second letter from a concerned reporter from the La Crosse, Wisconsin *Register*, the official paper for the area's Catholic diocese (A3). He was beside himself over a local performance by Elvis and dubbed it "the filthiest and most harmful production that ever came to La Crosse for exhibition to teenagers.

> Eye-witnesses have told me that Presley's actions and motions were such as to arouse the sexual passions of teenaged youth. One such eye-witness described his actions as sexual self-gratification . . . Although police and auxiliaries were there, the show went on. Perhaps the hardened police did not get the import of his motions and gestures, like those of masturbation or riding a microphone.

To prove his point, he sent along clippings from the La Crosse *Tribune* detailing the commotion caused by Elvis's visit.

Again, Hoover wrote back (A4) saying the problem of Elvis was outside his jurisdiction—and asked his agents to step up their information gathering on the singer. Even if his Bureau had no official leverage, that didn't mean Hoover wouldn't try to build his own personal case against the singer that could be put to possible use at another time.

The accusation that Elvis's dancing was a form of masturbating was not new. Elvis found it particularly embarrassing because he knew his mama was no doubt hearing it, too. Privately with me and Red, he'd make off-color jokes about it.

"Shows you just how much they don't know me. I wouldn't waste it on stage—I'd rather save it for one of those pretty young girls later."

But by and large, he found it just another indication of how little respect people had for him and his family. While he loved performing for his fans, the hassle and problems of touring became a constant source of irritation for Elvis. He understood the importance of appearing in person and those moments on stage were what he lived for. But the glory came at a price. Elvis always looked forward to coming home.

Whenever he was away from Memphis, Elvis felt more vulnerable and less self-assured. Unfamiliar surroundings heightened the clamor his presence caused and his uneasy response to it in large crowds. Back home, when he was with his entourage and felt safely insulated, he had a swagger and was the leader of the pack. Memphis was his home turf and mirrored his "country boy" soul. The people there spoke the same language he did. Even though he was followed by fans wherever he went just as much in Memphis as anywhere, he considered them neighbors, making the situation less threatening in his mind's eye. Out in the world, the sheer size of the crowds made him nervous. That's why over the years he began to take his entourage with him—they acted as a sort of traveling security blanket.

No matter the size of his fame, there was never a question that Elvis would make Memphis his permanent home. When he bought Graceland, it was first and foremost a gift to his mother. Running a close second in importance was the security it gave Elvis. It was the one place he could take a walk with no fear of being accosted, engage in affairs away from the scrutiny of the press, and just be himself. On the road, it was a different story.

La Crosse was a typical example of what life on the road was like for Elvis. As soon as he arrived, Parker introduced him to his police escort. Elvis was cordial and thanked each one for his help—although he could immediately pick up their disapproval by the way they looked at him. Once the personal appearances started, though, he'd be too busy to think much of it. Plus, he was getting used to it.

As much as he resented their judgmental stares, he was glad they were there. Elvis performed at the local auditorium and in their frenzy, thousands of teenagers descended on the building, beating on the windows and threatening to burst through.

"It sounded like a tornado was whippin' through the building," Elvis told me on the phone. "If they'd of gotten in, they'd of trampled all of us like bulls after a cow in season."

Elvis was scared and admitted it to a local reporter. Parker didn't mind the honesty but wanted to make sure it was kept in perspective. He didn't think it was good publicity to let fans know they frightened Elvis too much.

"You have to be their hero. They look up to you. Do you understand what I mean?"

Elvis listened, his head bent toward the floor, one foot twisting his toe into the carpet.

"There's a certain image you've got to project to stay on top. It's all right to show a soft side, but not a weak side, see? I said, do you see?"

"Yessir."

In the way only Parker could, he had managed to make Elvis feel small and insecure.

"He might as well have jus' come out and called me a sissy," he complained bitterly.

"Elvis, he's just trying to get good publicity for you, that's all. People can take things the wrong way if you're not careful," I told him.

"He thinks I'm stupid. Maybe he's right. I always seem to say the wrong things."

His words got him into a lot less trouble than his performing. Everywhere he went, swarms of frenzied fans followed his every move, and dozens of policemen and security guards were required to keep Elvis from getting swallowed up. And everywhere he went he had to endure hatred from people who called him evil. The magnitude of his popularity incited his detractors to curse him as loudly as they could in an effort to be heard over the screaming adoration of his fans. Looking back, I'm sure they were just frightened people who no doubt genuinely believed Elvis was promoting indecency. But I'm also sure they would have liked Elvis had they ever met him.

Naturally, Parker loved the controversy. Elvis was probably the main topic of conversation for much of the country—certainly in any city he visited. The more vocal his opposition got, the more his fans rallied behind him. And the more records he sold. Parker was smart enough to know that was the bottom line—keeping Elvis's name in the headlines and laughing all the way to the bank. But it was mildly risky. There was always the possibility some overly exuberant policeman could arrest Elvis on a local obscenity charge. The thought nearly gave Gladys apoplexy.

"Arrested for singin'—that's ridiculous. Don't they have anythin' better to do than bother my boy?" she asked Parker.

"Nobody is going to arrest Elvis. They are just trying to get their names in the papers so they can remind people of it next time they're up for election."

"How can you be so sure? Why can't he jus' make records instead of goin' places in person? It ain't worth goin' t'jail over."

Parker would skillfully calm Gladys, mostly by flattery and using enough double talk so Gladys didn't know whether she was coming or going. Parker also convinced Elvis there was no chance anyone would arrest him on stage. And Elvis loved performing so much, he never needed much coaxing and happily continued singing.

Still, it was virtually a guessing game trying to figure how much the local police would be inclined to interfere on behalf of the area's censorship codes. There were several instances where the town sheriff would tell Elvis to his face he couldn't perform because his act was too vulgar. As far as I know, Parker and Elvis ignored the tactics and performed on schedule. Still, it was nerve wracking and involved a lot of wasted energy.

What worried Parker more was Elvis's off-stage, extracurricular activities. Although hardly a ladies' man himself, Parker knew how many romantic opportunities a performer in Elvis's position was offered. Dancing on stage was easily defended. Parker publicized Elvis's unique stage style as the uninhibited exuberance of youth let loose by the purity of music. It fit with the image of humble southern boy made good.

But charges of statutory rape and paternity suits were not as easily defended or dismissed. Parker constantly preached at Elvis to be careful, especially when he was on the road.

"People love going after celebrities. Especially young girls who get carried away. It might be a casual date to you, but she'll come away expecting you to marry her. If you aren't one hundred percent positive how old they are, leave 'em alone. You got plenty of girls back home."

Once when Elvis gave a little smirk and muttered, "Aw, a little kiss is harmless enough," Parker went for the jugular. Elvis was shaking with anger—and worry—when he told me later what Parker had said.

" 'You listen to me—I've worked too hard to make you what you are. I'm not going to let you throw it away chasing after young girls all too willing to let you have your way with them.

" 'I'm sure it would break your mama's heart if she knew you were acting like a tomcat in heat. What do you think she would say? I'd hate to tell her, but if you don't listen to me you won't leave me any choice.' "

Elvis was furious at being scolded like a schoolboy but even more mortified that Parker might tell Gladys of his numerous affairs.

"You don' think he'd really do it, do you? It would kill mama—you know her. She don' understand how it is. I swear, sometimes I'd like to kill Parker. Jus' 'cause he handles my music business, he thinks he has the right to order me around 'bout everythin' else, too."

Elvis's tirade was feeble fist shaking. Parker did call all the shots. Even though Gladys didn't like Parker, she was convinced Elvis would be lost without him. Vernon admired his confident business savvy and hung on his every word. Any time Elvis made the mistake of complaining about Parker in front of his parents, they would dress him down as an ingrate. He quickly learned to vent his frustration only in the presence of a selected few. Elvis frequently threatened to fire Parker and we'd encourage him to do it—even though we all knew it was posturing. In his insecure heart, Elvis believed Parker was the only one who understood the business of music and stardom well enough to keep Elvis on top. For as much as he resented Parker, he feared being poor again twice as much. So he listened—to a degree. He selected his road affairs with extreme care, usually having one of his boys do the talking so nobody would see him with the lucky girl for the night.

"Parker worries too much," Elvis liked to say. "A little lovin' never hurt anyone."

It turned out Parker had good reason to worry. He was dead right when he warned Elvis about people who would try to take advantage of his fame and wealth. And it wouldn't be long before Elvis had to face a more terrifying truth—some people hated him enough to want him dead.

In August 1956, a postman, taking the liberty of reading mail intended for Elvis, intercepted a postcard that warned, "If you don't stop this shit we're going to kill you" (A5–15).

It's ironic that Elvis never knew about his very first death threat. None of us did until finding it in the FBI files. On one hand, perhaps we can assume the FBI didn't take the threat seriously. They were probably right in dismissing it as the harmless ranting of a kook whose wife was just too enamored of Elvis.

On the other hand, I have to wonder about their wisdom. Today, we are painfully aware that celebrities are often the targets of legitimate, deadly threats. It's only by the grace of God this one didn't follow through. It seems irresponsible not to notify somebody of a potentially dangerous situation. But that's the way they chose to handle it.

A longtime member of the Memphis police force claims the FBI did indeed contact them about the postcard, but it was considered a nuisance letter. They instructed the postman to keep an eye out for any additional postcards and put the whole thing on a back burner.

Even if the authorities had made us aware of the threat, I doubt anyone would have told Elvis or his parents about it straight away. No need burdening them with possible problems when there were enough concrete difficulties to deal with. There's only so much a person like Elvis could handle at one time without breaking into pieces.

Up until the mid 1960s, I oversaw Elvis's fan mail. In the early days, most of the letters were from people who just wanted a photograph. Some wrote to say they were disgusted with Elvis's sexy act, while others penned imaginative X-rated letters outlining in great detail just what they would like Elvis to do to them and vice versa. He also got dozens of letters a week from love-struck women announcing they were going to leave their parents, husbands, families, or boyfriends so they could come to Memphis and be with Elvis. One woman, whose desperation came through in her letters, was particularly sad.

Her first one was chatty and went on about how much she enjoyed Elvis's records and performances. As usual, we sent back a signed photograph of Elvis wishing her the best. That must have started the ball rolling in her mind. The second letter was more personal. She confided to Elvis how bad her home life was—her husband abused her and her parents turned a blind eye out of fear she would come back to live with them. She fantasized how wonderful it would be to come visit Elvis and be with someone who was so kind and gentle.

It's so hard to know what to do in cases like this. Part of you wants to contact the person and try to help but common sense dictates against it. Elvis enjoyed browsing through his fan mail sometimes, but I would make sure correspondence like this was removed. It would bother him to no end knowing this was happening. One thing the authorities told us never to do was answer fan letters, whether good or bad, with a personal letter. Making one-on-one contact like that could set somebody off into a fantasy world that could potentially lead to trouble. The best thing to do was ignore the letters, or if a series of letters got too strange or threatening, turn them over to the police or the FBI.

In this case, it was just sad to read one woman's fevered desires and dreams. Several letters later, the woman announced she couldn't stand her life anymore and was running away. She told Elvis the day and time she wanted him to pick her up—in Bakersfield, California. A bus would take too long and she didn't have enough money, anyhow. In her mind, she and Elvis were soulmates and had become intimates. More than that, he was her savior.

I didn't know what to do, so I called a friend on the police force who told me to just forget it.

"She'll eventually wise up and go home."

"But it's not safe for someone to be roaming the streets."

"Listen, if you become responsible for every nut fan of Elvis's, you're not gonna have time for anything else. It's not your problem—unless they mean any harm. Then it's our problem."

To my knowledge, Elvis never got another letter from her. My police friend was evidently right—she waited and went home completely disillusioned when Elvis didn't come get her. At least, that's what I hope happened. That incident really taught me that the dangers of celebrity come in a lot of different guises. It was suddenly easy to see how obsessive fan love could turn into murderous hatred and rage. The lady in the letters probably just went back home crushed. But someone else might have been filled with jilted fury and come after Elvis. People can turn so easily—and the star lives in ignorance, unaware of the effect he is making.

I remember once having to break up a fistfight in front of Graceland between two teenaged girls who were scratching and clawing each other bloody. Now, it wasn't unusual for there to be pushing and shoving between fans jostling for position down by the gate to get the best glimpse of Elvis coming and going from Graceland. But I'd never seen such a sight as this.

I jumped in between the two girls, ducking their wildly flailing fists, and tried to pry them apart. All the while, they spat insults at each other and argued over who Elvis liked the best.

"You're just jealous 'cause he smiles at me every time and doesn't give you the time a'day."

"He does so. He even touched my hand and asked my name. That's why you want my spot."

"I had it first . . ."

And on it went. We finally got them apart and restored order, but it was just another example of how close to the edge celebrity and stardom can drive people. The desire to be touched by fame, and thereby have your own moment in the reflected sun, is a powerful drug—for both performer and fan.

No matter how difficult his fans made it for Elvis, he never resented them for it. They were his reason to be and he respected them for making his wildest dreams come true. That's not to say his celebrity never frustrated him. It did, constantly. When he was drafted, Elvis was sent to Fort Hood, Texas, for boot camp. Shortly before he was to ship off for Europe, Elvis and I drove into Killeen to buy presents for some of the officers and their wives. Despite the nervousness he felt in being sent to Germany for so long, he was in relatively good spirits. But the day turned into a complete disaster. He was absolutely bombarded in the stores. Those who didn't ask for an autograph simply followed a few steps behind. Elvis got terribly self-conscious and claustrophobic. And as the crowd got bigger, a warning bell began to go off in his head—he knew this was a potentially volatile situation. Abruptly, Elvis politely waved to the people and quickly left, without buying a single present.

"Damn, can't even go shoppin' without raisin' a ruckus."

"Aw, come on, you'd feel a lot worse if everyone suddenly started ignorin' you," I teased.

"I guess I want it both ways. I wanna be famous but I wanna do what I wanna do like a regular person. It scares me when people start crowdin' in like that. Should scare you, too. God, I'm always so scared somebody with me's gonna get trampled.

Next time, I guess I'll have to drag Red along—even just to buy a few presents in the middle of nowhere."

Elvis's fear that somebody might get hurt on account of him was genuine. It was not unusual that his personal appearances sparked near-riots of fans swept up in mob emotion (A16–17, A20). Naturally, Elvis was held accountable by many of the local authorities, who found it irresponsible of him to do any live performances knowing the potential for pandemonium. His fans were not unaware, either—although they seemed to bask in the danger. One teenage girl who had been waiting outside a Brooklyn, New York theater to see Elvis breathlessly told a reporter,

> "It'll be a miracle if this theater is in one piece when we get out."

A Louisville, Kentucky official wrote Hoover asking the director to help prevent a similar riot in his city. Typically, Hoover was forced to refer the writer to the local law enforcement in areas where Elvis previously appeared but carefully logged the complaint in Elvis's file as yet one more example of his illicit influences.

Threats come in a variety of packages. Some are directed at your life and well-being; others are more subversive, aiming at your image. Like a slew of celebrities before him, Elvis was the target of numerous whispering campaigns. The ones that claimed he was dead or had shot his mother were more or less easy enough to disprove, but others were more insidious.

In 1957, we got wind of a wild rumor circulating about Elvis. Allegedly, Elvis had told a reporter during a radio interview that he would rather kiss three black women than one Mexican. As if that weren't enough, he supposedly went on to talk at great length about the unattractiveness of Mexican women in general.

Obviously, this rumor spread like wildfire—all the way to the FBI (A21–22). In an intelligence summary, the Bureau made note that Mexican authorities were trying to prohibit radio stations from playing any of Elvis's records and to ban him from appearing in their country. Echoing sentiments similar to American conservatives, the report noted that until Elvis, Mexican youth were too well brought up and too serious to be influenced by rock and roll. Until Elvis, that is. Authorities gave him almost single-handed credit for corrupting their nation's youth. Elvis created such a stir that one newspaper took out an ad that screamed "Death to Elvis Presley!" The story that Elvis had insulted Mexican women just fanned the fiery controversy.

It was a particularly frustrating, no-win situation. Elvis knew that if he denied it, he would inevitably sound defensive and guilty. If he didn't, people would automatically assume it was because he had indeed said it.

"Who the hell would have started such a thing?" he asked in exasperation. "I wouldn't say that."

"Hell, no, you ain't yet met a woman you didn' wanna kiss," Vernon joked.

Gladys shot him a look. "Ain't no time for jokes, Vernon."

She was right. The last thing Elvis needed was to be branded a racist. True, back then minorities hadn't developed the level of political clout they have today, so it wasn't as if Elvis was worried about a boycott. That wasn't the point. He found it very upsetting to be accused of something he didn't do, something that hurt people.

"They must really hate me to accuse me like this."

"Who's 'they,' son?" Vernon asked.

Elvis waved his hand, gesturing vaguely outside the door. "All of 'em. I worked so hard to get us here and they all wanna take it away. They have to make up bad things about me to try and turn my fans against me. It just ain't fair. You'd think they had better things t'worry about than me and my singin'."

The "Mexican girl thing," as it became known, didn't create as much of a long-term furor as Elvis had expected it to. But it did linger and periodically over his entire career questions about whether or not he really said it would arise. It was just one of dozens of controversies Elvis seemed to find himself in the middle of in those whirlwind first years. The steady stream of mini-traumas took a toll on Elvis because he could never completely remove himself from them.

What Elvis couldn't grasp was that it wasn't him

personally they were attacking. From the local high school principal to J. Edgar Hoover himself, it was what Elvis symbolized that had them in an uproar. America was going through a painful adolescence and making the break was going to be a painful transition with passions running high on both sides. Certainly, the tumult of the sixties would have happened with or without Elvis—he just presented a tangible imagery for young people to latch onto. And for the old standard-bearers to crucify. A syndicated columnist named George Sokolsky presented their case in response to a teenager who wrote proclaiming Elvis to be her generation's savior (A23).

> I heard Elvis sing and I believe that perhaps in five years or so, he might be able to carry a tune as well as Bing Crosby. But in 50 years, he could not make the chorus of the Metropolitan Opera.
>
> The fault no doubt is in a school system which gives the child so little cultural background, so little basis for taste and so little understanding of beauty. Rock-n-Roll, which is a musical reversion to the tom-tom of the jungle, can stir so many of our young to ecstasy only because they know no better. It is curious that in a Western country a child could write 'the greatest thing the world has ever known: Elvis Presley.' I used to hear them say that that title went to Jesus. How times have changed.

Which was exactly the point. In an effort to break free from the repression and conservatism of the 1950s, America's youth went in search of their own heroes and role models. If it hadn't been Elvis, it would have been someone else. But, it was Elvis, and he became the unwitting symbol of change. Which is particularly ironic, considering all Elvis wanted to do in his life was fit in.

Although McCarthy's stranglehold on the American psyche had lost its death grip by 1958, Communism was still seen as the ultimate threat to our society. Otherwise, the FBI would never have wasted any time or money accumulating documentation on the travels of two beauty queens (A24–26). Except that one was from Austria, a country tolerant of Communists—therefore a country not to be completely trusted.

During a brief stay in Las Vegas in January 1958, Elvis was introduced to Kathy Gabriel, the current Miss Ohio, and to Miss Austria, Hannah Melcher. It was hardly unusual for Elvis to meet other celebrities or personalities. Sometimes, it was strictly for publicity purposes—Parker wanted Elvis's face out there with all kinds of people. Other times, other public figures would personally request to meet Elvis. The opposite wasn't true, though. While there were dozens of performers Elvis admired, he could have never suggested an arranged meeting. He was too shy and too self-conscious. Not that he was any less nervous meeting an admirer of his—but if asked, it would have been unthinkably rude not to accommodate the request.

As far as public introductions go, getting to know these two beauty queens was one of the less painful experiences for Elvis. The three of them hit it off and spent an enjoyable day laughing, talking, and flirting in general. As he often did, Elvis told them to stop by Graceland if they were ever in the area. By the time he got back home to Memphis—and his girlfriend of the moment—the girls were pretty much just a pleasant memory.

To his surprise, they did show up a few weeks later, all smiles and anticipation. To their surprise, it was a much more subdued and preoccupied Elvis who hosted the girls during their visit. In fact, he was struggling not to fall apart. At the peak of his career, Elvis had been drafted. He was convinced his career was over and that all of his hard work and dreams had been yanked out from under him. Parker assured him there were enough songs recorded to keep him on the airwaves and in record stores for the duration of his enlistment. But to Elvis, two years might as well have been twenty.

Some photo opportunities with the girls were arranged and it was all Elvis could do not to cry in them. A caption in the files describes him as "nonchalant," but shell-shocked would have been much more appropriate. Beyond the potentially catastrophic consequences for his career, Elvis was horrified at the thought of being in the military. He would have to cut his hair, take absolute orders from some hard-nosed sergeant, and leave Graceland. Gladys was even more upset than Elvis at the idea he might be shipped overseas somewhere, half a world away from her watchful eyes.

This was the hornets' nest Hannah and Kathy walked in on. Not surprisingly, they left fairly soon, heading toward New York to audition for jobs as "show girls" at the Copa. All in all, it was one of the more innocent encounters Elvis had ever had—but don't tell that to the FBI.

Apparently, the FBI had Melcher under surveillance to make sure she wasn't really a communist agent of some kind. When Elvis struck up a friendship with her and Miss Ohio, little did he realize it would come to the immediate attention of J. Edgar Hoover. Elvis, to my knowledge, never saw either young lady again and they faded from his memory as the most casual of acquaintances. But in retrospect, it's frightening to think your own government is keeping tabs on your houseguests—behind your back.

CHAPTER THREE

Army Life and the Strange Case of Dr. Schmidt

Elvis came out of the shower still a little groggy from the sleeping pills he had taken earlier, but it was nothing a few cups of coffee and some Pepsis wouldn't cure. His suite was ablaze with light and there was a subdued flurry of activity now, the nightly pre-show rituals in motion. In the bedroom, a garish sequined jumpsuit hung on the closet door, with the rest of his clothes spread out on the bed. The television was off in favor of the radio, carefully turned to a "contemporary" station more likely to play Elvis and Sinatra than the Jackson Five and the Rolling Stones. His hairdresser chatted with a couple of bodyguards, who drank beers down like soda. Elvis walked by and grabbed a bottle for a quick sip. He didn't really like alcohol but it served a purpose when he had to lay off his tranquilizers. Elvis glanced at the empty dinner plate on the room-service tray and felt his stomach growl. He had just eaten a big cheeseburger, fries, and a milk shake and was still hungry. He was hungry all the time and no amount of food seemed to satisfy him. That's why he had to take diet pills. Elvis knew his system was all screwed up, and he promised himself to start exercising and get healthy as soon as this death threat business was over. Right now, it took all his effort not to break down and cry in terror.

Why would anyone hate so much to want to kill him? Whom had he ever hurt so badly? His whole life, all Elvis wanted to do was have people like him and accept him regardless of his unique style. That's why he wanted to be a singer. But he never imagined the dream could so often be turned to nightmare. For every person who embraced him there were ten who wanted to ruin it for him. Elvis had never been able to fully enjoy his success. Besides losing his mama, his entire career had been troubled by people wanting to use him, ruin him, or hurt him.

Elvis's greatest fear was that his fans would forget him while he was in the service. No chance. The volume of fan mail actually increased, most voicing strong approval of Elvis's decision to be in the infantry instead of using his celebrity status to transfer to the entertainment services. Not that he didn't want to, but Parker wouldn't hear of it. He didn't want Elvis to come across as even the least bit unpatriotic, even if it meant more personal and emotional discomfort for the singer.

For as rigid as military life was, it wasn't able to protect Elvis any better than civilian authority from obsessive, potentially dangerous fans. Without a doubt, the most curious incident was the strange case of a doctor I'll call Hans Schmidt, an alleged dermatologist from South Africa (A27–

34). "Schmidt's" real identity is not revealed due to legal considerations.

Elvis was stationed in Germany, still reeling from the sudden death of his mother while he was in boot camp, when Schmidt first wrote. Elvis had wanted me to join him overseas along with Red West and Vernon, but my parents wouldn't hear of it. So he hired a temp to handle some of his daily business affairs while there; Elvis's German secretary, Miss Stefaniak, was the first to read his mail.

Schmidt claimed to be a dermatologist who had developed a skin treatment that he swore worked miracles on crow's feet and other facial imperfections. Evidently, the good doctor noticed that Elvis was beset with little wrinkles around his eyes and wrote to offer his services. It was as if he instinctively knew exactly what to say to get Elvis's attention.

Elvis was just this side of being phobic about his crow's feet and the skin on his face. As a teenager, he had suffered through some pretty bad acne and had never gotten over being self-conscious about his face. He did have a few small scars from the acne, but nothing terribly noticeable to anyone else but him. Elvis was also the only one who could see the crow's feet he fretted over so much. But even then the thought of growing old bothered him—and he was only in his early twenties. Also, the emotional thunderbolt of losing his mother had left its tracks on Elvis's face in the form of blemishes, pallor, and a generally unhealthy appearance. All of this could have been easily remedied by proper food, rest, and exercise—but trying to get Elvis to eat properly was nearly impossible. If the food wasn't fried, he turned his nose up at it. His poor diet, combined with his aching heart, left him looking worse for wear. Elvis also knew that as soon as he got out of the service he was signed to do a movie—and he had to look his best for that. So either through accident or design, Schmidt hit a button that piqued Elvis's interest. When Miss Stefaniak mentioned the doctor and his special skin treatments, Elvis was intrigued enough to ask her to write back and get more information. Little did Elvis know the fire storm he had just ignited.

Hans responded with an exceedingly detailed letter intended to both impress and flatter Elvis. He extolled the virtues of his "aroma therapy," which he had developed in his Johannesburg salon.

> I have recently received the World Patent Rights of this formula and the treatments may be given advantageously to people of any skin type and I would say it is very acceptable to people suffering from oily skin, enlarged pores, acne scars and wrinkles—crow's feet, etc., and expect Mr. Elvis Presley to benefit from this Scientific Method and to receive Great Satisfaction as others have received. It has given me Great Pleasure to receive your enlightening and most welcomed letter and from the innermost recesses of my heart I would welcome the opportunity to treat Mr. Elvis Presley.

Schmidt was nothing else if not a salesman. While his pitch would have probably turned off a certain majority of people who can smell a quack a mile away, his scientific-sounding rhetoric elicited a different response from Elvis—one of impressed awe. As mentioned before, Elvis's education was limited. While it's true he graduated from high school, his ability to grasp certain subjects was limited. Talk to Elvis about mechanics or wood carving and he would know exactly what you were saying, but start showering him with phrases like "neuromuscular receptivity" or "epidermal elasticity" and his eyes would literally glaze over. If you sounded official enough, Elvis assumed you must know what you're talking about—especially if he didn't. Elvis was impressed by the complex-sounding treatment Schmidt preached.

> Through the odorous part of the flowers, aromatic plants and resins and that of Roses, Carnations, Orange blossoms, Mimosa, Camomile, Cinnamon, Rosewood, Sandalwood, etc., the treatments help to revitalize the skin cells and structure beneath the epidermis—which is continuously being discarded . . .
>
> Those electrons which are responsible for the odor of certain perfectly organized molecules can penetrate the epidermis and by infusing the epidermis with ordoriferous molecules one injects Biological Energy—i.e., or in other words, 'New Life'. Mr. Elvis Presley can thus rest assured that his treatments will be individualized—that is to say—adapted to suit his skin type or epidermis. I am now busy preparing the treatments and composing mixtures of the essential oils . . .
>
> If Mr. Presley decides to follow a certain routine or . . . make use of my Special Aromatherapy Mix-

ture & Elixir House Method he will not age but instead become as handsome as I would like him to be.

Schmidt claimed this cosmetic line would soon be on the public market but that until then, he had a couple of free weeks during which he would be glad to fly to Germany to administer treatments. Schmidt also assured Elvis he understood the need for confidentiality, which had been made clear by Miss Stefaniak. Elvis always kept his vanity in the closet. To the outside world, he was unconcerned about aging, but those who lived under the same roof knew it was one of his magnificent obsessions. As a rule, it drove Vernon crazy.

"Elvis, you lookin' bad is better than most people in their Sunday best. You're gonna worry yourself into the very wrinkles you're worried over."

"If you had a camera in your face showing every hair you'd care, too. It don't matter how you look," Elvis retorted.

"I look jus' fine—'cause I don't worry about it."

Needless to say, Elvis didn't mention his interest in Schmidt's treatments to Vernon; only his secretary was privy to it. But while he was intrigued by the "Method," he was not obsessed with the treatments. There were plenty of other things going on to occupy his thoughts, not the least of which was his new sixteen-year-old girlfriend, Priscilla Beaulieu.

But for Schmidt, the chance to personally administer his treatment to Elvis became his raison d'etre. In her initial reply, Miss Stefaniak had been authorized to tell Hans that if he came to Germany, his travel would be paid for as part of his fees. To Schmidt, this meant it was a done deal. In a lengthy postscript, he offered the secretary the option of either depositing the money necessary to book passage in his bank account or, preferably, to merely make the arrangements herself and send him the tickets when complete.

Less than two weeks later, Schmidt wrote again. He still hadn't heard back from Elvis or his secretary, but undaunted, he took the bull by the horns and made his own arrangements—using his own money. Schmidt was probably worried Elvis had lost interest, but it's more likely that neither he nor Miss Stefaniak had gotten around to replying. The sheer volume of daily paperwork that surrounded Elvis was hard to imagine for anyone who hadn't experienced it firsthand. Plus, Elvis was a soldier and did have a certain number of duties he was expected to perform.

Regardless, Hans was not to be denied. It's interesting to note that his second letter was already very familiar in tone—no more Mr. Presley, now it was "Dear Elvis."

> May I inform you that I have cancelled many new bookings and that I have completed all arrangements for my departure to Germany . . .
>
> I feel honored and very privileged in having been chosen for this important task . . .
>
> Please convey to your very good and charming secretary my sincerest thanks for all her kind at-

> tentions.—As you would say with your sense of humor "Miss Postage Stamp" must be overworked what with all the mail. —Bless her.

Like a lot of obsessed fans, Schmidt believed he knew Elvis as an intimate—"as you would say with your sense of humor"—there was no way Schmidt could really know the intricacies of Elvis's humor. The Elvis he "knew" from magazines and radio was ninety percent image and publicity hype, with the real man buried among his commercial appeal. Not only did Schmidt presume to know Elvis, he also imagined they were already friends with a defined relationship. Just how defined would come as a major shock to Elvis later on.

Schmidt waited impatiently, and in vain, for a reply. Two weeks later he wrote again, this time to Miss Stefaniak, unable to resist pointing out in his very first sentence he hadn't gotten a reply to his last correspondence. The familiarity begun before continues here.

> Enclosed is a photo of our Elvis out of an Italian periodical . . .
>
> Post Script,
>
> Attached please find a few nice pages all about Elvis—the "STAR OF THE CENTURY." I would not like to see him grow older and who would. (page 7) I clearly noticed the wrinkles on Mr. Presley's forehead and made a note of it to you.

Charm hadn't succeeded in expediting Schmidt's trip to Germany, so he turned to emotional button pushing with the comments on aging that he hoped would spur Elvis on. It didn't. With words reflecting increasing desperation, Schmidt wrote one last time. For the most part, his next letter tried to be upbeat and chatty, but signs of strain were still obvious, and in retrospect, seeds of the dissension to follow are easy to spot.

> Elvis, once again I beg you to let me be of great service to you and let me know when to come.
>
> Concludingly, I wish to let you know that I have given up my business and cancelled many new bookings in order to do you. So Elvis, please don't disappoint me as I won't be able to get over it easily.

Just how poorly Schmidt handled disappointment would be the basis for one of the biggest scandals Elvis had faced to date.

Unable to contain himself any longer, Schmidt took the initiative and left South Africa for Germany in late November. Armed with his line of emollients custom designed for Elvis's skin tone and texture, Schmidt arrived in Bad Nauheim full of misguided hopes and fantasies.

At first, his plan worked beyond his wildest dreams. After settling into his hotel, Schmidt made his way to Elvis's house. As fortune would have it, Miss Stefaniak answered the door and the self-described doctor introduced himself. The secretary was momentarily taken aback by his sudden arrival, but she assured Schmidt she would let Elvis know he was in town. She took his hotel number and promised to call him later that evening.

When Elvis got home, he too was surprised—but not unpleasantly so—that Schmidt was in Germany. The worst part was having to admit to Vernon who the doctor was and why he was there. Vernon was typically skeptical.

"You got some doctor flyin' all the way from Africa for some skin cream? Ain't they got enough 'round here?"

"This is stuff he makes special for each person."

"Flower therapy—I heard it all now. Boy, you're a salesman's dream. I swear, you're even more gullible than your mama was, God rest her soul."

"It ain't bein' gullible. You jus' don' understand."

"I understand you'll throw away money on any harebrained idea you think will keep you young forever. For Christ's sake, you're only a boy and you can stop worrying about bein' an old man."

Miss Minnie, Vernon's ma, stood up for her grandson.

"Vernon, let the boy alone. Ain't nothin' wrong with takin' care of yourself, regardless how old you are. I wish you'd take better care of yourself. Besides, for Elvis it's business."

"I still say it's a waste of money."

"Well, I guess it's my money to waste," Elvis said, bitterness creeping into his voice. Money, and how Elvis chose to spend it, was an endless sore spot between father and son. Paying to have some quack, as Vernon liked to think of any doctor, put ground up flowers on your face made as much sense as setting the bills on fire.

Despite his father's skepticism, Elvis had his secretary contact Schmidt to set up his first treatment. Schmidt arrived positively beaming. In his bag, bottles clinked together sounding like chimes. When Elvis walked in to meet Schmidt, the South African's face flushed and his hand quivered as he thrust it out to shake the hand of his idol.

Much to Elvis's irritation, Vernon ambled out to take a look at the skin doctor. What he saw was a nondescript, nervous, fortyish-year-old man who seemed to be burning with adrenaline. Vernon had seen awestruck fans before and didn't doubt that regardless of his treatments, Schmidt was there first and foremost simply because he had wanted to meet Elvis.

Elvis decided to have the treatments in the den—with the door closed. The last thing he wanted was for Vernon to come in and start hassling him. Two ladies who also worked as secretaries under Miss Stefaniak were in the room as well. Getting Elvis sitting in one place for any length of time was rare, so the women took the opportunity to have him sign autographs and take care of any other little business that needed his attention. But in truth, by this time, Elvis had very little hands-on input into the daily running of the business that was "Elvis." More than anything, he invited the ladies in because from the first handshake, Elvis was inexplicably uncomfortable with Schmidt and didn't really want to be left alone with him.

"It's those eyes—he stares at me so hard like he's trying to see inside my skin. And I hate it when people are too anxious to please. Makes me nervous when someone's jumpin' all around me."

Schmidt became a semi-fixture at Elvis's German home, bustling in with his bag filled with the secrets of youth. He would attentively massage the lotions onto Elvis's face, neck, and shoulders. Typically, Elvis loved being surrounded by friends, so it wasn't uncommon for other service guys to come around for a visit. Schmidt's officious manner raised a few eyebrows, but since Schmidt was sworn to secrecy about the reason for his visit, most non-family members assumed he was an oddball Elvis had befriended. When asked, Elvis was evasive and brief.

"Just a family friend here for a visit."

Had Elvis been halfway astute, he would have seen what lay in store by Schmidt's reaction to Priscilla. Elvis had been dating the young beauty for a while and was in the throes of young love. Maybe that's why he didn't notice that behind Schmidt's beaming smile toward Priscilla, his eyes were cold with jealousy. To compensate, he went overboard on his compliments to the point where they smacked of obvious insincerity. Still, Elvis and the others just put it off to Schmidt being a "foreigner."

A couple of weeks into the treatments, the tone of Schmidt's visits began to change and he began taking liberties. He would come early for appointments and while waiting for Elvis, would try to ingratiate himself with Miss Minnie, Miss Stefaniak, Red West, and especially Vernon, who for the most part tried not to give him the time of day. Hans also attempted to include himself among Elvis's army buddies—which is where the saga of Dr. Schmidt took a dark turn.

In quieter moments when he wasn't going overboard with nervous energy, Schmidt tended to be somewhat flamboyant. The more comfortable he felt in Elvis's house, the more fey his mannerisms and behavior got. Again, Elvis initially dismissed it as traits particular to Schmidt's culture—until a number of his army buddies told Elvis that his "family friend" had made blatant homosexual passes at them. According to the soldiers, Schmidt had suggestively touched or tried to touch various parts of their bodies, and in one case offered to perform a certain sexual act. Elvis was so stunned he didn't know how to respond, other than promise to confront Schmidt.

Obviously, this was not a conversation Elvis could have in front of ladies, so he took Schmidt aside privately. On one hand, it was rare for Elvis to take such an initiative, but there really wasn't anyone else to do it. Parker was back in the States and he didn't want to have to fill Vernon in on this latest development, so he was stuck.

When he finally stammered out, "My buddies say you been way out of line with them," Schmidt didn't exactly admit to the specific charges, but he did take the opportunity to open up to Elvis.

"While I'm sure they misinterpreted my intentions, it is true that I have had past relationships with men as well as women. I hope that doesn't shock you?"

Whenever confronted directly like that, Elvis would always defer. This case was no different. Although he was very surprised by Schmidt's admission, Elvis mumbled an unformed sound to indicate he wasn't shocked.

Interpreting Elvis's muteness as acceptance, Schmidt launched into a personal history. He claimed to have been raised in an orphanage, under almost unbearable conditions. He painted a bleak picture of childhood hopelessness and loneliness, exacerbated by a lack of personal contact and love. Schmidt said he was still trying to overcome the scars of his upbringing and had even taken the extreme measure of shock treatments.

Schmidt told Elvis he had first homosexual experience in the orphanage and blamed that encounter for his adult tendencies—although it was said as more a fact than a regret. Schmidt did apologize, though, about Elvis's friends.

"I sincerely hope you believe me. Please don't think I meant to offend anybody. Because of the way I am, people mistake my intentions sometimes. It would hurt me to think you doubted me."

Schmidt was genuinely worried that Elvis would think badly of him and that concern softened Elvis's resolve. Instead of telling him to never come back, which had been his original intention, Elvis let Schmidt off with a mild warning.

"Jus' don't go botherin' my friends anymore. Don' even talk to 'em."

Schmidt readily agreed. But in some strange way, Elvis's calm reaction must have set his mind into an illogical motion. Maybe Hans's entire sales pitch to Elvis had been a smoke screen for the real reason he had flown half the length of the globe to meet him. Or I suppose that Elvis's undeniable appeal up close in person was too irresistible for a gay man to ignore. Whatever the motivation, Schmidt was driven to try and make his greatest fantasy come true. But his vision of desire backfired disastrously.

Shortly before Christmas in 1959, Schmidt was giving Elvis a treatment, still concentrating on the face, neck, and shoulders. Elvis sat in a chair, shirtless, lulled nearly to sleep by the rhythmic motion of Schmidt's massage. The two secretaries who usually sat in during Schmidt's visits had left, probably to do last-minute Christmas shopping, so Hans found himself untypically alone with Elvis. He took particular care with this treatment, applying the lotion with studied care. As Schmidt worked his shoulder area, Elvis tilted his head forward, shutting his eyes. He later told me he might have even drifted off for a second but was aware of being massaged on his chest. Before he could wonder why the treatment was being expanded, he was jolted to attention—Hans had reached down and slipped his hand between Elvis's legs in a definite, unmistakable caress. Elvis literally jumped out of his seat and halfway across the room in one motion.

Schmidt was equally startled by the violent reaction and curled his hands into his chest as if they had touched something hot. Still, he was so love-struck he forged ahead, stammering out his feelings for Elvis in a rush of impassioned words. Elvis stood against the wall, glistening with cream, too shocked to be angry—fortunately for Schmidt. When he regained his breath and his wits, Elvis ordered Schmidt to leave.

"Don't be afraid of me, Elvis. Nobody cares for you like I do."

"If you don't get out, I'll have Red throw you out."

The surprising calm Elvis displayed in the minutes after Schmidt's pleading grope didn't last. Instead of seeing it for what it was—a desperate attempt at romance by a love-struck fan that was ultimately harmless—Elvis attached more and more significance to it. It wasn't the first, nor would it be the last, time Elvis was the object of another man's attentions. To be honest, sometimes Elvis toyed with the attention, knowing he was the one who controlled the outcome. The rest of the time, he ignored it or sneered at it. But for some reason, Schmidt's proposition struck a nerve out of proportion to the event itself.

On Christmas Eve, Schmidt came to wish everyone a happy holiday. His ebullient manner had been thoroughly chastised by rejection and he was the picture of dejection. Amazingly, though, he asked when Elvis wanted his next appointment. Elvis was dumbfounded and told Schmidt in no uncertain terms the treatments were over. But he couldn't leave it at that. He felt the need to humiliate Schmidt in front of Red, Vernon, and another friend named Lamar.

"I'm afraid my daddy was right—I threw away good money after bad on your worthless treatments that don' even work. I only let you keep comin' back 'cause I felt sorry for you. Then you go and try to do things to my friends. Man, you're just a joke around here—a sick joke."

More than the words, it was the contempt in Elvis's voice that skewered Schmidt to the bone. But instead of folding up and skulking away, the South African flew into a spitting rage, fueled by the pain of dreams lost. Schmidt flailed wildly while shouting back at Elvis.

"You think because you're the famous Elvis Presley that you can treat me like dirt. Well, you're not invincible, Mr. Elvis Presley. You can be broken like this."

Schmidt grabbed a photo album on a nearby coffee table and in a display of unexpected strength he tore it in half. Once again everyone was stunned into inertia.

"First you lead me on, then act as if I did something terrible to you. Don't think I couldn't ruin your career—I know what's going on. You think I don't see, but I've come around at night and stood nearby. I hear what goes on between you and your young girlfriend. I know how to protect myself—I have taken photographs and made recordings of what you do with that young, young girl. Or maybe

I should just send it to her parents, then the American press."

It was Vernon who broke out of the reverie first and cut Schmidt off.

"I think I've heard jus' about all I can take from you. Get outa our house and if you come sneaking back, I'll have you tossed in jail. Red, get him movin'."

Schmidt let himself be herded out but he hurled insults and threats the entire way. Once he was gone, the room was abuzz with the electricity generated by violent confrontation. Uppermost on everyone's mind were the alleged photographs and tapes, but the only one with enough nerve to ask was Vernon.

"He was jus' talkin' hot air, right, son?"

"I can't believe you're askin' me that. Who's side're you on?"

"I jus' wanted to make sure there wasn' some things we needed to take care of, that's all. Don' go gettin' all riled like usual."

Except for that exchange, Elvis refused to talk about what had just happened. It was Christmas Eve and he had plans to spend it with Priscilla. He wasn't going to let anyone, especially Schmidt, ruin that.

"It's over and done with—I gotta go get 'Scilla. See you later."

But it wasn't over and done with, not by a long shot. Before Elvis managed to get out of the house, Schmidt was back, demanding financial compensation.

"I gave up everything to come and be with you."

"I never asked you to do anything," Elvis said, genuinely shocked.

"You knew what I was leaving behind because I told you in letter after letter. You never told me not to come. Now you're turning me out like some dog."

Even with his lack of business savvy, Elvis could smell trouble brewing in a big way. So could Vernon. Together they sat down with Schmidt and worked out a compromise. Elvis would pay him $200 for the treatments and give him an additional $315 for a plane ticket to London. Schmidt had decided he couldn't face going back to South Africa and wanted to spend some time in England. Elvis didn't care where he went, as long as he left Germany. The only thing Elvis demanded was that Hans leave immediately.

"I will be on the plane and out of your life tomorrow," he said solemnly.

He might have meant it at the time, but overnight Schmidt changed his mind. The day after Christmas, Schmidt shocked the entire household when he called and asked to speak to Elvis.

"What's that son of a bitch want now? He's supposed to be long gone by now."

"I told you from the get go he was up to no good, but you wouldn't listen."

"I don't need lectures from you right now. I got enough problems without having you on my back, too," Elvis snapped.

He picked up the phone and listened to what

Schmidt had to say. The conversation was short and to the point. When Elvis hung up, his face was pasty white with what could only be fear.

"He says he wants $2,000 to make up for losing his business comin' here. He says if I don', he's gonna ruin me in the papers."

Vernon waved his hand in dismissal. "Ain't nothin' he can do to hurt ya. I wouldn' worry over it."

"You would if it were your career. Who knows what this guy can do? You know the kind of stuff they write about me anyway—even if it ain't true, there's enough people who'd want to believe it. What difference does it make whether it's true or not? I gotta do something before he takes everything away from me."

There was no calming Elvis down. Schmidt had tapped into Elvis's rawest nerve, his fear of losing everything and being poor again. It was an irrational terror that overwhelmed him, regardless of what his bank account might say to the contrary. Anyone else might have ignored Schmidt and dared him to pursue his ridiculous claims, but Elvis panicked. His reaction was so strong that even Red and Vernon silently wondered to themselves if Elvis wasn't hiding something. Why get so distraught over threatened blackmail unless you had something to fear? But Elvis steadfastly denied Schmidt had any dirt on him—he was simply worried about his career.

His concern was strong enough to make Elvis turn to the most unlikely source for help—the

United States Army. While Elvis had been pleasantly surprised at how well the other soldiers had treated him, he hated the whole structure of existence of army life. He resented the strict chain of command and the fact that the army had robbed him of two vital years of his youth and career. But now he looked to the army to use its considerable authority to save him from Schmidt. It was a big step because now the whole affair would become a matter of official record.

Had Elvis followed his dad's advice and just sat tight, the matter would have died a natural death. At the same time Elvis was calling his commanding officer and making an appointment to come in and talk, Schmidt was in his hotel room writing a letter to Elvis. In the heat of impassioned emotions, Schmidt had consulted a lawyer who advised him to put his financial demands in writing to Elvis. Despite the hurt and betrayal Schmidt felt, his feelings for Elvis managed to win out.

> I wrote the attached letter on a solicitor's instructions here in Bad Nauheim.
>
> But, I have decided since this morning Sunday the 27/12/59 not to take action against you.
>
> I am deeply sorry for you and know I feel that you miss something Big in life, then too, it's unchristian to take anyone to court. I will just have to make up the loss and make the very most of a bad situation and start all over again with a new salon . . .
>
> Since you have had to go through so much in life I sympathize with you and forgive you . . . yes, we

must be forgiving to one and another—that's how it goes . . .

I am leaving Bad Nauheim for a better clime and wish you every success and happiness in the future.

The next afternoon, Schmidt added another letter as post script, before sending them all at once to Elvis.

> Don't worry about this letter now.
>
> I have been very hurt because things did not turn out the way I expected and you had more time for the other things which interest you most. I could not carry on and get results. Well, as I've said, there is no ill will and I wish you well.

That same day, Elvis was interviewed by military police concerning the "Schmidt incident" and related the chronology of how the doctor ended up in Germany treating him. Elvis was particularly indignant when detailing Schmidt's sexual advances to his friends—but he neglected to mention his own encounter with Schmidt. He decided it was too embarrassing—besides, if it ever got out, someone could somehow misconstrue it and use it against him.

Within hours of the interview, military police picked up Schmidt for questioning. Ironically, he had just come back from posting his letters to Elvis, but naturally, nobody really believed him when he swore he had decided against suing Elvis. Schmidt also denied he had tried to blackmail

Elvis—he was merely asking for what was rightfully his for services rendered. Whatever else he might have been, Schmidt wasn't stupid. He knew better than to take on both Elvis and the United States Army.

The Army ordered Schmidt to stay in Germany while they investigated the allegations. They did a background check on Schmidt and confirmed he was misrepresenting himself as a doctor. When confronted with this, Schmidt asked why he was being persecuted—all he wanted was to leave and start rebuilding his life. The Army was inclined to agree that would be the best course of action. They wanted a scandal involving Elvis Presley less than anyone except Elvis himself. So when they consulted with Elvis and Vernon on what they wanted to do, both were inclined to drop the matter.

"I jus' want him outa my life—I don' even want to hear his name again, sir," Elvis said.

On January 6, 1960, Hans Schmidt boarded a plane for London. Before leaving, he placed one last call to Elvis's house and spoke to Miss Stefaniak. He told her he was leaving and that he thought he might even go on to America, where he was sure his treatments would be a smashing success. Before he hung up, he asked her to please say good-bye to Elvis—he would never forget him.

By the time the Army passed on their report to the FBI, a month had elapsed. The Bureau's attempt to locate Schmidt in the States proved unsuccessful, nor were they able to pinpoint his whereabouts through English or South African authorities. It seemed as if he had mysteriously disappeared off the face of the earth. To this day, nobody knows whatever became of Schmidt. Most likely he simply adopted another name to protect himself from the past catching up with him and tainting whatever new life he was trying to build.

Elvis, naturally, saw it in much more sinister hues. Only a few months away from discharge, he was convinced Schmidt was setting a trap.

"He's probably gonna be waiting for me when I get back home. I'll walk in to find a dozen letters, each one demanding more money than the last."

But Schmidt never showed up in Memphis, nor did he ever contact Elvis again. I never heard Elvis refer to the whole Schmidt saga except for one time, the day after he got home from Germany. When Vernon made a crack about keeping an eye out for the South African, Elvis shot him a look.

"I don't ever want to hear him brought up again."

When I asked what was going on, Elvis told me the whole story, including the pass Schmidt made at him. My initial thought was that Elvis totally overreacted—and was still too touchy for no apparent reason. But ever since his mother died during his boot camp training, Elvis wasn't always on solid emotional ground, so I put it off to that. I have to admit, though, it is curious that Schmidt claimed to have photographs and recordings of Elvis in compromising positions. Because a short time after coming back to Graceland, Elvis spent several evenings making X-rated movies of himself and groupies selected from the dozens regularly posted at Graceland's front gate. Maybe Schmidt just gave him the idea for it—or maybe the would-be doctor really did know something we didn't.

The FBI files contain a memorandum dated February 3, 1960 that gives a brief sketch of what happened, but something is missing. All I know is that the strange circumstance of Hans Schmidt and Elvis's paranoid response to it didn't ring completely true—but it was one of the few secrets I feel Elvis took to the grave.

Although it was the most intriguing, the Schmidt case wasn't Elvis's only encounter with military authority. There were a couple of incidents that drove home to Elvis just how powerful government agencies can be in hiding the truth or fabricating "the official story"—which made him that much more leery of Big Brother and the powers that be.

His first taste of military whitewashing came after Elvis nearly managed to create an international incident. One of Elvis's constant joys was driving his cars. In Memphis, he loved heading out of town to cruise the country roads, going as fast as the car would take him. Germany was no different and he would take off whenever the chance arose, either in his own rented car or in a military vehicle assigned to him.

One Sunday, Elvis and another Army buddy decided to go for a joyride. Armed with a map and a compass, they turned off the main road and explored the country byways, which were often little more than dirt paths, barely wide enough for two cars. Elvis navigated his jeep on the winding lanes that took them past rustic farms, quaint cottages, and an occasional beer garden.

Being out in the country away from his life as a soldier thrilled Elvis and his mood was light. He regaled his buddy with stories of life on the road, with pretty girls dying to meet you at every stop. Knowing Elvis, he must have punctuated his escapades with naughty details that would have made Gladys roll over in her grave.

Between the glorious day, the reverie of reliving past conquests, and the feeling of being momentarily free from the constraints of Army life, Elvis lost complete track of where he was going. It wasn't until near dusk that he realized he didn't have a clue where he was. They pulled over to the side of the road and took out their map and compass. After a few minutes of calculating and double-checking the map, Elvis's companion sucked his breath in sharply.

"Elvis, we're across the border—we're in East Germany."

Elvis snatched the map away to see for himself. Somehow they had found an unpatrolled rural area and had driven unnoticed into Communist Germany. Headlines immediately formed in Elvis's brain—SINGER DETAINED BY EAST GERMAN GOVERNMENT and PRESLEY COURT-MARSHALLED. Even though it was an honest mistake, Elvis automatically assumed he would be severely reprimanded by military authorities—if the East Germans didn't capture him first.

"We gotta get the hell outa here," Elvis said. He turned the jeep around and pushed the gas pedal to the floor, fishtailing wildly down the road.

As it turns out, they were less than three miles into East German territory and were back across within five minutes, the way Elvis was tearing down the road. But his erratic driving attracted the attention of several locals and Elvis was convinced someone would turn them in—even on the East German border, people recognized Elvis. To avoid facing the music later on, Elvis and his friend went directly to their commander when they got back and told him what had happened.

Rather than be put in the position of explaining why Elvis Presley, U.S. soldier, had been in East Germany, his superiors decided to cover up. Elvis and his friend were ordered to say they had spent the day in town. The log entry showing Elvis had used the jeep was erased. Officially, the whole day didn't happen. Now, in the days of glasnost and the reunification of Germany, the story seems trivial. But back then the cold war was raging and insignificant events could be blown out of proportion. So any potential trouble or controversy had to be sniffed out and snuffed out before it had a chance to ignite. Elvis gave the Army more than its share of headaches.

In March of 1959, half a year before Laurenz Landau came into the picture, RCA Victor asked the FBI to investigate a letter sent to their office by a woman in Canton, Ohio (A36–37).

> Dear Sir
>
> I have just received a letter from a relative in West Germany.
>
> Plans have been made and already in the hands of a red soldier in East Germany to Kill Elvis Presley . . . This red soldier will be wearing an American uniform—he is to leave East Germany slip in to West Germany some time between Mar 14 and 22nd. He has been given orders to kill him even if he has to blow up the Hotel or home where his Father lives . . .
>
> Please, please don't take this as a crank letter . . . "I can not give my name . . . the people in West Germany would be in danger and of course the sister would be killed . . .
>
> I am not a teenager. I am a mother and Grandmother . . .

As soon as the FBI notified Elvis's superiors of the threat, he was put under immediate house guard. It wasn't the first time his life had been threatened, but this time it seemed more real and foreboding. Part of it was being so far from home in a foreign country among people with different language and customs. Getting a letter from an angry American upset with your dancing seemed tame compared to possible political assassination.

At first, Parker tried to reassure Elvis by telling him the letter was obviously from a woman in Ohio who had previously harassed Elvis, both threatening his life and trying to extort money from him.

In that particular case, authorities were able to track the woman down, but Elvis decided against pressing charges after the woman agreed to seek psychiatric help. Still, it was a big coincidence to get another letter from the same part of Ohio, leading Parker to a natural assumption. Parker told the FBI why he suspected the former culprit, whom he labeled "nuts."

Despite Parker's assurances, the FBI continued their investigation. Letters from the first woman were compared to the most recent missive and a number of differences were found (A38, 40, 42). For one thing, the original series of letters contained direct threats against Elvis of the "I will kill you" type, and demands for money. The last letter merely warned of an alleged plot by others. But what convinced the Bureau the authors were different was an analysis of the two sets of handwriting samples (A37). Feeling they were at a dead end, the FBI kept copies of the letters on file but considered their investigation over. It was up to the Army to keep an eye on Elvis.

This hardly instilled confidence in Elvis. Part of him had been hoping it was his old nemesis. At least he knew where she was—fifteen thousand miles away—and that her ravings were basically harmless. Not knowing the person behind the new warning—and the terrifying thought it could be true—was enough to make him a nervous wreck. Elvis stepped up his personal security, seldom going anywhere without at least Red at his side, while the Army also kept an especially close eye on him. But after a month or two, the fear dissipated and the threat felt more remote. Nobody ever heard of a red soldier trying to slip across the border, nor did Elvis ever receive another letter from the anonymous writer. Like a lot of the things Elvis had to deal with, this event had no neat, tidy conclusion. The passing of time merely gave the illusion of security and of yet one more danger passed.

I was at Graceland wading through stacks of fan mail when Vernon called. Normally, he would want to gossip and hear how everything was going at home, but this time his voice was strained.

"Earl, you got to tell the press over there that Elvis has to go into the hospital to get his tonsils out."

"His tonsils? Isn't he a little old for that?"

"You think it's okay to talk?"

Even Vernon was getting paranoid.

"Why wouldn't it be?"

Well, I soon found out why. Elvis had nearly been killed the night before while out on military maneuvers. It had been frigidly cold and Elvis was so frozen, he couldn't think, much less sleep. Probably against regulations, he sneaked away from his troop and walked to where the military vehicles were parked. He climbed in, started the ignition, and turned on the heat. For the first time all night, Elvis felt the chill begin to leave his body. He only meant to stay just long enough to get warm but it was so comfortable, and he was so tired, he fell asleep. Elvis was so exhausted, he didn't notice that exhaust was seeping in from a hole in the floorboard.

It was only a miracle that saved Elvis from dying of carbon monoxide poisoning. One of the other soldiers noticed Elvis was missing and went out looking for him. It was getting close to reveille and he didn't want Elvis to be in hot water for missing it. Beyond that, he was worried because Elvis never wandered off on maneuvers—he was very much a team player who pulled his weight.

The sound of an idling engine caught his attention. When he opened the door to see what was going on, exhaust billowed out and he found Elvis slumped in the seat. He dragged Elvis out and yelled for a medic.

"They woke me up at dawn to tell me Elvis was in the hospital—I ain't stopped shakin' all day. I don' know how he could do somethin' so stupid," Vernon said, his fear coming out as irritation.

"Is he going to be all right?" It's a terribly helpless feeling to get bad news half a world away.

"The doctors say he'll be fine but they want to keep him a day or two just to make sure. But Parker doesn't want this to get out—makes Elvis look kind of foolish. And the Army sure don't want it gettin' out Elvis almost died in one of their cheap trucks.

"They told us all we're not supposed to say anything to anybody. Hell, they'll prob'ly toss me in the brig for tellin' you. Lord, I'll be glad t'get home."

I put out the press release here while the Army

issued their own in Europe to the Armed Forces outlets. By the time everyone heard the news about Elvis's "tonsillectomy," he was out of the hospital. He was still shamefaced about it when he got home the following year.

"It ain't bad enough that I get caught leaving the camp like some sissy 'cause of the cold, but to almost get myself killed doin' it was plain embarrassing. Thank God they didn't want anyone to know. I'd never live it down."

Elvis shook his head. "Man, whatever they say, that's what goes. Nobody tells Uncle Sam what to do. You can't breathe without them knowin' about it. You can't go to the bathroom without askin' first. I never hated anything so much in my life as I have these last two years. If it weren't for having everyone there with me, and meetin' 'Scilla, I'd of died."

Elvis swore as long as he lived, he didn't want to have anything to do with anyone in government ever again. It proved to be a painfully unfulfilled wish.

CHAPTER FOUR

Visions of Doom

Elvis draped the cape over his shoulders and took one last look in the mirror before pulling the sunglasses down over his eyes. Up close, the makeup didn't completely cover his puffy eyes, but it would fool an audience. It was time to put on his stage face and get psyched up to perform. With a conscious effort, Elvis let himself be cajoled into talking and even making some jokes. As he warmed up, the atmosphere in the room noticeably relaxed—he was pulling it together. Some nights, it was a nerve-racking race to see if Elvis could be sobered up in time for the show. His moods swung wildly, depending upon the drug—or combination of drugs—of choice that day. Tonight would go smoothly, backstage at least. Unless some gun-toting wacko was sitting in the audience.

Elvis stood in the wings, shadow boxing, pumping himself up for the nightly tryst with his audience mistress. He kept his head down, trying to ignore the extra security force patrolling nearby. As the time drew near to make his entrance on stage, he could feel adrenaline coursing into his limbs, racing his heart, and clearing his brain. The ache in the pit of his stomach was the same now as it was before stepping up to the tinny microphone at the county fair when he was six years old. Nothing thrilled him with equal parts fear and exhilaration as offering himself up to an audience. Elvis suddenly thought about his first Las Vegas gig back in the fifties. Parker insisted Elvis try to expand his audience beyond the teenage crowd and booked him into the New Frontier Hotel. It was a disaster. So much so that Elvis refused to play Vegas for the next thirteen years. Until his career had turned 180 degrees. Until Parker had mired him in bad Hollywood movies and mediocre album selections, leaving him only Las Vegas with aging tourists in the mood for nostalgia. And maybe one madman bent on destroying him.

A burst of orchestra music jolted Elvis out of his melancholy reverie. A couple of his boys tossed him curious glances, which he deflected with his patented down-home smile. He smiled even more widely when told he could still change his mind and not perform tonight. Then he walked steadily on stage without a beat of hesitation.

Elvis returned home from the Army at emotional loose ends. The encumbrances of military duty and of being stationed halfway around the world had helped him deflect the overwhelming grief of his mother's death during boot camp. Postponing the grief simply magnified its intensity when he walked through the door of Graceland and was greeted by her echoing ghost in the rooms and hallways she once walked.

Elvis also suffered a delayed reaction to Army life. Although he had hated every minute of it with a consuming passion, he had typically kept it tightly bottled up inside. To the casual observer, he had accepted the rigors and authoritarian lifestyle of the service in stride. But once free from its yoke, he vented his anger at having been forced to give up two years of his life and career by lashing out at people at random. Nobody was safe, except perhaps Parker. Elvis kept his hostilities in check with the Colonel, but only out of fear that if Parker had "made" him, Parker could just as easily "break" him.

Elvis was a volatile mix of emotions, and the mental anarchy made clear thinking more difficult than normal for him. The only release he seemed to get was through casual, anonymous, and frequent sex. That's another thing the death of Gladys let loose. When his mama was around, Elvis had to conduct his affairs discreetly. With her watchful, possessive, and disapproving eyes gone, he indulged himself to the point of exhaustion. But even here, it was easy to see that something inside Elvis had changed. His attitude toward women was antagonistic and occasionally emotionally abusive. He treated his "dates" for the night little better than one might a street hooker—which for all intents and purposes was how he saw them. Sex with these one-night stands was often tinged with anger, with a fair dose of paranoia thrown in. But his suspicion of women wasn't confined to groupies. He assumed every woman he dated, whether it be Juliet Prowse or the girl next door, was in some way out to use him—either financially or to get their name in the paper. He thought so little of himself that he couldn't believe anyone else might simply love him for him. That distinction went solely to Gladys, and she took it with her to the grave.

Put everything together and you have one angry, unstable young man setting himself up for a truck-load of potential misery. Which Elvis did.

One of the more curious byproducts of Army life was that it convinced Elvis of the government's omniscience and subtle malevolence. When he told the stories about crossing over into East Germany or the time he almost killed himself with carbon monoxide, his voice filled with a hushed awe at how easy it had been to keep the incidents a secret.

"If they can do that, there prob'ly ain't nothin' they can't do."

He extrapolated that theory onto a number of people, the first and foremost being Parker. The story has been told in detail elsewhere about Elvis foolishly making X-rated home movies with underage girls. For someone who firmly believed in Big Brother, it was a rather daring—and stupid—thing to do. And he paid dearly for it. Although Elvis didn't tell anybody until shortly before his death, and we only have Elvis's word for it, Parker somehow found out about those orgy sessions and managed to confiscate the film, putting Elvis completely under his thumb. Jerry Lee Lewis's career had been ruined for simply marrying an underage cousin. What would porno movies do to Elvis?

In retrospect, it helps explain Elvis's conviction that Parker was spying on him. As time passed, he added more people to the list, but in the beginning it was Parker who haunted Elvis.

"I can't see nobody or get a phone call that he don' somehow know about. He prob'ly even knows when I go to the bathroom. I hate it but I don't know what to do.

"It's got to be somebody here in this house, but what do I do, kick everyone out and shut myself in all alone?"

Elvis once made the mistake of confiding to Vernon, something he seldom did—and for good reason, it appears. Vernon immediately dressed Elvis down and turned the tables on him.

"You ain' got no cause to be accusin' Parker of some low-handed trick. That's jus' your own guilty conscience peekin' through, boy. If you didn't go 'round makin' a spectacle of yourself, you'd have no cause to worry."

Elvis clenched his jaw but walked out of the room without saying another word. He didn't let loose until he had closed himself off in the music room.

"I should know better than to think he'd ever take my side about anything against Parker. And he sits there high and mighty judgin' me—at least I didn' go steal someone's wife."

Elvis was still seething over Vernon's relationship with Dee. Dee had been married to an officer stationed with Elvis in Germany. They started a torrid affair and ultimately Dee left her husband to come back to the States with Vernon.

As soon as her divorce was final, she and Vernon got married; Elvis boycotted the ceremony. He hated his father for not grieving more over Gladys and for finding a "replacement" so soon after her death. Any argument between Elvis and his dad inevitably wound up a discourse on Dee. The sad part was, Dee is a lovely woman and if Elvis had only given her a chance, he would have loved her, too. But the specter of Gladys was just too powerful—as every woman, including Priscilla, eventually discovered.

Adding to his woes was Elvis's own miscues. Shortly after being discharged, Elvis was back in Hollywood filming *G.I. Blues*, a blatant attempt to capitalize on his recent Army stint. The only memorable thing about the film was his costar, Juliet Prowse. She was the kind of woman Elvis had always dreamed about—and felt unworthy of. But Juliet adored Elvis and their affair continued after the movie was done. The only glitch was that Juliet was already romantically linked with Frank Sinatra. Elvis abruptly cut off the relationship after Frank—and two large, brutish "friends"—stopped by in person to chat with him. But even after he refused to take Juliet's calls anymore, Elvis spent months looking over his shoulder.

One night we went out late to grab a cheeseburger. As we pulled out of Graceland, Elvis jerked in the seat and clenched the steering wheel so tight I could see his whitened knuckles in the dark.

"Did you see that?"

"What?"

"In that car back there."

I turned around and saw a lone car parked on the roadside.

"There's someone in it."

"I didn't see anybody."

"That's cause when they saw me lookin', they scrunched down in the seat, hidin'."

Forget pointing out that in the pitch dark, nobody parked a hundred feet away could see where your eyes were looking, or that the security guard was on duty and would notice somebody sitting in a car across from Graceland in the middle of the night. When Elvis got an idea in his head, it was glued there.

"It's got to be one of Sinatra's guys, checkin' up on me. Parker wouldn't be so obvious."

Like Sinatra would. All you could do was let Elvis talk himself out—or in this case, drive himself out. He took every conceivable side road to the hamburger joint to make sure we weren't being followed. Never mind that we were the only car on the street.

We ate in the car but Elvis was too nervous to go home, in case "Sinatra's" car was still there waiting for him. Instead, we took a ride on the outskirts of town, then parked so to admire the stars and pick out the constellations we knew. This was an old game from childhood that Elvis often reverted to when he was feeling anxious or sad. We stayed out until the stars began to dim with the dim brightening that comes on the horizon before dawn. When we drove up to Graceland, it was light—and the suspicious car was gone.

"Guess I outsmarted them this time," Elvis said with grim satisfaction. It wasn't rational but at the time it seemed more eccentric than anything. This evening's paranoia was a psychotic seed that would flourish later in his life under the adverse nurturing of drugs.

In the early sixties, Elvis had already started relying on sleeping pills to a certain extent. He first took them during the days following Gladys's death and found he liked their ability to shut off his mind and let him rest. He didn't use them much at all in the service but when he came home, the pressure of getting back into the flow of being "Elvis Presley"—and the stresses that came with it—sent him scurrying back to his doctor for more. He also added tranquilizers, but in both cases he was still using them as directed and hadn't yet begun abusing the prescriptions.

It's ironic that the very drugs that were supposed to calm him actually made him more unnerved. The rebound effect sleeping pills and tranquilizers had on Elvis was significant. Elvis never liked getting up, but when his sleep was artificially induced, waking up became almost painful. And his mood was as ugly to match. The same was true for the tranquilizers. When one wore off, it left Elvis more edgy than he'd been before taking it. He was stuck in a revolving door that was slowly gaining momentum, and one that nobody but Elvis could stop—and he either couldn't or wouldn't. While it's easy to see the progression looking back, it went virtually unnoticed in the beginning. Even if anybody had tried to intervene, Elvis would have gotten defensive and probably done twice as much.

If any one event sent his paranoia into overdrive and captured his macabre fascination, it happened on November 22, 1963.

Even though he continued to have affairs, Priscilla's presence at Graceland had given him some anchor. His lashing out at people continued, the turnover rate among his hirelings kept rising, and taking pills to help him relax was now habitual, but a reasonable status quo was being maintained. Then President Kennedy was murdered.

Understand that Elvis was one of the most apolitical people you could imagine. To my knowledge, he never once voted in his life and I doubt even he really knew whether he was Republican or Democrat. He barely paid attention to the Kennedy–Nixon debates, nor did he particularly care who won. But when Kennedy was killed, the assassination consumed him.

Elvis sat glued to the TV set, digesting every convoluted report. He had a radio playing softly beside him, in case they had a shred of news the broadcast journalists somehow missed. He was so agitated, he could barely sit still, and so stricken that his face was a sickly gray. He was getting on everyone's nerves, especially Vernon, who muttered,

"If he don' stop pacin', he's gonna be next."

Elvis stayed up late into the night, turning the day's events over and over in his mind.

"Don't you see what this means? It means nobody's safe. If they can kill the President of the United States, there ain't nobody they can't get to. If some Commie really wanted to come over from East Germany and shoot me dead, not even the Army could stop it.

"Everyone always tells me not to worry. But if there ain't nothin' to worry about, how come I need people protectin' me—and how come the President is dead? Nobody on this whole earth is safe. Boom, just like that, and your brains are all over the street."

The first live broadcast of a murder, up close and personal, awed Elvis into near reverence over the ease of violence.

"Did you see Oswald's face, right before he got shot? It's like he was beggin' for someone to help—and they all just stood watchin'. Hangin' him out to dry."

Elvis and a couple of buddies argued back and forth over whether the Dallas police offered him up like a sacrificial lamb, or whether Ruby was an overwrought citizen avenging Kennedy's murder. After they left the room, Elvis shook his head knowingly.

"I don' care what they say, it ain't no accident Oswald's dead. They set him up so he couldn' talk.

You know the police could've stopped it if they wanted to. You just can' trust anybody. People are just out to get you one way or another."

He seemed very sad talking, as if he saw his own doom foretold in Kennedy's. Naturally, in the year following the assassination, with rumors of conspiracy refusing to die, Elvis latched on and became an earnest believer. And he personalized it. It wasn't a matter of "if" someone would try to hurt you; it was simply a matter of "when."

Whether because the country was in such turmoil or because the sixties bubbled toward a boiling point, Elvis's file at the FBI showed less activity than in the fifties. Certainly his swiveling hips suddenly seemed tame compared to the free love and LSD trips being touted by the younger generation. In fact, his act was downright dated.

The sixties even ignited change in the film industry's censorship code. The irony wasn't lost on Elvis.

"They wouldn't let me dance on TV but now it's okay to show people naked and screwing in movies. That ain't right."

As promiscuous as Elvis was, he had a curious double standard. It didn't matter what you did as long as (1) you did it in private and (2) you didn't get caught. But more and more, Elvis felt his privacy, and what little security that came with it, slipping away.

Elvis had a love–hate relationship with the "boys" in his entourage. On one hand, he desperately hated being alone when out and about. Plus,

Elvis enjoyed being lead rooster, head cock of the barnyard. But on the other hand, he basically mistrusted them all, except for Red West and a few others. When his career was new and exciting, having a few bodyguards was a small price to pay for fame. In those days, the boys practically lived at the house and Elvis welcomed them like family. But as his paranoia grew, he began to suspect they were only using him and he came to consider them a necessary evil. With fair regularity, starting in the early sixties, Elvis would fire one or another guy for any number of reasons. Once, when he misplaced a ring, he was convinced he knew who stole it and fired him with no explanation. Even though Elvis found the ring wedged in the headboard of his bed a few days later, he refused to rehire the employee or even to apologize.

"Just 'cause he wasn't guilty this time don't mean he didn't steal from me before."

In all fairness to Elvis, though, he wasn't round-the-clock paranoid or a constant basket of nerves during these years. For the most part, Elvis was a fun-loving, warm, vulnerable man with a good heart. Just because we're concentrating on a certain aspect of his life, I don't want to give the impression he was miserable to be around. But every now and then, irrational ideas erupted from him. Nor was Elvis necessarily always wrong. More than most people know, he had reason to be paranoid because many times he was being robbed blind by some of those who worked for him. Some cash here, a few pieces of jewelry there—it added up. And, it was said, several guys over the years were paid extra by Parker to help "keep an eye" on Elvis for him.

While Parker was his manager, Elvis drew the line at his doorstep. Very seldom was Parker a guest at Graceland except to conduct business. It was his one sanctuary and Elvis guarded it jealously. It was one of the few things concerning Parker that Elvis stood firm on, too. But if the Colonel wanted to find out what was going on behind closed doors, he knew he only had to pay for the information. Other than Red and a few others like Charlie Hodge, none of the celebrated entourage really cared about Elvis—only what they could make off of him. So if Elvis jumped the gun on occasion, or overreacted, it wasn't completely without reason. The real problem was the way Elvis indiscriminately lashed out, attacking the friends who truly did love him in the same breath as the users who didn't. He couldn't discern between the two—drugs surely contributed to his nearsightedness—and that was his fatal error. He slowly but systematically cut off people who had his best interests at heart, turning himself into a sitting duck for the vultures a celebrity is sure to attract.

In the aftermath of the Kennedy assassination, Elvis was more sensitive to any mail that carried a threatening tone, however vague. To a large degree, he still considered the writers of these letters kooks. But on a more primal level, he sincerely believed a kook could make good if he really wanted to. In light of his anxiety over the issue, Vernon and Parker tacitly agreed to keep as much from Elvis as possible.

"Like in the Army, it's on a need-to-know basis," Vernon told me.

Not that Elvis had ever paid too much attention to his fan mail anyway, except to ask for the X-rated letters, but they didn't want to upset him unnecessarily over letters that usually amounted to nothing. Even though Parker and Vernon dismissed the letters as harmless snipes, the FBI was required to take them more seriously.

In January of 1964, a postcard addressed to "Presdient [sic] Elvis Presley, Memphis S, tennessee," was delivered to Graceland(A43–45). On the back in a childlike scrawl was the ominous message:

> You will be next on my list
> 1. Elvis Presley
> 2. Johnny Cash
> 3. Tommy roese
> 4. presdient JBJ
> 5. George C. Walluse

The secretary in charge of sifting through the mail brought the card to Vernon, who shook his head in wonderment.

"Lord, they spell even worse than any of us. Looks like someone was half crocked when they wrote it. I bet . . ."

Then Vernon noticed the postmark and stopped short. The card had been sent from Huntsville, Alabama—Dee's hometown and the place where they had gotten married. More than likely, it was just a curious, funny coincidence. But Vernon didn't see it that way. Suddenly, he was parroting Elvis's paranoia.

"My God, it's prob'ly one of those relations still upset with me and Dee stealin' off together from her husband."

If that were the case, one would think they would be coming after Vernon, not Elvis. But Vernon disagreed.

"Ain't no better way to hurt me than go after Elvis."

Maybe so, but that didn't explain why the writer would also pick on Johnny Cash and the others.

"Just tryin' to throw me off track."

It is interesting that when the shoe was on the other foot and Vernon had even the slightest reason to feel he was a target, he let his imagination run wild—just the thing he always accused Elvis of doing.

The next day Vernon delivered the postcard in person to the Memphis branch of the FBI. He introduced himself and asked that the matter be given the highest priority, and that the Bureau keep him apprised of their investigation.

More than Elvis, what piqued the agent's attention was the reference the "Presdient [sic] JBJ." It was close enough to Lyndon Johnson's initials to warrant concern, cspccially to a country still reeling from the murder of its last commander-in-chief.

For the next two months, the Bureau went through the motions. The Memphis office forwarded copies to the Birmingham division and sent the original to Washington, D.C. for analysis. Vernon religiously called once a week for progress reports, only to be disappointed. After a two-month investigation, the Bureau had no more idea who sent the card than they did on day one. Since Elvis hadn't received any similar correspondence, the Bureau considered it an isolated incident and stashed their reports away in Elvis's secret file (A46–48).

Vernon was duly disappointed. He was convinced the card had something to do with him and was desperate to find out who sent it. Naturally, he neglected to share his suspicions with Dee, since it was someone in her family, albeit unknown, he was accusing. But his brush with potential danger left its mark and it altered his previous critical attitude toward Elvis.

"It might have been addressed to Elvis, but sure as I'm sittin' here, it was meant for my eyes. I never knew how nerve-rackin' somethin' like that could be. No wonder that boy gets so riled up over little things sometimes. You never know if some loony letter writer is waitin' for ya outside somewhere.

"It's enough to make anyone crazy, 'specially someone like Elvis."

As mentioned before, early in his career Elvis was the victim of numerous pranks and hoaxes started by Lord knows who. Most were of the rumor variety; the real Elvis Presley had died and the record company was using a fake or Elvis had been arrested for shooting his mother—the stories were not too unlike the Rod Stewart stomach-pumping tale. Stories like these had died down as Elvis's career evened out and settled into a certain status quo—until the most elaborate ruse surfaced in 1968 (A49–52).

In September of that year, Elvis's aunt Lorraine Smith received a frightening call. An unidentified man claiming to be from the Manning-Dunn Funeral Home in Louisville, Kentucky, telephoned to say that Elvis had been killed in a plane crash on the outskirts of town and that his body was interred in their morgue.

Lorraine and her husband, Travis—Gladys's brother—lived in a small cottage on the back grounds of Graceland in exchange for doing various work. Travis was a gate guard and Lorraine helped in the house. They were both simple people unaccustomed to the complexities of celebrity existence. So it didn't occur to Lorraine that the call might be a cruel joke. She took it at face value and hung up the phone in a state of shock. Grief set in at once and she sank into a nearby chair sobbing over the tragic "accident." She was so upset, it took her a few minutes to call down to the gate for Travis and even then she could barely get the words out.

Travis ran to the cottage to see what was wrong, and when he heard the news, he too was stunned into inertia. Finally, he pulled himself together to go break the news to his brother-in-law.

Vernon was startled at how bad Travis looked. "Better lay off the bottle, Trav," he joked.

When Travis stuttered out the news, Vernon was taken aback momentarily, but only by its blatant lack of credibility.

"For Christ sake, Trav, Elvis is fine—I jus' talked to him no more than five minutes ago. He ain' been anywhere near Louisville. It's jus' some goddam kook havin' fun. No need to go and get all worked up."

Travis was so relieved, he needed a shot of whiskey to calm his nerves—all the while forgetting poor Lorraine grief-stricken back at the cottage. After letting the liquor relax him, Travis went back home and told Lorraine it was all a prank. Bolstered by his liquid pick-me-up, Travis called the Louisville Funeral Home and gave them a piece of his mind.

The receptionist at Mann-Dunning must have thought there was a lunatic on the other end of the line.

"Elvis Presley here? Is this some kind of joke?"

Travis's bravado turned to confusion. "Well, ain't that what you jus' called to tell us?"

"Called who? Who are you?"

Travis finally started from the beginning and the funeral home employee eventually understood—all too well. Mann-Dunning had recently been beset with a number of crank calls. Several times they had received calls to pick up recently deceased bodies at specific locations, only to arrive and discover they had been sent on a wild goose chase. At first glance, it seemed that this was just another in that series.

The FBI wasn't so sure. Because Lorraine had received a phone call across state lines, local authorities informed the FBI of their investigation. Upon closer examination, there were important differences in the pranks. First, the calls plaguing Mann-Dunning had them racing around town in search of nonexistent corpses, all within the city limits of Louisville. The call to Lorraine was from out of state and of a distressing nature. Also, in this case Mann-Dunning had not been contacted. It was a subtle but important difference. And there was this intriguing question—how did the caller get the Smiths' phone number, which was actually listed in Elvis's name?

As fortune would have it, an operator had seized the line used for the first call because she suspected the caller might be attempting to defraud the phone company by giving a false telephone number from the phone he was using. The last four digits of the number he gave were designated for commercial pay phones only. So the FBI discovered the first call had been placed outside a convenience store in Louisville. But after further investigation, they hadn't found anyone with any information as to who used the phone to call the Smiths. Unless the caller phoned again, there wasn't much authorities could do except keep the operators on alert.

The next day, they got lucky. Lorraine picked up the phone to hear the same man's voice telling her a terrible accident had befallen Elvis. She kept him on the line as long as she could, until the caller got suspicious and abruptly hung up. But he was too late. The FBI was able to trace the call to a phone in Louisville registered to a middle-aged woman. When the operator dialed the traced number, the woman answered and told the operator she had just returned home, flatly denying any involvement with crank calls. She also claimed her back window had recently been broken, making it easy enough for anyone to sneak into her house to use the phone. Since it was a man who apparently called, the lady was questioned about any relationships she might be involved in. She admitted she lived with a boyfriend, an occasional itinerant farmer currently working out of state and unreachable.

Despite intense grilling, she held firm to her story. The Louisville police confirmed a window in the back door was broken, indeed giving anyone easy enough access to the house and phone. Other than tracing the call back to her residence, authorities had no proof—certainly nothing to back up a felony charge of phone harassment. So the Louisville branch made a final report to the Washington Bureau and came to the conclusion the call was a hoax perpetrated at the expense of the funeral home. End of story, sort of.

The question that still nagged was how the caller knew the Smiths' unlisted phone number. And why call them instead of the main house? Something didn't add up and Vernon smelled a rat. Or maybe it was just a case of "It takes one to know one."

A few days after authorities closed the investigation, Vernon strolled down to the front gate to chat with his brother-in-law. As he was leaving, Vernon invited Travis up to the house after his shift for a drink, which he readily accepted. Travis was an extremely likable fellow with a definite eye for the ladies. He was actually a wonderful choice to work down at the gate because he enjoyed talking to the people who would gather out in front hoping to catch a glimpse of Elvis. Sometimes Travis did more than just talk and this is what Vernon wanted to hear about.

Late that afternoon they sat on the porch, braced against the chilly air by the spreading warmth of the bottle they shared. Once he had Travis relaxed, Vernon prodded him to own up.

"Come on, Trav, how did anybody come to have your number, lest you gave it to 'em? Come on, you can tell me."

Travis stared guiltily into the bottle then took a long, sputtering swallow.

"Aw, you know how it is, Vern—all those ladies down there. I know the only reason they're hikin' their skirts up at me is 'cause I know Elvis, but hell, what's the diff'rence? Sometimes I take one or two out for a drink and tell 'em stories 'bout Elvis, you know."

Vernon nodded because he did know. After Gladys died and he went back to Texas with Elvis for boot camp, he had taken plenty of ladies out, thanks to his son. If they couldn't get the real thing, many were quite happy to take the next best, or third best, thing.

"Had some trouble with one, huh?"

Travis nodded morosely. "I didn't mean for it to be anything, it just sort of got outa hand 'fore I knew it. I told her I was married and that it was jus' s'pposed to be friendly, you know? I mean, I knew she was jus' visiting in town and would be leavin' and thought we saw things the same way."

"Was she from Louisville?" Vernon asked.

"I swear, I don't know for sure. Coulda been, maybe."

"You know how much trouble you caused—not jus' to poor Lorraine who got scared half to death, but to Elvis?"

"But Vern, we don't know for sure who it was—the police said it had to do with the funeral parlor, you said."

"That's only 'cause they couldn' pin it on anyone else. You know they hate not havin' an answer and havin' to admit they're stumped. But considerin' it was your number got called, I think it's pretty clear."

Vernon was firm but quietly so. Travis looked so miserable. Vernon supposed there was the chance it didn't have anything to do with Travis's dalliance, but his gut told him otherwise.

"I think you best go talk to Elvis 'bout this."

"Why?" Travis's voice was suddenly fearful. "I don' want him mad at me."

"Jus' to put his mind at rest—you have no idea how these things eat at him."

Rather than put it off—and bolstered by the liquor—Travis trudged off like one of the condemned to face his nephew. Elvis listened to his confession with a mixture of amusement and pity, but kept an even disposition while Travis was there. He thumped his uncle on the back gently and thanked him for telling him. Later, Elvis had to smile over the revelation that Travis was conducting an occasional side romance on the job.

"I didn't think ol' Trav had it in him. God help him if Lorraine finds out—she'll skin his hide and hang it outside the cottage for all the world to see."

Elvis also thought it had been mean of Vernon to make Travis come hat in pitiful hand.

"Vernon ain' no better. I've seen him do the same thing. He coulda told me himself instead of sending Trav in, half crawling. He was prob'ly just jealous that anyone but him was workin' the gate. He can really be a son of a bitch at times."

Travis kept a very low profile for a while after that, no doubt terrified Lorraine would somehow get wind of it. But neither Vernon nor Elvis brought it up again. As far as Elvis was concerned, it was the least of his worries and besides, it was a relief to know he hadn't been the target again. Vernon's assessment of Elvis had been painfully on the mark. Little by little, each crackpot Elvis encountered left a long-festering wound. While this most recent incident wasn't inherently any more troublesome than most—probably because from the outset it was about him, not directed at him—it still weighed on his mind. When he first heard about the call, Elvis merely shook his head.

"Where do they come up with this stuff? It would be different if it was somebody I knew, they might have cause to hassle me, but not a perfect stranger. It's depressing."

A lot of things depressed Elvis as the sixties wound to a close. While there were a few strident conservatives (A53) who had never forgiven Elvis his risque dance moves of the fifties, the days of his white-hot popularity and controversial appeal seemed a world away in light of the cultural revolution consuming America. Elvis wallowed in self-pity over a career he felt had been curtailed by a sudden and drastic change in our country. The irony, of course, is that many credit him with heralding the change. The power of his sexuality and sensuality signaled the beginning of the end for the old guard and its Victorian mores. Unfortunately for Elvis, the vanguard stallion was put out to pasture before his time. Not that Elvis lacked fans—his records still sold and the number of people gathering in front of Graceland remained constant. But they weren't the hormone-intensive ingenues of years past. More and more they tended to be young mothers and middle-aged housewives looking to recapture their youth, the springtime of their lives embodied in Elvis.

Elvis was caught in a vortex on other sides as well. The box office draw of his movies, which he put down as travelogues, dwindled as Hollywood changed gears and opted for a grittier reality. *Midnight Cowboy* left Elvis slack jawed and offended.

"I can't believe they made a picture 'bout queers—little kids could get in and see that. It ain't right."

The overt sexuality of films also made it clear to

Elvis his travelogues were as dated as his swiveling hips and lacquered black hair. But change terrified Elvis and his self-doubts bubbled to the surface at the thought of moving ahead with the times. It was more comfortable to play it safe and stay with what got him there, even if it meant resigning himself to nostalgia.

Elvis's fear was natural but it could have been balanced with encouragement and a buildup of his confidence. But none was forthcoming. Whatever interest Elvis expressed in taking on a more challenging acting role, Parker squashed. He subtly convinced Elvis he had neither the range nor the talent to stretch as an actor. "Travelogues" were the only things he was good enough for.

Elvis also felt constricted musically. By and large he hated the songs picked for him to sing but felt powerless to fight over it. He would comply, then throw heaving tantrums behind closed doors trying to exorcise his frustration and fury. He also turned more and more to tranquilizers and downers of all kinds to soothe his agitated soul.

"I thought when I got famous I'd be able to do all the things I ever wanted, but I ain't no better off than if I'd of bought me a gas station back in Tupelo."

He felt trapped emotionally as well as physically. But if nothing was going the way it was supposed to it was only because Elvis still hadn't grasped the basic truth of life—he had to take control of his own life and not leave it in the hands of others. But he had so little confidence, and was so conditioned to listen to Parker, and to a lesser extent Vernon, he let himself be led along like a sacrificial lamb.

Adding to Elvis's angst was a growing distrust of his hired help. On several occasions he mentioned his personal mail was being tampered with.

"Not fan mail, my mail. I swear, Earl, I go to open letters and can see plain as day they've already been opened then resealed."

"Mail from who?"

"Lots of people, and not just ladies if that's what you're thinkin'. And I know 'Scilla would never think of such a thing, if that's what you're thinkin', too. It's got to be Parker or one of the boys he's hired to spy on me. I don' know—maybe even the police."

When asked why the police would be opening his mail, Elvis shrugged and turned evasive.

"Tryin' to catch me at something, anything—to make me look bad."

"You got somethin' to be guilty about?"

" 'Course not. I guess it's easier to think the police are spying on you than the guys who say they're your friends. I know Parker is behind it—he's afraid I'm gonna up and fire him. And I'm gonna, as soon as the time's right. I promise."

His belief in the power of conspiracy had been cemented forever in June of 1968 when Robert Kennedy was shot and killed at the Ambassador Hotel in Los Angeles. Elvis simply could not accept it was a tragic coincidence that both brothers were dead. And again, the murder of a very protected public figure filled him with tingling personal dread.

"When they decide they wanna come get you, there's no stoppin' 'em."

Adding to his horror was his conviction the conspiracy included Kennedy enemies within our government.

"How else could they get away with it so easily this time? The poor guy was set up—he didn't have a chance. He pissed off the wrong people and paid for it. It was probably someone closest to him that set him up," Elvis said, devoutly subscribing to the Judas theory.

To say he was personalizing it would be an understatement. He felt so vulnerable to people and events beyond his control he couldn't help but see through blood-colored glasses. There was little to offer him relief or salvation. He kept Priscilla on such a high pedestal as to make her unreachable from his lowly grasp, isolating himself from one of the few people who might have made a difference. He treated her as an icon instead of a warm, living being needing love as much as he did. His paranoia built a wall between them as well, condemning Priscilla to her own solitary confinement.

Drugs, random and sometimes callous sex, and the love of his fans were the fuels on which Elvis ran. Those and fear. Fear of being a has-been, fear of his boys spying on him, fear of Parker totally controlling and ruining what career he had left, fear of impotence, fear of getting murdered, fear of getting caught.

The surest sign Elvis's drug problem was starting to get the upper hand was his vain attempt to deny and hide it. More than once, Vernon made a feeble attempt to confront Elvis, only to hear sincere-sounding protests.

"Aw, I'm okay. You know I've had trouble sleepin' ever since mama passed away. And sometimes I jus' need somethin' to steady my nerves. No diff'rent than you taking a few shots after dinner."

"I'd hate for people to think you was some kind of druggie—you could kiss your career goodbye, then."

Regardless of what line he gave Vernon, Elvis did feel guilty. Not enough to stop using drugs but enough to worry about getting caught. He knew the power and omnipotence authorities could muster—if they wanted to get him they would. He had to go out of his way to stay on their good side and divert any suspicion. Suddenly, Elvis became a champion of the police and the FBI, extolling their virtues to all who'd listen. His simple mind didn't see that such sermons merely attracted more attention, bemusement, and suspicion. All he knew was that if he ever got busted, his fans would never forgive him. They would abandon him, leaving him truly alone.

While drugs and sex offered temporary release from his pain and fear, only the love of an audience gave his soul enough sustenance to survive. He would do whatever it took to keep them happy—even risk his life if need be.

CHAPTER FIVE

Death Threats and Legal Headaches

Man, he felt good. No, better than good—he felt GREAT. Everything was clicking into place this Saturday night, in that rhythm that put the audience in the palm of your hand. His body ached from lack of sleep and too many cheeseburgers, fries, and Pepsis, but it was a good hurt. No, it was a GREAT hurt. The sweat pouring off his forehead stung his eyes. In the audience, women probably assumed he was batting lazy bedroom eyes instead of trying to see through the sweat. Elvis laughed at the thought, feeling downright giddy. He hadn't expected tonight to be so right on. But he learned a long time ago you never knew for sure how it would go on stage, how the audience would react, whether they would be flirtatious or hard-to-get lovers. Tonight, they had opened wide for him and he embraced them with all he had. No matter how many times he got up on stage, the thrill never waned. This was the most addictive drug of all—if they could bottle this feeling, everyone would be a junkie. And he wouldn't have to try to duplicate the sensation off-stage, where just waking up could cause a stab of pain in your heart.

Elvis was so wrapped up in his performance, he barely noticed the watchful, wary men stationed in the showroom, their bodies taut with tension. Hidden by the shadows, their eyes scanned the room, examining each face, looking for some clue that might give away the face of a killer.

The lights went down as Elvis eased into a ballad. Leaning back on the stool, he let the darkness caress him and made every man and woman in the room feel he was singing directly to them. Elvis knew he was attractive to men and intentionally seduced them along with the women. It was a private power game he loved playing because he was in direct control of its outcome. Whatever purity his voice had lost over the years was more than compensated for by the poignant richness in feeling it had gained. The pain and longing was real, transformed into musical pleas that offered a glimpse into his troubled and needy soul. It was that "little boy lost" quality that grabbed his fans by the heart. He made them want to take him home and tuck him in, not to mention one or two less innocent activities. For those who "got" Elvis, it was a devastating combination.

When the lights came back up, Elvis strolled the stage as he sang the next song. Out of long habit, he cruised the audience, looking for a pretty face that might catch his fancy. He hated sleeping alone. And tonight he felt strong, up for a second performance after this one was over. Sometimes he was too worn out to face the challenge. Even though they didn't admit it, he knew every woman he slept with expected to see stars. Half the time he was lucky to get it up at all—thank God for Doc's bottle of instant energy. But tonight he didn't need any help and he scanned the audience with prurient intent. Hell, he felt so good, maybe he'd find him two girls and make them perform for him.

Elvis's mind raced along on its own course, while his body sang and performed to a slightly different beat. When it was good on stage, that's how it was. He didn't think about what he was doing, it just came naturally, leaving his mind to free-fall, except when it came time to talk them up a bit. During a brief lull in the music, he made small talk, making eye contact with two young ladies in particular. It looked like they were together, which made it that much better. Everything was going his way tonight. He turned around to signal his band to start the music when suddenly a man stood dead center in the audience and called out, "Hey, Elvis."

Elvis froze and the sweat on his body chilled and made him shake. He had been so high, he'd actually forgotten. Before the guards could make their way to where the man stood, Elvis slowly turned to face the executioner, his shoulders slumped in sad, expectant resignation.

Elvis was not sorry to say goodbye to the sixties and hello to the seventies. The birth of the new decade filled him with momentary hope of a new beginning in his own life. It was time for a change—to get out of the rut swallowing him up. Everything was out of synch—his singing career, his films, his health, even his marriage. Elvis knew his relationship with Priscilla could be better but he didn't know how to improve it. He had kept her on a pedestal for so long, he couldn't truly relate to her as a flesh-and-blood woman, if he ever had. He wanted to start over on so many fronts but didn't know how.

"I wish I could just go away for a while and think things through. It's hard to keep my thoughts with so many people talking at me and tellin' me what to do," he complained.

"Maybe I'll just go by myself to Hawaii and hole up there until I don't feel so tired anymore. Take 'Scilla and Lisa Marie so we can jus' be by ourselves. Away from everyone."

Disappearing was a favorite fantasy, but one that nobody ever believed Elvis would make reality. His only escape was his daydreams and the numbing effects of drugs. His rosier outlook upon entering the seventies faded within a matter of weeks as Elvis's continued inability to make any concrete changes depressed his spirit. The decades marched on but Elvis could only stand and watch the parade go by without him.

The 1970s proved to be no panacea for Elvis and his career. No string of hits to catapult him back to the top of the charts on a consistent basis materialized, nor did Hollywood offer him a script that could breathe life into his quaintly stereotyped movie image. With the other areas withering, live performances became the necessary cornerstone of his career. The rigors and stresses of living out of a suitcase on the road on a long multicity tour were beyond Elvis now, so he was left with painfully few options. Financially, there was really only one viable answer—the Vegas–Tahoe circuit. Elvis resisted at first but finally agreed to end his thirteen-year boycott of Las Vegas. The bad aftertaste of the ridicule he suffered during his first disastrous engagement at the New Frontier in 1956 had never been rinsed clean. So what that he had earned $12,500 a week for a month-long gig? It had been the wrong kind of crowd. He played to half-empty rooms. Those fans who didn't walk out sat listlessly, anxious for the final song. So this is the new phenom—nobody got it. As if that memory weren't painful enough, even the landscape depressed him—colorless, humorless, arid flatness filled with slick high rollers with loud laughs and unsmiling eyes. All heat and no warmth. It was a place where a soul could die of thirst, a place where nothing could ever happen. But it was all Elvis had. Besides that, Parker loved Vegas—and all the perks he managed to finagle for himself. The Colonel had a weakness for gambling and loved being seen as a high roller himself. Beyond what Vegas meant for Elvis's flagging career, it was where Parker himself didn't mind being.

Initially, Las Vegas was not the last stop before hell Elvis anticipated. While still a safe haven for the polyester-clad tourist reveling in an adult Disneyland atmosphere, it had changed. There were more hotels and more emphasis on glamour over glitz—although glitz still won out hands down. In a way, that actually suited Elvis better. His flamboyant taste in clothes and personal style lent itself more readily to a velveteen mentality. Still in all, it was hardly his favorite place on earth and the only thing that made it bearable was how enthusiastically his showroom audience embraced him.

His naysaying aside, Elvis enjoyed a certain stature in Las Vegas he hadn't commanded in a while. In a way, he was caught in a time warp, playing to audiences composed mostly of his original fan peer group. The faces were more weathered and the waistlines were thicker, but the adoration still flickered through. They were adults in a gambling playground reliving the sweet memories of another day. It was a winning combination—much to Elvis's chagrin. While he thrived on performing regularly, he felt himself being drawn into a career quagmire that terrified him. This was an okay *temporary* situation, but he didn't want it to be his final resting ground. He had so much more to offer if only people would let him. He dwelled on his cursed quandary during the interminable days and sought to quiet his raging thoughts with drugs.

Like a lot of addicts, Elvis continually devised ways to fool himself. Since the drugs he took were prescribed, it was OK. He was under "doctor's orders" and therefore not guilty of anything. At least that's what he told himself, but I know deep down he never really believed it. At the core, he was ashamed of how he was throwing away his health and youth, but he was too weak to confront the problem head on. He hoped that if he ignored it, somehow everything would eventually work itself out.

Being ensconced in the middle of nowhere gave Elvis a false sense of security that his isolation meant (1) his behavior was under less scrutiny and (2) his personal safety was greater. Neither belief was true.

It seemed that every time Elvis turned around, he was embroiled in a lawsuit of one kind or another. What was particularly frustrating was that although he was named a defendant in a case, half the time he had been nowhere near whatever event had transpired. At least twice Elvis was sued over car accidents one of his boys was involved in. In one case, the driver of the other car was killed and Elvis, even though innocent of any wrongdoing, was deeply troubled by it.

"Even though I wasn't drivin', it's still my car. Maybe I shouldn't let anybody but me drive my cars anymore. Maybe sometimes those guys get carried away showin' off a nice car and don't pay enough attention to what they're doin'. If I was drivin', it probably would of never happened."

Being responsible for people in his employ was bad enough, but Elvis sometimes couldn't keep himself out of trouble, either. In the summer of 1970, a woman named Patricia Parker—no relation to Elvis's manager, Colonel Tom Parker—filed a paternity suit against Elvis in Los Angeles Superior Court. At the time she was approximately seven months pregnant. Parker claimed she had had a brief affair with Elvis in Las Vegas the previous

January and that she had gotten pregnant as a result.

Elvis, naturally, swore up and down he had never slept with Parker. In court documents, Elvis's attorney claimed Elvis had met Parker just once as a fan at the Las Vegas International Hotel and that the only contact he ever had with her was to pose for a photograph. But Parker was determined and was pursuing Elvis doggedly in court, pushing to have him take a blood test to help determine her unborn baby's paternity.

Elvis never admitted one way or another to me whether or not he had ever really slept with Patricia, although I will admit it wasn't unusual for him to pick out some lucky female fan for an afternoon or evening's diversion. But even if he did have a one or more night stand with her, it still doesn't mean the baby was his. Elvis was a wealthy, internationally famous star and more than one woman tried to get him to admit being the father of her baby.

Although Elvis never publicly ackowledged any illegitimate children, he apparently suspected he may have fathered more children than Lisa Marie. In his will, he mentions other "lawful issue," which seems to indicate Elvis was making provisions for any other child who might be his. While nobody other than Lisa Marie has yet been recognized as a legal Presley heir, the inclusion of his other lawful issue phrase keeps the door for such a possibility open.

Guilty or innocent, the looming court battle cast

a pall over Elvis, although he did his best to believe his attorney, Gregory Hookstratten, who assured him the case would quickly resolve itself and ultimately go away. He was still on edge over the paternity suit in August of 1970 when he suddenly found himself in the middle of a more ominous threat than any before it (A100–108).

In the late afternoon of August 27, an anonymous caller phoned Colonel Parker's Vegas office and left a brief, chilling message before hanging up: Elvis was going to be kidnapped that weekend (A54). The voice was apparently that of a man, and it had a distinct southern accent. Nobody knew quite what to do; it was more than likely some crackpot having warped fun. But what if it wasn't? As Parker tended to do, he decided to just sit on it—besides, the weekend was a few days away.

At six-fifteen the following morning, Jane Smith (not her real name) was awakened by the phone. She assumed it was her husband, who was in Las Vegas with Elvis. He'd probably stayed up all night and was calling with beer-soaked levity. Her amused smile faded as soon as she said hello. The voice on the other end told her he had to get in touch with her husband and asked for the phone number where he could be reached.

Jane demanded to know who was calling and why he needed to reach her husband so desperately. The caller refused to give his name but explained that Elvis was going to "get it tomorrow night." When she refused to give a number, the caller hung up.

The call left her unnerved, but she decided to wait a bit before calling her husband—she didn't want to wake him over what was probably some nut's idea of a joke. But less than an hour later, the man called again (A55). This time the warning was more specific and deadly: Elvis was going to be shot by a man with a gun. The gun had a silencer and the would-be killer was a madman. Smith asked why anyone would want to hurt Elvis.

"Elvis done him wrong about a year ago."

The caller claimed he knew who and where the killer was but unless he was paid $50,000, he would let the fatal scheme be carried out. The caller pointed out that he was doing Elvis a favor, after all, so why shouldn't he get compensated for it?

Smith kept the conversation going, hoping to glean more information. It struck her as curious that in the course of their talk, it became clear the caller knew her husband. But before long, the caller got impatient, demanded payment one last time, said he would call back at noon, and hung up. Jane immediately called her husband, who in turn called Colonel Parker. Faced with this new information, he had no choice but to bring in the police. But before they could mount much of an investigation the caller phoned Mrs. Smith again at noon (A56).

Sounding more desperate, the man sweetened the pot by revealing he had the license number of the would-be killer's car in addition to the name. According to the mysterious southern voice, the killer was on his way to Las Vegas from Los

Angeles, and he already had reservations for the Saturday night show. He also made it clear that the killer was mentally deranged, possibly as a result of taking too much LSD. All the caller wanted was a token of gratitude—what was $50,000 to Elvis in exchange for his life? Again, the caller abruptly ended the conversation by saying he would call back with details of how to leave him the money.

A little investigation revealed that the caller had phoned other people besides Jane Smith. Two days earlier, a security guard at the International Hotel was phoned by a man calling himself Jim Reeds, who said he had information that Elvis would be kidnapped that night by two other men he happened to meet. The duo claimed they had cooked up the plan during a party they had attended in Elvis's honor prior to this recent Vegas engagement. Reeds claimed he was asked to participate in their scheme. He declined and wanted to alert security to the danger. Reeds hung up before the guard could ask any questions. When asked later, the security man couldn't be sure if the caller had an accent but he said the call sounded to be long distance.

Elvis slumped into a chair when he heard the news. His initial reaction was sad exasperation. "Christ, the kooks even follow me here. There just ain't no place where I can go and not be harassed."

The first thought that ran through nearly everyone's mind was that the threat might have something to do with the paternity suit—an idea that demoralized Elvis even more. While Priscilla had been publicly supportive, Elvis confided that the strain was taking its toll behind closed doors.

"It don' matter that I swear it ain't my child, she just looks at me so hurt. I can see in her eyes it pains her just to look at me. I know if she could, she'd crawl into the ground and not come up for a year. I'm just thankful Lisa Marie's too young to understand what her daddy's goin' through. It jus' never ends, never eases up for me."

What bothered him more about the current threat was how it filtered down to Priscilla and three year-old Lisa Marie, who were living at the house in Beverly Hills. Memphis held no fascination for Priscilla and unless she was there with Elvis, she preferred life on the West Coast. But the tranquility of her life was abruptly shattered with a knock on the door by police. Priscilla and her daughter found themselves with round-the-clock police protection and life was once again a fishbowl.

Authorities reached Patricia Parker's attorney to ask if there was any possibility his client or someone close to her could be involved. With a shrug in his voice, the lawyer said it was possible but since there were no facts to back such an idea up, it remained pure speculation.

While it might have been the easiest solution, it didn't ring true—and Elvis knew it. Even if Parker felt Elvis "had done her wrong" a year ago, a phoned threat was out of character for someone pursuing the case so actively through legal channels. Elvis instinctively sensed it was darker than that.

"I'm worried they'll be so busy following her around, the real killer will slip in right under their noses," Elvis said.

"It ain't safe anywhere anymore. I don't care how many police you have coming in and out, if they want to get me, they will. The only chance I have is to protect myself. I can't depend on anyone else to do it for me. It's me that's got everythin' to lose."

Looking back, Elvis's fascination with firearms should have set warning bells off. While he had grown up familiar with rifles and such, he had never been interested in them the way a lot of southern boys are. Elvis was not one to pick up a gun and go out in search of rabbit to shoot for dinner. Nor was he anti-gun, either—he just didn't think much about firearms one way or another. Until he began spending more and more time in Las Vegas.

Seemingly overnight, Elvis latched onto the security and power afforded by holding a killing weapon in his hand. Considering the other hand was often popping pills, it was a potentially deadly combination—but of course nobody dared suggest it. You don't argue with a man carrying a gun and now Elvis always seemed to have one nearby. He would hold it in his hand and study the detail for hours, taking fake aim at people and things in the room. It drove Vernon crazy.

"Don't you go pointin' that thing at me. One day you're gonna pull the trigger jus' to see what happens. It ain't the toy you seem to think."

It wasn't unusual for Elvis to literally sleep the day away, particularly in Vegas. Molelike, he shied away from the same sun he used to crave just a few years before. The dark was a shield and comfort. But on those days when sleep eluded him, he would pace his hotel suite, anxiety keeping him on the move. Sometimes he would peer out the window and pretend to take practice shots at people he saw walking by.

"See how easy it would be? They'd be walking along and never know what hit 'em. I tell you nobody's safe. Especially someone like me."

As a matter of course, Elvis was normally shielded from the majority of daily nuisances hurled his way. Insulting mail and obscene or harassing phone calls from people who simply didn't like his persona were carefully kept away from him. On one hand, he dismissed these disturbances as coming from "kooks" but on another level, they still hurt. His nearly obsessive need for acceptance left him vulnerable even to anonymous strangers. Everyone knew this and tried to protect Elvis from unnecessary hurt. But something on the scale of this new threat couldn't be swept under the carpet. He had to be told and the potential danger of the situation emphasized.

Elvis sat and listened. When his initial surprise wore off, he reviewed the events in his mind. Guided more by instinct than intellect, the realization hit him that something was off. When the answer came to him, an ache perforated his chest. Elvis forced himself to tune back in to what the others were saying. He shook his head now when the suggestion was made again the calls must be intertwined with the paternity suit.

"How can you be so sure?" one of his boys asked.

"I just am. I can feel it in here. I wish it were just that but it ain't. It's more than that."

When asked what, Elvis shrugged and clammed up. In his heart, he knew the threat wasn't from the outside—it was much closer than that. There was a Judas in his midst—Elvis could almost smell him. How else would someone have known to call Jane Smith and know she had direct access through her husband to Elvis? It was definitely an inside job. Even though he was already sitting down, Elvis suddenly felt lightheaded. Images of the Kennedy brothers flashed through his head and he felt icy-hot pinpricks of stinging fear. Elvis excused himself to go lie down.

His head was pounding and his nerves were short circuiting. He took a tranquilizer to help him calm down—he needed to think. He had always known it would be this way. When the ultimate betrayal came, it would come from within the very group he counted on to keep him safe. That's why he refused to consider canceling any of the shows. What difference would it make? When Elvis talked about this later, he was almost unnervingly philosophical. He held up his dead mother and infant twin brother as examples.

"I learned from them that destiny is gonna find you regardless of how good you are. When it's your time, the Lord's gonna take you. It's not so much the thought of dyin' that bothers me 'cause I know Mama and Jesse'll be waiting for me.

"But what scares me is how dyin' comes about. It ain't supposed to come at the hands of someone close to you. It could be any of 'em. I don't think any of 'em give a damn about me, only the money I give 'em and the girls they can get usin' my name. They're just pretendin' to be something they ain't. I don't know why I don't fire all their asses—I'd feel safer by myself."

But moments of clarity were becoming fewer and farther between for Elvis. Most of the time he felt confused and unsure, unable to stand up and make a firm decision to take the first step toward the control of his own destiny—Especially where Parker was concerned. Somehow, it was long forgotten that Parker worked for Elvis, not the other way around. Any time Elvis made any kind of attempt to take the reins back on his life, Parker knew just the buttons to push that would make Elvis meekly back down and do his manager's bidding once more.

Elvis had a hard time standing up to anyone, though occasionally he did win out. After the series of calls prompted the Beverly Hills police to station officers near the house, Priscilla called to tell Elvis she was coming to Las Vegas to be with him. Elvis told me later that he absolutely did not want her there.

"It's too dangerous. If there is some madman running around wanting to shoot me, I sure as hell don't want 'Scilla and Lisa Marie anywhere nearby.

I told her I'd personally feel better knowin' she was home with the police guardin' her. I mean, it's kinda sweet, but for once I begged her to listen to me. Unless they shoot me, she can come after the weekend is over."

About the only other time Elvis could stand up and be counted on a regular basis was when it came to his fans. Against everyone's advice and pleas, he steadfastly refused to cancel any show, including Saturday's.

"D'you realize some of these people might o' been saving up for a year or more jus' to come and be in Las Vegas and see this show? How can I just not go on 'cause some kook has been makin' phone calls? I won't do that. I can't."

"But what if somethin' goes wrong?" Vernon asked.

"We'll just have to make sure it don't."

Parker wasted no time (A58). Later that same day, with the help of Elvis's attorney, Hookstratten, an off-duty L.A. police officer was hired to be an additional—and armed—bodyguard. He flew to Vegas within hours and by the time Elvis was being prepped for the show, he was outside the door warily watching every person passing by. The officer would stay on duty full time until Elvis finished his engagement, which was scheduled to end September 7.

Saturday arrived hot, dry, and dusty. It was impossible not to dwell on what might happen later that night. Nothing distracted Elvis for long—not the pills he had taken the night before nor the groupie who secretly shared his bed. With all the added security around, that had been tricky but he'd done it. He hated sleeping alone, although he had been glad upon waking to see she was already gone. She was one of the good ones who understood the daylight brought a night's passion to an abrupt close, especially when the place was swarming with security guards.

Later, Elvis admitted he couldn't shake the morbid fascination with what it would feel like to be shot and killed.

"Will it hurt so bad you'd go crazy, or do things just suddenly start getting dark and all far away? I hear you're supposed to see a bright light and people'll be there to help you. What if it's not like that, what if it's just awful and cold and you die and that's it?"

He pushed aside his momentary doubts and latched onto the faith of Gladys. She taught him to believe in a hereafter and he had to. If there wasn't one, he would never see his mama again. That ephemeral reunion was a source of constant solace and longing. To question it was an act of betrayal to Gladys's memory.

Elvis found himself looking at the most ordinary objects in a new light, wondering if it would be the last time he'd get to watch water spray from a faucet or appreciate the softness of a down pillow. He picked up a picture of Lisa Marie and Priscilla and when the thought of not being there for his little girl flashed through his mind, Elvis felt a sharp pang. Lisa Marie gave him a reason to stick around and put off joining his mother and brother waiting for him in heaven.

"If I weren't so dumb, I know I could figure it out," Elvis told me. "I don't know why nobody else can see. They're prob'ly in on it, too. Think about it, Earl, I know I can't always think straight, but it don't add up."

He was right. First, was Elvis going to be kidnapped or killed? The caller presented both options. Second, it was very strange that the caller knew Jane Smith's husband. The Smiths had been friends of the family for years, which meant if the caller knew them, then Elvis probably knew the caller. The southern accent bothered Elvis from the start, because added to the other questions, it pointed in only one direction—the caller was somebody very close to him. Probably from right in his entourage. And the threat was probably a big lie, an elaborate hoax conjured up for one reason and one reason only—to get money out of Elvis.

"If the caller really knew of two guys tryin' to kill me, he'd ask for a damn sight more than $50,000. Even I know that I can come up with that much cash pretty fast, but much more than that would take some wheelin' and dealin'. I know they tie up my money as fast as I can earn it so I can't spend it. And so would people workin' for me. Daddy loves talkin' about my money enough, anybody with ears would know.

"When you look at it that way, and how they just happened to call Jane, it suddenly makes sense, don't it?"

When you least expected it, Elvis could be a shining beacon of sense. But because he'd probably never be able to prove it, he kept his mouth shut except to one or two people. It just meant that if there were traitors in his midst, he'd have to be even more careful and suspicious. He was caught in a catch-22—he needed some security to protect him, he absolutely hated being alone, and yet he distrusted nearly everyone around him. It was an exhausting emotional treadmill that Elvis was powerless to stop.

His conviction that the kidnap-murder threats were an inside job gave Elvis a strange sense of comfort. For the most part, he knew he had little to fear if it was all an elaborate hoax. He chose to ignore the possibility he was wrong and approached the night wearing rose-colored blinders.

Elvis was particularly intense that night on stage and he gave an inspired performance. The adrenaline that must have been working overtime served to kick Elvis into a special gear. At first, the guards stationed strategically in the showroom were rigid with taught nerves, looking for the slightest sign of trouble. As the evening wore on and nothing out of the ordinary happened, and as Elvis took charge on stage, everybody visibly relaxed.

During a break in the music, put in so Elvis could catch his breath—he was pretty out of shape and performing on stage takes more out of you than most people know—Elvis was chatting to the audience and cracking little jokes. As he turned to walk back toward his musicians, a man abruptly stood up in the center of the showroom.

"Hey, Elvis!"

Elvis froze and a curious hush draped the showroom. Before the security men could make their way to where the man stood, Elvis slowly turned around, looking suddenly fatigued—and resigned.

"Yeah?"

"Could you sing 'Suspicious Minds'?"

It took a moment to sink in, then Elvis laughed and laughed.

" 'Suspicious Minds,' of all songs," he said later. "I thought for sure I was a dead man—I even saw myself lying there in a heap. I tell you, Earl, I was never so happy to sing a song in my life. I'd of sung it twice if he'd asked."

And that was that. Elvis finished the performance and got a thunderous ovation, sucking it in like pure oxygen. In his heart, he knew for sure now he'd been right about everything. He was alive to prove it. Not surprisingly to Elvis, the mysterious caller was never heard from again. The Las Vegas and federal authorities kept the investigation open for several more weeks, but when no more threats were received, they dubbed the file inactive and effectively closed the case.

The whole experience served to further isolate Elvis emotionally. Nobody in his family or circle could ever truly understand the strain and terror of being a victim of one's fame—only someone in a similar circumstance would appreciate what Elvis felt he suffered. Elvis's misery longed for company, and this need to commiserate on his lot in life was the basis for his strangest alliance and most secretive friendship, with the notorious Las Vegas recluse—Howard Hughes.

CHAPTER SIX

Elvis and Howard Hughes

The backstage was a bustle of relieved activity, the nervous tension from earlier in the evening dissolving into giddiness. Elvis laughed over and over about the man who shouted out his request, but his good cheer was tinged with a subtle mania. Even though the night had been ultimately uneventful and the threat an apparent false alarm, Elvis was still quietly shaken by his belief the entire incident had been perpetrated by someone within his very own circle of associates.

As the adrenaline from performing wore off, the weight of the week's emotional roller coaster ride finally settled in and anchored itself around Elvis's heart. Suddenly, despite being in the middle of this roomful of people, Elvis felt completely alone—just like a cliche in one of his bad movies. The thought of his dead-in-the-water film career further depressed Elvis. His mind began wandering toward a dangerous mental quicksand that he spent half his time trying to avoid—a black swamp that could swallow him up if he ventured too near. But sometimes it was impossible not to inch closer out of morbid fascination and gaze at the remains of his once-shining self. As far as Elvis was concerned, the days and nights in Las Vegas were indistinguishable from one another and as time slipped by he felt frozen in suspended animation. The rest of the world passed Elvis by while he became further entrenched in Las Vegas, sustaining his career through musical nostalgia. Oh, sure, he still drew crowds, but he wasn't attracting a new generation—Elvis knew he was riding out his career on the coattaiis of a time long gone by and the truth of it hurt. He knew better than to try and talk about it—to the people in his sphere, Elvis had everything anyone could want and more. Any complaint was dismissed as the whining of a self-indulgent star. They just didn't understand. When he was first starting out, Elvis fantasized about having the time and money to party when he wanted with as many women he wanted where he wanted. And for a while it had been fun. Then it inexplicably became a chore. More and more lately, the pills and the women were done out of habit and compulsion, even though neither gave him much—if any—joy or thrill. Elvis looked in the mirror and stared at the people in the room around him. None of them had a clue what he felt inside. They were content to take his smile and bravado at face value, ignoring what his eyes screamed out at them. Elvis was inching ever closer to the brink of the quicksand. He knew if he didn't muster the courage to pull away, it would eventually drown him.

But it was hard. Elvis knew that as the night went on, the old feelings would start and he would dread the thought of sleeping alone. So he would either stay up with his boys until the daylight erased away the terrors of the night or he would take his pick of the never-ending pool of available women willing to share his bed. All he really wanted to do was get in his car and drive until he felt clean again. Away from Parker and his boys and Vernon and all the people who wanted a piece of him in exchange for nothing. It was a comforting vision and one he could lose himself in for hours at a time, a make-believe existence far preferable to the road he was really on.

Elvis suddenly focused on his reflection in the mirror and realized with a start that the room was nearly empty. His faraway, lost gaze had apparently caused the others to give him a wide berth—sometimes he got so wrapped up in his daydream that if interrupted, Elvis would fly into a rage, furious at being dragged back into the reality that was his life. So they learned to leave him alone when he drifted off, making him feel that much more desolate when he returned. Elvis pulled on his cape to leave, only half-listening to the conversations buzzing around him. He didn't feel like going to his room yet so he walked outside, his entourage trailing behind him obediently, the camaraderie mere shadow boxing.

The night air was dry and cold, cutting through his clothes. Even through the garish neon lights spotlighting the night, the stars flickered brightly above Elvis, reminding him of other nights from another life he once knew as a little boy. Staring past the stars towards heaven, Elvis wondered for the thousandth time how differently things might have turned out if his mama were still alive. He could always talk to her and know that whatever happened she would never stop loving him. Elvis had never been alone while she was alive, but since her death nobody had come close to filling the void she left behind. But . . . Elvis picked out a star. It was funny how when he least expected it, somebody had come into his life—as if sent by heaven. Not a buddy like Red West nor a mentor like Parker—but a special, secret friend, a soulmate. Whether by instinct or superstition, Elvis didn't share his new friend with anyone lest he vanish forever. As it was, Elvis always wondered if each good-bye would be the last but tried not to dwell on it. Elvis didn't understand why, but he believed their destinies were inexplicably tied together—mirror images trying to keep from shattering.

Elvis scanned the lights of Las Vegas. Aware his boys were restless, he turned and suggested they all go get some food. He was tired and didn't want to think anymore, didn't want to peek ahead and glimpse where his life and career were headed. It was just too scary to contemplate.

It's hard to say whether Elvis ever fully appreciated the surreal nature of his bizarre connection with Howard Hughes. By the time Elvis returned to Las Vegas in 1969, Hughes seemingly owned half the town and led a mysterious existence on the top floor of the Desert Inn casino hotel. He had long been an enigma and was already immersed in the private paranoias that led him to obsess over "germs" and cease cutting his hair and nails, among other eccentric quirks. A notorious recluse, Hughes refused to go out in public anymore and what contact he had with the outside world was achieved via sporadic phone calls. Although Elvis was anxious to meet Hughes again, their contact was relegated to late-night conversations on the phone, always at Hughes's discretion. While Howard knew how to reach Elvis, the businessman had never given Elvis the same option in return.

According to an actress and former mistress of Howard Hughes, Elvis first met the billionaire in the mid-to-late 1950s, after Hughes arranged a brief, private meeting in Hollywood.

"I know it seems odd that a worldly, sophisticated man like Howard Hughes would be intrigued by someone like Elvis, but he was," says the woman. "Howard found the Elvis phenomenon fascinating and wanted to see what the hoopla was all about firsthand.

"Howard was a strange man who would do the most unpredictable things. But once he set his mind on something, he did it. I had no doubts he would meet Elvis, which is exactly what he set up.

"I remember Elvis as looking so very young—and nervous. He was also incredibly polite, calling Howard 'Mr. Hughes.' What struck Howard most about Elvis, I think, was this aura of simplicity he had about him. Despite being thrust in the spotlight as the country's biggest, hottest new star, Elvis still came across like he was fresh from the hills. Maybe simple isn't the right word—maybe purity is more fitting.

"Considering the people who normally surrounded Howard, Elvis was very much a breath of fresh air. Typically, he asked Elvis to keep their little chat just between them and Elvis promised he would, with the most serious expression in his big eyes. I could tell Howard got the funniest kick out of him, especially when he told Elvis they'd be talking again. But after Elvis left, Howard stared out the window a moment then said, 'I feel sorry for him—he has no idea what's out there.' "

The actress says to her knowledge, that was the only private face-to-face meeting Hughes had with Elvis.

"Although, who ever really knew with Howard? But even though Howard shied away from being in public or seeing people in person, when I knew him he had no aversion calling someone. Out of the blue, he would pick up the phone and touch base with a person who might not have heard from Howard in years. Elvis was one of those people Howard kept in touch with that way."

As Elvis got older and more disillusioned with the trappings of his success, his fascination with Hughes grew. Elvis wondered how someone managed to cope with being Howard Hughes. What Elvis, and most of the world, didn't realize was how much Hughes didn't cope. But it wouldn't be until years later that the billionaire's macabre existence would be uncovered, so to Elvis, the disembodied voice over the phone was a would-be mentor who might help guide him through the jungle of celebrity.

When Elvis became a fixture in Las Vegas, his personal downward spiral was already in steady motion, with drug taking par for the daily course. Even though he hadn't heard from Hughes in years, he wasn't surprised when the phone rang and it was the billionaire on the other end, making the first of what would amount to probably just a handful of calls made over the next couple of years. Mostly Hughes talked and Elvis listened—about the boredom of being unable to move about as freely as he wanted, about the dangers of "subversive" types infiltrating our country, about endless inaccurate stories and speculation about him, when all he wanted was to be left alone. Hughes talked about creating your own world, where you didn't have to answer to others and where you had the freedom to do what you wanted—whether it be choosing what time you could go buy an ice cream cone or deciding whether or not to cut your hair. What rang clear was Hughes's distaste for being answerable to anyone or anything. To Elvis, this was a sermon on how to survive—you had to take control of your own life. From where he stood, Elvis saw Hughes as a man controlling his own destiny, in charge. He didn't have a Colonel Parker telling him what to do—he'd *crush* someone like Parker.

Elvis hung on every word, convinced Hughes embodied some mystical talisman. Besides, he relished the idea of having a secret that nobody else could share in. Unfortunately, it was more a case of the blind leading the blind, sharing skewed views of the world surrounding them. Hughes's obvious paranoia was contagious, especially to someone like Elvis, who was already halfway there. When Hughes advised Elvis to be most wary of those closest to him, it confirmed his suspicions, which were already heightened by his accelerating drug use.

Even though Elvis outwardly deceived himself with the belief that if a pill was prescribed, it wasn't really "taking drugs," it was medicinal, he acted like a guilty man. His drug use was carefully guarded and hidden by those around him and he worried incessantly that his habit might be found out. What would Priscilla or his fans think if they knew? While it was painfully clear to those in his entourage that Elvis was in deep trouble, it was amazing how well the fact was hidden from the public at large. Still, when in a public arena, Elvis often over-compensated out of a fear of being found out. Especially if he was in the presence of someone in an official capacity. More than once Hughes himself had warned Elvis that the government loved to spy on people so they could try to blackmail and control them. Elvis decided the best way to protect himself was to ingratiate himself whenever possible. There was incentive on a deeper level, too—Elvis was desperately trying to assuage the guilt he no doubt felt over squandering his life the way he had been.

In December 1970, Elvis began to fret over Hughes's warning of Big Brother and what would happen to his career if the government decided to brand him a junkie. Not that Elvis admitted to himself he was an abuser, mind you—but the government could use his need for special medication in a twisted way that would make it appear to his fans he was some low-life druggie.

Elvis became virtually obsessed with making the FBI "his own." He started reading anything and everything he could find about Hoover and the Bureau. It was as if he believed that by immersing himself in it, Hoover and the FBI would magically come to accept him in return.

Whether it was a conscious attempt at diversion or a subconscious form of self-protection, Elvis decided he wanted to take a somewhat official anti-drug stand. Close to Christmas of that year, he called Senator George Murphy of California and asked if he would help Elvis arrange a trip to Washington, D.C. to meet both J. Edgar Hoover and Richard Nixon.

"I think it's about time some of the higher-ups find out I'm not who they prob'ly think I am," Elvis said. "I want 'em to know I support what they do all the way."

In fact, there were some things Hoover stood for that Elvis did support. One conversation with Hughes that had particularly hit home concerned the threat of "foreign enemies." Obviously, they were more dangerous than our own governmental Big Brother because when it came to keeping America free for Americans, Elvis was behind Hoover all the way. Beyond that, there was the little matter of Elvis's deep-seated resentment of the musical British Invasion that had effectively pushed him out of the spotlight and into the shadow of nostalgia, although I doubt that he was consciously aware of the connection. In his heart, Elvis considered himself a patriot.

To show you the kind of pull Elvis did have, Senator Murphy agreed to help him. Along with Bill Morris, the former county sheriff of Memphis, Senator Murphy accompanied Elvis and several of his bodyguards on the flight to the nation's capital and once there, arranged an appointment between Elvis and John Ingersoll, Director of the Bureau of Narcotics and Dangerous Drugs, and called both the FBI and the White House to facilitate the meetings Elvis requested.

In December 1970, while waiting for the FBI and White House to open their collective arms to him, Elvis wrote then President Nixon a long, often rambling letter, offering to help in the nation's war on drugs.

Elvis said his sole motive was to help the country and that he could do the most good if Nixon would make him a special drug agent. He goes on to tell Nixon where he is staying in Washington, D.C., what alias he is using and the phone number, promising to stay as long as it takes to be made a special agent. To bolster his case, Elvis boasts that he was named one of the country's Ten Most Outstanding Young Men, and says his communication skills with people will help him reach the nation's youth.

He ends the letter with a chart listing all his various phone numbers in Memphis, Los Angeles, and Palm Springs—and by telling Nixon he has a personal gift for him.

While the Bureau took its time deciding, Murphy had better luck with President Nixon, who in 1970 was trying desperately to gain favor among the nation's younger generation. With the help of the White House media people, it was quickly arranged for Nixon to present Elvis with the badge of an honorary agent of the Bureau of Narcotics and Dangerous Drugs. You would have thought Elvis had been pinned sheriff he was so excited by the prospect—unfortunately the day ultimately left a sour taste in his mouth.

During a brief chat after the badge presentation, Nixon made an off-the-cuff comment to Elvis about his lifestyle, suggesting that perhaps Elvis could do more good by setting a better example. All the old, bad memories of a life full of put-downs flooded back. *Beneath the smiles and ceremonies, they still consider me trash*, he thought. Elvis looked down at the badge before answering with measured control.

"Why don't you stick to what you do best and I'll do what I do best?"

Even though it was a minor thing, Elvis let it engulf his spirit.

"Just 'cause you're the president doesn't give you the right to go around insulting people and bein' disrespectful. I thought people like him were supposed to know how to act. He ain't got manners better than a sharecropper back home. Maybe less."

The FBI visit went slightly better, at least as far as Elvis was concerned. The Bureau saw it more as a dilemma, as made clear in an in-house memo penned by M. A. Jones (A59).

> According to Senator Murphy, Presley, whom he described as being a very sincere young man, is deeply concerned over the narcotics problem in this country and is interested in becoming active in the drive against the use of narcotics, particularly by young people . . .
>
> Presley noted that his rise to prominence in the entertainment field is evidence of what can be accomplished in this country by the poor and the deprived. He said that his relative youth and his background in the entertainment industry has helped him establish rapport with the younger generation and that in gratitude for all this country has done for him he would like to be of service. In this regard he indicated that should the Bureau ever have need of his services, he can be reached under the pseudonym of Colonel Jon Burrows . . . Memphis, Tennessee.

When Elvis decided he'd like to go undercover for the FBI, he also decided he needed an alias.

"No spy goes by his real name—it's too dangerous for others if they ever get caught."

Elvis was so caught up in his burgeoning fantasy that he neglected to consider that fake name or not, half the world would recognize him on sight. He was a grown man playing make-believe, but his proposed playmates were the real thing. And they were not amused.

It's obvious the FBI was not overly thrilled with the proposed meeting. At the bottom of the memo is a brief summary of the FBI's view of Elvis (A59).

> Bufiles reflect that Presley has been the victim in a number of extortion attempts which have been referred to the Bureau. Our files also reflect that he is presently involved in a paternity suit pending in Los Angeles, California, and that during the height of his popularity during the latter part of the 1950s and early 1960s his gyrations while performing were the subject of considerable criticism by the public and comment in the press.

A second memo dated 12-30-70 from M.A. Jones put it more bluntly (A60).

> Presley's sincerity and good intentions notwithstanding he is certainly not the type of individual whom the Director would wish to meet. It is noted at the present time he is wearing his hair down to his shoulders and indulges in the wearing of all sorts of exotic dress. A photograph of Presley clipped from today's "Washington Post" is attached and indicates Presley's personal appearance and manner of dress.

The recommendation by Mr. Jones was for someone at the Bureau to grant Elvis and his party a special tour of the FBI facilities on New Year's Eve while passing along the news that it would not be possible for them to meet Hoover. In truth, the tour was fairly boring, considering the reduced holiday staff. But what it lacked in real drama, Elvis augmented with his fertile imagination.

"I felt like a regular Eliot Ness walking through them halls. Makes you feel important just being there," he would say later.

During the tour, Elvis took the opportunity to do

a bit of grandstanding and let some of his wounds ooze in the process. In his last memo on the subject, Mr. Jones outlined Elvis's professed opinions (A62).

> Presley indicated that he has long been an admirer of Mr. Hoover, and has read material prepared by the Director including "Masters of Deceit, A Study in Communism" as well as "J. Edgar Hoover on Communism." Presley noted that in his opinion no one has ever done as much for his country as has Mr. Hoover, and that he, Presley, considers the Director the "greatest living American" . . .
>
> Presley indicated his long hair and unusual apparel were merely tools of his trade and provided him access to and rapport with many people particularly on college campuses who considered themselves "anti-establishment" . . .
>
> Presley advised that he . . . from time to time is approached by individuals and groups in and outside of the entertainment business whose motives and goals he is convinced are not in the best interests of this country and who seek to have him lend his name to their questionable activities.

Elvis was probably acting out his best performance in years. The subversive groups he left mysteriously unidentified were various peace and antiwar organizations, all very above board and public, who phoned to ask if Elvis would contribute money, time, or public appearances. But the hippies who preached "Make love, not war" were alien to Elvis and in many ways threatening. They represented a changing of the guard, and Elvis stood to be left behind. Like the parents of the youngsters who propelled him to the top, Elvis mistrusted what he didn't understand.

Jones's memo continues:

> Presley indicated that he is of the opinion that the Beatles laid the groundwork for many of the problems we are having with young people by their filthy unkempt appearances and suggestive music while entertaining in this country during the early and middle 1960s. He advised that the Smothers Brothers, Jane Fonda, and other persons in the entertainment industry of their ilk have a lot to answer for in the hereafter for the way they have poisoned young minds by disparaging the United States in their public statements and unsavory activities.

The irony here is so profound as to be farcical. The man who was the corruptor of a generation was casting stones at others who exercised their freedom of speech. When someone pointed out to Elvis, only half-jokingly, that he was going establishment, Elvis got angry.

"That ain't it. All I ever did was sing, but these others are underminin' the country. They got no right doin' that."

To Elvis, freedom of expression was limited to rock-a-billy. He genuinely didn't see how the freedoms were different sides of the same issue and how they nurtured one another.

Before leaving, Elvis took the FBI representative aside, showed him the agent's badge he was carrying in his pocket, and reiterated his offer to be an undercover agent in the battle against drug use.

Or, for that matter, he'd assist them on any mission for which they might need his services. They politely thanked him, then no doubt shut the door behind him with a sigh of relief.

The trip left Elvis vaguely unsettled. It hadn't turned out the way he envisioned and an uneasy tug of melancholy settled in on him during the flight home. Had Elvis been a truly introspective man, he would have seen his pensiveness as an outgrowth of guilt and self-loathing. Regardless of what the others chose to see or think, Elvis knew he was dishonoring himself with hypocrisy. His shame made him shirk away from the truth even more.

By the summer of 1972, Elvis's grip on reality was painfully suspect. His paternity suit with Patricia Parker lingered on and on, with Patricia pursuing the case with suspicious resolution. Even though a court-appointed doctor determined that in his opinion Elvis was not the father, Patricia insisted he was. Blood tests in hand, she scraped together the money to get a second opinion, which in fact supported her claim that Elvis could be the father. Buoyed by this information, Patricia sought to order yet another series of blood tests with a third doctor. Now, science has evolved to the point where a DNA assay can determine paternity with 99.9 percent accuracy, but in the early 1970s, all the tests could indicate was the probability a man was *not* the father.

Naturally, Elvis didn't want to take any more blood tests and through his lawyer fought to have the whole case dismissed. But Parker's refusal to just go away like a nice little lady was a constant source of agitation for Elvis—and a painful reminder of the problems his marriage suffered. Eventually, after four years, the court indeed dismissed Parker's claim and she lacked the money to pursue an appeal. But in 1972, she was still hot on Elvis's trail, adding to his overall misery.

At that point in his life, he was already a man hanging on by the barest of threads when he suffered the emotional blow from which he never truly recovered. Elvis was performing in Las Vegas, the days passing with numbing sameness. Assuming Priscilla was tucked safely away in their Los Angeles home, Elvis conducted business as usual—sleeping away most of the day, rising at dusk, eating, performing, eating, staying up partying with the boys or finding comfort with a one-night stand, then closing the blackout curtains and starting the cycle all over again. Elvis knew his relationship with Priscilla wasn't exactly where he wished it to be, but his way was to ignore the problem and hope it would go away. It never occurred to him that he was at risk of losing his wife altogether. Not until the night she showed up in Vegas unannounced and told Elvis she was leaving him. Just like that.

While most people thought Priscilla particularly cruel in telling Elvis just minutes before he was to perform, it was probably a blessing. Having to go on and entertain his audience gave Elvis a diversion during those first hours of confusion and loss. On stage, he could pass his breaking heart on to his fans—their compassion and response eased his suffering, even if for just fleeting moments. It wasn't until the backstage area finally cleared after the night's performance that the full weight of Priscilla's words caved in on Elvis. He put on a brave front at first, alternating between confidence that she would change her mind and fury at the thought of another man touching her. But inside, his heart was shredding.

Whatever feeble grip Elvis had on controlling his drug dependency was broken when Priscilla left. He really had nobody to answer to anymore. Without a wife or genuine authority figure, Elvis was now free to party and womanize with impunity. Between the drugs and his unhappiness, Elvis became subject to wild mood swings and increasingly irrational thought. Blackouts weren't uncommon, either. He'd wake up in the morning not remembering where or with whom he'd been the night before. Money and jewelry turned up missing with alarming regularity. While those around him claimed Elvis must have lost the items, in his heart he believed they were picking him clean, assuming he wouldn't remember. The agony of it was, he didn't.

One morning, however, Elvis nearly turned his Las Vegas suite upside down with rage. One of his favorite rings was missing and somehow, Elvis remembered who had come into his room. He tore through the suite, screaming the man's name, only to discover he was nowhere to be found. Elvis ordered everyone there to find him, no matter what.

Within a short time, Elvis was told the guy was at the airport, preparing to catch a flight. No doubt someone had warned the fellow the gig was up. Elvis jumped into his car and broke every speed limit driving to the airport, but he arrived seconds too late—the plane had just taxied onto the runway. In another show of amazing pull, Elvis called the head of security and told him why he wanted the plane brought back. A few minutes later, the plane was back at the terminal and Elvis's terrified former employee was being escorted off by airport personnel. After cooling down and getting back his jewelry, Elvis decided not to press charges but told the guys still working for him that the next time, he would.

All the incident did was make the other guys who tended to lift cash and jewelry that much more careful. Elvis was simply outnumbered. The obvious question is why didn't he just fire everyone and start all over.

"Different faces, same result," he'd say, shrugging. "Half the time I feel like I pay those guys to keep them from completely robbin' me blind."

Because of his debilitating lack of self-confidence, Elvis absolutely had to have his entourage, even though it came at such a huge cost. The parallel here to Hughes is obvious—and quite sad.

While Elvis normally was able to pull it together to perform, some nights were exercises in Russian roulette. More than once Elvis nearly started a riot by offering the audience some jewelry or scarves.

"Hey, y'all in back—why dontcha come on down in front so you can get a little, too?"

Afterward he would laugh at how they all came running, evidently oblivious to the danger he had caused. On a couple of occasions, people were hurt, but they were quietly taken care of so as to preclude any nasty public lawsuit.

Elvis nearly gave the management of the Las Vegas Hilton Hotel a heart attack after he told an audience in a conspiratorial whisper that his black backup singers' breath smelled of catfish. These were the ramblings of a mind poisoned and sodden with chemicals. Never in his life had Elvis been prejudiced—nor do I believe he really was then. Part of it might have been a naughty boy trying to get a rise out of people, but more than anything, it was a tormented scream for help.

The resentment of other celebrities he had shown when dissecting the Beatles to the FBI official got worse. He would blast everyone from Robert Goulet to Pat Boone to the Rolling Stones to the current crop of country stars—anybody whose career was basking in the sun seen only at the top. Quite frankly, anyone who wasn't relegated to playing Las Vegas. It is very telling that neither Parker nor Vernon made any honest effort to step in and force Elvis into sobriety. Apparently, they liked him just the way he was—malleable, vulnerable, and weak.

The more out of control Elvis became, the wilder many in his entourage got—a grown-up, desert version of *Lord of the Flies*. On several occasions, people claimed they had been attacked for no apparent reason by men in Elvis's employ. Sometimes the accusations were ignored and other times men were effectively paid off. In at least one instance, Elvis found himself a defendant in yet another lawsuit when four men filed a civil complaint for damages after Elvis and several of his boys allegedly beat them up.

Not surprisingly, Elvis flew into a rage. This one particular thing—his belief that everyone wanted to take advantage of him because of his money—festered like few others. Second only to the frustration of not being able to live a normal life and having to be a prisoner in his own home, this was something he felt only Hughes had truly understood. They had commiserated with one another about the leeches that bellied up to them or sought them out. Life was a never-ending struggle to protect yourself from those who wanted to share a piece of your action. Everything Howard had talked about was coming true—it was as if Hughes had gazed into a crystal ball and could foresee events in Elvis's life before they happened.

As in many of the other lawsuits brought against Elvis, the attempt by Kenneth MacKenzie, Roberto MacKenzie, Mario Martinez, and Marcelo Elias to receive damages fizzled out. And for a common reason—the plaintiffs ran out of money. It is the ace in the hole of the wealthy that often, they can simply outlast the other party until the finances are dried up. But even though the legal suit came to naught, the underlying forces that allowed it to happen in the first place swirled with ever-greater velocity. Elvis was not in full control of his faculties—too many days and nights were consumed and tossed aside in a drug-induced haze. This is not to say Elvis never had a lucid or sober moment—he did. Nor is it to say his personality was only that of an embittered man—it wasn't. Elvis still had days when he laughed and felt hopeful or optimistic. He was still generous and tender. He looked forward to visits with Lisa Marie and always got himself together for them. In addition to the numerous one-night stands he still pursued, he also courted special girls and treated them kindly, showering them with gifts and attentions while the affair lasted. But the good traits and qualities were often overshadowed by his dependency on drugs because of how severely it handicapped him emotionally and mentally. The insidious ripple effects of long-term drug abuse continued to erode his personality even on days when he left the pill bottles unopened.

By the mid-1970s, Elvis felt anchorless. His divorce from Priscilla was final and it was obvious she would never come back. His last shot at a real movie career had been torpedoed by Parker when he negotiated Elvis right out of costarring with Barbra Streisand in the *A Star is Born* remake. He wanted to be rid of Parker but didn't know how to go about it. His boys couldn't be trusted and he knew instinctively he had lost Hughes.

Elvis had followed the Clifford Irving story with intense interest. Regardless of what anybody said, Elvis believed Irving, based on his own strange dealings with Hughes. Maybe Howard had been bored and simply set the guy up just for sport. Or maybe he had warmed to the idea of telling his life story then just as suddenly cooled to it. Elvis didn't know, but suspected Irving had been a fall guy of some sort. The one thing Elvis did know is that he never heard from Hughes again after the Irving debacle. The nighttime phones were silent and he knew they would continue to be. Like a kid who suddenly learns there is no Santa Claus, Elvis felt mournfully bereft. His secret friendship was gone. He knew they had been an odd couple but they shared enough common ground—not the least of which was their paranoia—to bridge the cultural gaps. Elvis had felt so honored to be singled out that it made the end that much more sad.

Howard Hughes died in 1976, his death shrouded in even more mystery than his life. Now that the recluse was dead, there was no real reason to keep their late-night friendship a secret, except that Elvis sensed that if he told anybody within his inner circle, most of them would think he was making it up. Rather than subject himself to ridicule among the guys, Parker, and Vernon, he simply mentioned to them that he had talked to Hughes a few times and thought he was a great man when he heard the news of his death. Every now and then, though, Elvis would open up more to other people, but never in too great detail and usually with a vagueness that would have made Hughes smile. At least Elvis hoped so.

Through Vegas friends, Elvis heard the whispers

and rumors that swirled around Hughes's death. Stories of him being kept a virtual prisoner by greedy underlings turned Elvis cold, as did the picture painted of Hughes at the end—so fearful of germs he refused to go out, dirty hair down to his waist, unclipped fingernails so long they curled at the end, giving him an evil warlock appearance, days spent in a mental haze. Elvis tried to block the visions but they kept creeping back to haunt him to a degree he couldn't fathom. Had Elvis been capable of deep introspection, the parallels between himself and Hughes would have sobered him. Two self-made men who were considered pioneers in their fields who wound up isolated from the outside world. Except in Elvis's mind, Hughes was a recluse by choice, while Elvis believed he was kept from living a "normal" life because of various outside forces. It wasn't until the stories began circulating after his announced death that it occurred to Elvis that maybe Hughes was just as much a victim as he was. The thought thoroughly depressed him—if a man like Hughes with so much intelligence and money was powerless to protect himself from those around him, Elvis was doomed. The magic talisman had suddenly turned deadly. If someone had told Elvis he only had a year or so to live, he probably would not have been too surprised.

Much of the last year before Elvis's death was marked by turmoil within the confines of Graceland. Many longtime employees were unceremoniously fired, including Red West, who was dismissed without explanation. Some of it was Vernon's doing. He had never liked the men who comprised his son's entourage and considered them all a waste of money. Vernon was constantly filling Elvis's already-reeling head with notions that he ought to completely clear house. By this point, Elvis couldn't have differentiated between a real friend and a poacher if his life depended on it. Nor did he seem to care most of the time.

How he met Ginger Alden is an example of how low Elvis had sunk. One evening, a hanger-on who knew Elvis and always sought out his favor brought two sisters to meet him. They made it clear that Elvis had his choice. Elvis was out of it that night and wasn't in the mood to make a decision of any kind so he shrugged and left it up to the others to make the decision for him. Ginger got the nod and ended up staying with him up until he died. Despite that loveless beginning, Elvis treated Ginger kindly and was grateful for the company. He had grown weary of waking up every morning and wondering what the name of the girl beside him was. Not that Elvis was ever completely faithful to any of his girlfriends, but having a steady definitely cut down the one-nights stands.

The most tragic element of Elvis's death is that in the weeks preceding it, he appeared ready to make a solid attempt at turning his life around. For the first time in years, he said he could see a way out of his funk. The first order of business was to sever his ties with Parker, followed by getting back in shape and going back on tour and seducing a new generation of music lovers. He never got the chance. He died looking over his shoulder, always worried that someone, somewhere was out to get him. Finally they did—and more than anything else, they were his own demons. Like Hughes before him, Elvis died under curious, murky circumstances, a victim of his celebrity, his upbringing, and his own hedonistic nature.

Elvis stepped out onto the porch at Graceland and looked up at the star-drenched sky. The stars were harder to see now than they were when he and his family first moved to Memphis. He always marveled, though, that no matter what tragedies happened on earth, the stars stayed the same.

Elvis sat on the step and hunched his shoulders to ward off the slight chill he felt. He felt oddly at peace for once—maybe it was 'cause Lisa Marie was sleeping upstairs in her room. Maybe it was because he finally had a plan after so many years of flapping about blindly. Where did the years go? Half the time he felt as if he'd missed most of his life. Although he shouldn't complain—there were lots of good things to be grateful for and it wasn't too late to start enjoying them more.

Elvis was tired but knew he wouldn't be able to sleep on his own. His body ached from the exercises he'd started doing, but it was a hurt of accomplishment. Wouldn't they all be surprised when Elvis came back, healthy, clear-headed, and strong as ever. He looked forward to having the last laugh. But more than anything, he looked forward to not being so afraid.

Elvis picked out his special star, the one that shone for his mama and brother. I'll make you both proud of me again yet, I promise I will.

Maybe tomorrow he would take Lisa Marie somewhere special, just the two of them. Or just walk around the grounds and play with the dogs. Elvis looked at his watch—if he was going to do anything, he'd better get to bed soon. He sighed at the thought of the nightly struggle looming before him. Easing off his sleeping medication had been harder than Elvis ever dreamed, but he had turned a corner and was winning the fight. Pretty soon, a hot glass of milk would be all he would need. Soon, but not just yet. Elvis felt his body getting chilled and a dull throb pulsed his temple. He stood stiffly and stretched his out-of-shape muscles. Man, he was looking forward to a good night's sleep. Maybe tonight would be the last night he'd ever need pills at all.

Epilogue

On August 16, 1977, Elvis was found dead in his bathroom at Graceland. The speculation on what really happened to cause his untimely death began before his body was even laid to rest, and it has continued since. Some say it was suicide, some an accidental overdose, and some even hint that it was murder. From what I've uncovered over the last several years, they're all correct in one fashion or another—and they're all wrong, too.

For a good portion of his adult life, Elvis abused his body in ways he wasn't even aware. From childhood, his diet oozed with fat, his taste for southern fried food becoming a near-addiction. Considering his family on Gladys's side had a history of heart disease, his sky-high cholesterol and fat intake were open invitations for trouble.

Once he hit thirty-five or so, Elvis's weight began to balloon, but only partly because of the amount and kind of food he ate. Even though he loved karate, he didn't exercise enough to keep in shape.

His body turned soft with flab that became ever more difficult to lose the older he got. Also, certain drugs he took inspired great eating binges followed by unconsciousness. The sheer physical abuse he subjected himself to was a form of long and drawn-out suicide that started the night his mother died. That was the first time he ever took a drug and the immediate but very temporary relief it offered hooked him from the start. It was no secret back then that Elvis lost a lot of his will to live when they buried Gladys and he never stopped looking forward to the day they would be reunited. He often mentioned it wouldn't matter if he died—at least then he'd be with his dead twin and his mother in a place where he wouldn't hurt anymore.

Shortly before his death Elvis announced to certain close friends that he was changing his ways. He had started exercising for a planned tour and was building the courage to once and for all fire Parker. The last time I talked to him he sounded hopeful and clear-headed. Despite his unresolved agony over Gladys's death, Elvis realized he had something very important to live for—a little girl named Lisa Marie. He worshipped his daughter and often felt great pangs of remorse over his drug-laden nights and hazy days. He worried over what effect his lifestyle might have on her. When Elvis told me he was going to straighten up, he also made it clear that Lisa Marie was the great incentive. She had given him a goal to work for and he wanted to reach it while there was time to make good.

But even if he was tapering off and trying to

cleanse his system, it was obviously too little, too late. Laughing in the face of his hopeful purpose, the years and years of abuse took their final, terrible toll just as he seemed capable of turning his life around.

I know for a fact Elvis wanted to dry out but it's also true, once an addict, always an addict. Despite his good intentions and determination, it would be naive to think he would stop cold turkey or never slip. So it's easy for me to believe he was still taking pills, especially to help him sleep. It was also no secret that Elvis had a weak will if tempted—just like a little boy. If somebody offered him drugs enough times, I doubt he would be able to resist. Which brings us to the question—was Elvis murdered?

If his drug abuse played an integral part in bringing on the heart attack that killed him, the question has to be asked why the people around Elvis allowed the drug abuse to carry on for as long as it did. The most obvious, and ominous, answer is that a lot of people had more to gain from a whacked-out, sickly, and ultimately dead-before-his-time Elvis than from one who was in complete command of his senses and life.

Elvis had been told many times by many doctors to change his diet and take better care of his body or face dire consequences. Many of these discussions put the fear of God into him—for a few days, anyway. Then it would be back to business as usual. Considering his family medical history and the state of his own health, it was a safe bet that a drugged-up Elvis would at best be unable to conduct his own affairs and at worst be setting himself up for an untimely death. Elvis was a heart attack just waiting to happen, and yet nobody around him tried to intervene. Not his entourage, not Vernon, and especially not Parker. I blame myself, too. Even though I was living in California, could I have done something to make a difference? I'll never know.

To be fair, it was hard to tell Elvis what to do. He would fly into rages. But Vernon and Parker both were in positions of authority to do something. Or at least to try. To let somebody push himself to the brink of the grave without making an attempt to intervene could be construed in dark moral terms, particularly if that person had something to gain.

Some of Elvis's entourage certainly stood to gain by his addictions. Regardless of the rampant distrust he felt for them, many of the guys, who had rather cushy jobs doing practically nothing, succeeded in robbing him blind. Vernon used to call them leeches and resented almost every one of them.

The story is told by many in both Las Vegas and Memphis that Parker was up to his neck in debt. The Colonel had a weakness for gambling and owed close to a million dollars to various Vegas casinos. He certainly stood to lose if fired by Elvis because he suddenly would have no way to recoup his gambling losses. And as it turned out, outside of the estate, Parker gained the most by Elvis's death.

Within hours of his dying, shops in Memphis were filled with memorial T-shirts, hats, and other Elvis memorabilia that were snatched up by grieving fans as fast as they were put in stock. One business associate of Parker's estimates that the Colonel reaped nearly a million dollars in the month following Elvis's passing.

Despite the personal and financial gains made, nobody is suggesting Parker or anyone else somehow injected or forced a lethal dose of anything into Elvis. In truth, Elvis was worth more to everybody alive. As long as Parker kept his high-percentage contract, he would rake in hundreds of thousands every year from residuals and endorsement money—*if* he stayed manager. Elvis had begun telling more and more people he wanted Parker out, almost as a way of forcing himself into finally doing the deed. But Parker was not the type to go without a fight. Another associate of the Colonel claims that Parker was paying one of Elvis's entourage extra money under the table to make sure Elvis was kept well supplied with drugs of all kinds. The mole saw to it that Elvis was "medicated" as much as possible, even if it meant getting high with him, too. As long as Elvis was not in control of his faculties, he could not be in a position to let Parker go. Parker needed the money too badly to be cut off now. When emotionally pulverized by drugs, Elvis was helpless to stand up and overcome Parker.

In a legal sense, manslaughter is the unintended killing of one at the hand of another. But in a moral sense, the crime can take on far more colors and implications. If he indeed is guilty of intentionally feeding the addiction through inaction, Parker contributed and possibly hastened Elvis's death. Motivated by sheer greed, the Colonel quite possibly put his client's well-being second to a need and desire to have him as a meal ticket. Nor were certain members of his entourage any more loyal, blithely spying on Elvis and keeping him drugged for personal profit.

Suddenly, Elvis's paranoia doesn't seem so irrational. He might have been functioning at half-speed but instinctively he sensed danger lurking within his very group. His inability to protect himself makes his demise all that more tragic. It also draws ironic and eerie parallels to his would-be mentor, Howard Hughes. Elvis once said he felt he understood Hughes as if he'd known him all his life.

"It's like lookin' in a mirror and seein' myself down the road twenty years older and twenty years richer. I jus' know what he means when he talks 'bout things."

Their money was lifeblood for those around both Hughes and Elvis, who fed like frenzied, starving sharks. The men had ample reason to mistrust and fear those who were the very closest to them—vultures jostling for position to swoop down and fight each other for the spoils. Even Vernon, Elvis's own father, got caught up in the gold rush.

For a long time, the events during the hours following the discovery of Elvis's body were a mystery. But over time, more and more people are quietly speaking out and within the old circle, the news has traveled slowly but steadily. All who hear are saddened but hardly surprised.

When Elvis was found collapsed in his bathroom, it was obvious he was already dead. Since there was nothing anyone could do to help him, several people in his employ set out on a mission to help and protect themselves. Parker was the first person called and he gave out a list of instructions. First and foremost, since Lisa Marie was visiting, the news of her daddy's death and surrounding activity had to be kept from her until Priscilla could come. This was achieved with relative ease—the house was plenty big to find a place to sequester her and Lisa Marie wasn't used to seeing her daddy early in the morning anyway.

Next, evidence of Elvis's ghastly history with drugs needed to be eradicated as much as possible. A few prescriptions were acceptable but not the drawerful of old pill bottles and other "medicines" that had controlled Elvis for so many years. Parker wanted to promote Elvis as a fallen hero who died before his time. The public would be more willing to gobble up memorabilia for a hero than for a virtual junkie in greater or lesser degree responsible for his own demise. Image had always been a number-one priority—even more so in death.

While certain members of the entourage scurried about preparing Graceland for the onslaught that would surely follow as soon as the news of Elvis's death was announced, Vernon embarked on his own private mission. Not long before he died, after his resolution to try and straighten up his life and take more control, Elvis decided he wanted to write a new, updated will. He told more than one person that he had actually done it, hand-writing in the changes he wanted made on a copy of the old will. While the bulk of his estate would still go to Lisa Marie, Elvis intimated he had included many more people and had slightly changed the distribution of wealth. Elvis left his father in charge of getting the changes to the lawyers to officially update the will.

For whatever reason, the revisions never made it to the lawyers' hands. Several eyewitnesses, who spoke on conditions of anonymity despite being disassociated from Graceland for years now, claim Vernon pulled the updated will out of a drawer and burned it within the hour after Elvis was found dead. Although it's only speculation, his motives don't seem hard to understand. From the time Elvis began making money as a journeyman singer, Vernon thought he squandered too much of it. Vernon was constantly bickering with Elvis over money "wasted" on excessive jewelry, cars, planes, and other luxuries. Before some of his entourage became a source of pain and fear, Elvis lavished gifts on his boys and their girlfriends or wives. His mistresses often walked away from a relationship with Elvis with new cars and expensive furs—all of which burned Vernon's sensibilities. Odds are, Vernon simply didn't like the number of new people Elvis had included in the revised will and took it upon himself to see to it Elvis didn't "squander" any more of his money in one last gesture of *largesse.* But it's indicative of how everyone around Elvis had their own agenda, while disregarding and disrespecting the star's wishes. Once it sunk in that the meal ticket had paid his last fare, it was every man for himself—the vultures finally came to roost.

Negligence, aiding and abetting a potentially lethal drug addiction, emotional manipulation, and blackmail—while these are certainly immoral and amoral deeds, they are probably not criminal. While the idea of an out-and-out murder or an intentional suicide is sure to grab more headlines, the truth is actually more insidiously dark and damning, especially because it was played out over a long course of years for reasons that amount to no more than pure and simple greed. Elvis was sacrificial gold calf.

It was a fact of life he'd grown to unhappily accept. Toward the end of his life, Elvis believed nearly everyone around him wanted a piece of what he had, but wanted nothing to do with him.

"I'm only good for the checks I can sign," he once sighed.

It's not a unique position for any wealthy, famous celebrity. But Elvis was an example of extremes. His near-clinical lack of confidence, combined with his personal and professional isolation from the outside world, made him more susceptible than most to the deceits and machinations of hangers-on, which tragically for Elvis included some intimates and longtime business associates. It was the dismal reality Hughes tried to convey—that celebrity and vast wealth turns a man into a commodity that other men will sell their souls to own a share of. And there's no power or authority that will change that fundamental law of man's base nature.

Even complete strangers wrangled ways to make money off of Elvis after his death. The FBI files include a lengthy investigation of a 1955 Corvette allegedly once owned by Elvis sold for $35,000 by a very enterprising man. But after the buyer discovered the sale had apparently been a fraud, the FBI was brought in to verify once and for all if in fact the car had ever belonged, even for a moment, to Elvis. It had not, meaning the buyer paid close to $10,000 more for the car than it was really worth. Had Elvis been alive, they could have simply asked him, but after his death, his estate was so riddled in legal affairs that it took the FBI four years to complete their investigation and determine that Elvis had not owned the car. Even dead, Elvis was vulnerable to exploitation. And while he was alive, he made the mistake of granting others the power to sway his destiny while relinquishing nearly all of his own control.

For most of his life, Elvis was an extreme: his family was the poorest of the poor as a child; in adolescence his far-out personal style made him the butt of jokes; as an up-and-coming young singer his unique, uninhibited joy of performing made him the ground-breaking symbol of a generation breaking free. His hedonism resulted in too much food, too many women, and far too many drugs. He was also overly emotionally dependent and critically insecure. Elvis didn't know moderation in any form and ultimately paid the price. Yet at the same time, he lived out his dreams and scaled heights others can only imagine. But his full potential as both performer and human being was cut short by his deference to those in positions of perceived and actual authority over him. If there is any legacy of his life's story to be gleaned, it's found there—to turn over more of our destiny to the control of others than life already necessitates is to ensure the loss of self-respect in the least, and at worst, the loss of a significant portion of our soul.

One can only hope that Elvis rests in greater peace now.

APPENDIX A: FBI Files

Covering the years 1956 to 1972, the Appendix contains exhibits, correspondence, FBI investigation files, and interoffice memos detailing both the Bureau's professional aboveboard dealings with Elvis and the secret dossier kept on his "subversive" activities.

A1–A2

Correspondence from a concerned citizen to J. Edgar Hoover concerning the writer's opposition to Elvis's indecency.

Hoover responded with a polite but noncommittal letter.

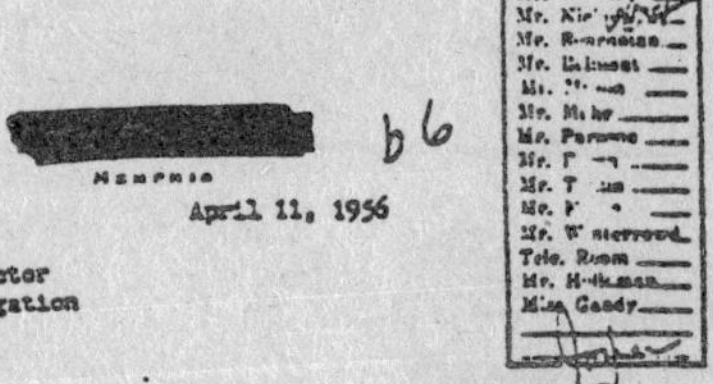
[redacted] b6

Memphis

April 11, 1956

Mr. J. Edgar Hoover, Director
Federal Bureau of Investigation
Washington, D. C.

Dear Mr. Hoover:

By way of introduction to you, will say that I knew Don Hostetter when he was in Memphis, and thought a great deal of him. Believe he will remember me, in our association together on occasions.

Am attaching a few clippings for your perusal. They are sent to indicate a trend with which you may already be familiar.

It is essential that some agency with sufficient organization and influence do something toward better censorship in our country. There are minds who will scarcely stop short of complete indecency to exploit their wares upon the public, and youth is not able to discriminate between the right and wrong of it.

We have had a struggle here on the local front in Memphis, a city of 453,000 people, in retaining a censorship, when a committee appointed had suggested that it was not necessary.

Have personally talked with members on the local censorship board, and have their testimony of the terrible pictures that would be released for showing here, had it not been for censorship.

Most of this entertainment becomes interstate, and hence should become a Federal Government problem. The fine work that our Churches and some of our Schools are attempting to do is offset by the freedom exercised in this country of licentiousness. The Apostle Peter warned in his 1st letter about our not using the new liberty for a cloke of maliciousness, but as the servants of God.

If there is something that your excellent and very fine organization is able to do concerning these problems facing us today, you will find that many citizens will deeply appreciate your effort.

May I take this occasion to thank you most sincerely for your own exemplary record and for preserving a great America for us at the risk of your life and that of your agents.

63-3064-X

Cordially yours,

[redacted]

b6 [redacted]

Enclosures 2 ENCLOSURE

b6

APR 12 1956

4-17-56
R

CRIME REC

April 17, 1956

63-3064-X

INDEXED - 45

81982

EX. - 107 Mr. [redacted]
Memphis, Tennessee

b6

Dear Mr. [redacted]

Your letter of April 11, 1956, and its enclosures have been received, and I can appreciate the concern which prompted your writing. I would like to advise you, however, that the FBI is strictly a fact-gathering agency, and it is not within the scope of our authority to make suggestions as to legislative matters.

I am most grateful for your generous remarks concerning the FBI and assure you of our desire always to merit your confidence.

Sincerely yours,

J. Edgar Hoover

John Edgar Hoover
Director

APR 17 5:38 PM '56
RECEIVED 11:42 AM FROM
F B I

MAILED TO
APR 17 1956
COMM.-FBI

NOTE: Letter from SAC Memphis in 1940 indicated that correspondent was then [redacted]

b6

(94-1-18228)

JUL 5 1956

PCE:jh
(3)

APR 26 1956

A3–A4

More correspondence, this time from a La Crosse, Wisconsin, reporter outraged over the hubbub among the city's youth caused by Elvis's appearance.

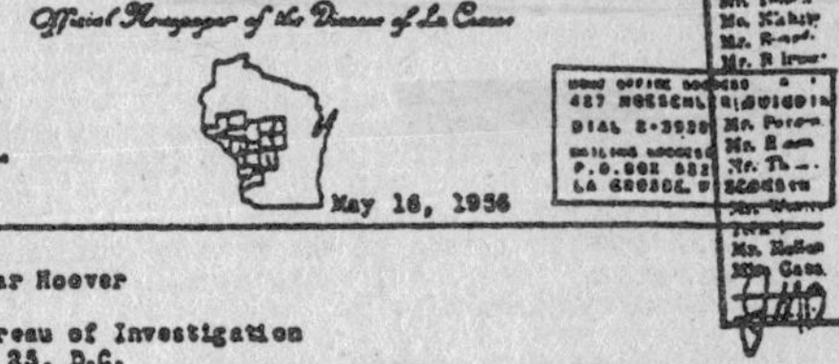

LA CROSSE REGISTER

Official Newspaper of the Diocese of La Crosse

May 16, 1956

Mr. J. Edgar Hoover
Director
Federal Bureau of Investigation
Washington 25, D.C.

Dear Mr. Hoover,

Elvis Presley, press-agented as a singer and entertainer, played to two groups of teenagers numbering several thousand at the city auditorium here, Monday, May 14.

As newspaper man, parent, and former member of Army Intelligence Service, I feel an obligation to pass on to you my conviction that Presley is a definite danger to the security of the United States.

Although I could not attend myself, I sent two reporters to cover his second show at 9:30 p.m. Besides, I secured the opinions of others of good judgment, who had seen the show or had heard direct reports of it. Among them are a radio station manager, a former motion picture exhibiter, an orchestra player, and a young woman employee of a radio station who witnessed the show to determine its value. All agree that it was the filthiest and most harmful production that ever came to La Crosse for exhibition to teenagers.

When Presley came on the stage, the youngsters almost mobbed him, as you can judge from the article and pictures enclosed from May 15 edition of the La Crosse TRIBUNE. The audience could not hear his "singing" for the screaming and carrying on of the teenagers.

ENCLOSURE

But eye-witnesses have told me that Presley's actions and motions were such as to rouse the sexual passions of teenaged youth. One eye-witness described his actions as "sexual self-gratification on the stage," - another as "a strip-tease with clothes on." Although police and auxiliaries were there, the show went on. Perhaps the hardened police did not get the import of his motions and gestures, like those of masturbation or riding a microphone. (The assistant district attorney and Captain William Roma also stepped in for a few minutes in response to complaints about the first show, but they found no reason to halt the show.)

SE 15 64

After the show, more than 1,000 teenagers tried to gang into Presley's room at the auditorium, then at the Stoddard Hotel. All possible police on duty were necessary at the Hotel to keep watch on the teenagers milling about the hotel till after 3 a.m., the hotel manager informed me. Some kept milling about the city till about 5 a.m.

Indications of the harm Presley did just in La Crosse were the two high school girls (of whom I have direct personal knowledge) whose abdomen and thigh had Presley's autograph. They admitted that they went to his room where this happened. It is known by psychologists, psychiatrists and priests that teenaged girls from the age of eleven, and boys in their adolescence are easily aroused to sexual indulgence and perversion by certain types of motions and hysteria, -- the type that was exhibited at the Presley show.

There is also gossip of the Presley Fan Clubs that degenerate into sex orgies. The local radio station WKBH sponsors a club on the "Lindy Shannon Show."

From eye-witness reports about Presley, I would judge that he may possibly be both a drug addict and a sexual pervert. In any case I am sure he bears close watch, -- especially in the face of growing juvenile crime nearly everywhere in the United States. He is surrounded by a group of high-pressure agents who seem to control him, the hotel manager reported.

I do not report idly to the FBI. My last official report to an FBI agent in New York before I entered the U.S. Army resulted in arrest of a saboteur (who committed suicide before his trial). I believe the Presley matter is as serious to U.S. security. I am convinced that juvenile crimes of lust and perversion will follow his show here in La Crosse.

I enclose article and pictures from May 15 edition of the La Crosse TRIBUNE. The article is an excellent example of the type of reporting that describes a burlesque show by writing about the drapes on the stage. But the pictures, to say the least are revealing. Note, too, that under the Presley article, the editor sanctimoniously published a very brief "filler" on the FBI's concern for teenage crime. Only a moron could not see the connection between the Presley exhibit and the incidence of teenage disorders in La Crosse.

With many thanks, and with a prayer for God's special blessing on your excellent and difficult work for justice and decency,

Sincerely yours,

b6

RECORDED 91
INDEXED - 91
63-3064

May 23, 1956

81081

[redacted] Wisc b6
La Crosse Register
Post Office Box 822
La Crosse, Wisconsin

Dear Mr. [redacted] b6

Your letter dated May 10, 1956, with enclosures, hasbeen received.

While I appreciate the interest prompting you to write, the matter to which you refer is not within the investigative jurisdiction of the FBI.

I want to thank you, however, for your most generous remarks relative to the work of this Bureau.

Sincerely yours,

John Edgar Hoover
Director

COMM — FBI
MAY 24 1956
MAILED 26

b6

NOTE: Bufiles contain no reference to [redacted] [redacted] Elvis Presley is referred to in a newspaper clipping in Bufile 66-0-3465 only. Correspondent describes the antics of Presley, a popular singer, as vulgar and suggests action by the Bureau.

CEN-sak
(3)

JUN 12 1956

A5–15

FBI investigation into a postcard sent to Elvis that threatened to kill him.

O B S C E N E

Postcard postmarked Niagara Falls, N. Y., 8 PM, 8/30/56

Addressed to: "ELVIS PRESLEY, Memphis, Tenn"

Containing message: "IF YOU DON'T STOP THIS SHIT WE'RE GOING TO KILL YOU."

It is noted this card was handprinted in pencil.

O B S C E N E

9-30861-2

BU 9-532-3

ADMINISTRATIVE

A copy of This report is being sent to the Memphis Office for their information inasmuch as the AUSA at Buffalo, New York, has advised that in the event the victim receives any additional threatening letters or postal cards from Niagara Falls, New York, he would reconsider the facts of the case and furnish his prosecutive opinion.

REFERENCE 30861-4

Buffalo airtel to Bureau 49-14356.

ADMINISTRATIVE PAGE

REPORT
of the
FBI
LABORATORY

FEDERAL BUREAU OF INVESTIGATION
WASHINGTON, D. C.

To: SAC, Buffalo

September 24, 1956

To: UNKNOWN SUBJECT:
ELVIS PRESLEY - VICTIM
EXTORTION

J. Edgar Hoover
John Edgar Hoover, Director

YOUR FILE NO. 9-New
FBI FILE NO. 9-30561 - 1
LAB. NO. 3-236568

Examination requested by: Buffalo

Reference: Airtel 9/14/56

RECORDED - 10

Examination requested: Document

EX-117

Specimen:

Q1 Post card postmarked "Niagara Falls, N.Y. 8 PM AUG 30 1956" addressed to "ELVIS PRESLEY MEMPHIS, TENN" and bearing message beginning "If you don't..." and ending "...going to kill you."

REPORTS OF EXAMINATION:

The questioned hand printing on specimen Q1 was searched through the Anonymous Letter File without identifying it with a prior submission. A photograph of this specimen will be added to this file for future reference.

Specimen Q1 is returned Herewith.

Enclosure (1) - Registered Mail 9 - 30861 - 1

1 - Memphis

MAILED 10
SEP 30 1956
COMM. FBI

6 (6-21-55)

FBI

Date: 9/14/56

Transmit the following message via AIR TEL

AIR MAIL

(Priority or Method of Mailing)

From SAC, BUFFALO (9-New)

To: BUREAU

UNSUB; ELVIS PRESLEY - VICTIM
EXTORTION

Re NY airtel to BU, 9/12/56. Re airtel is quoted as follows:

"Enclosed herewith is an anonymous postcard addressed to ELVIS PRESLEY at Memphis, Tennessee, postmarked 8:00 p.m. 8/30/56 at Niagara Falls, New York, and letters of transmittal by Postmaster, Memphis 1, Tennessee and Postal Inspecter in Charge, Chattanooga, Tennessee."

A copy of the postcard referred to above is enclosed to the Bureau and Memphis in the attached envelope marked "Obscene." The original postcard is being submitted to the FBI laboratory by separate communication.

From the enclosures furnished with re airtel it appears this postcard was intercepted by [redacted] Postmaster, Memphis 1, Tennessee, and was forwarded to the Postal Inspector in Charge at Chattanooga 1, Tennessee, by their communication 9/4/56. Postal Inspector in Charge at Chattanooga thereafter furnished the postcard to our New York Office by communication dated 9/6/56. Nowhere in the enclosures is it indicated whether the postcard in question was ever delivered to the addressee. b7C

Inasmuch as the postcard, as indicated by the enclosed, contains a threat to kill the victim, Memphis should make inquiry of the Postal Authorities, Memphis 1, Tennessee, to ascertain details of the receipt and handling of this postcard.

Buffalo will consult with USA for a legal opinion and thereafter conduct any appropriate investigation.

ENCLOSURE

ROCHE

3 - Bureau (Enc. 1)
2 - Memphis (Enc. 1)
1 - Buffalo
WIG:KKC
(6)

Mr. Rosen

RECORDED - 71
EX-117

9-30861-2

Approved: [signature]
Special Agent in Charge

SEP 24 1956

FEDERAL BUERAU OF INVESTIGATION
UNITED STATES DEPARTMENT OF JUSTICE

Laboratory Work Sheet

Recorded 9/17/56
EAB

LAB FILE

Re: UNKNOWN SUBJECT:
ELVIS PRESLEY - VICTIM
EXTORTION

File # 9-30861-1
Lab. # D-236561

Examination requested by: SAC, Buffalo (9-New)

Date of reference communication: Airtel 9/14/56 Date received: 9/17/56

Examination requested: Document

Result of Examination: Examination by: [redacted]

No ident ALF U.C. Ap.: N.Y. Vt. Mass. Conn. Penn. Tenn. Ky. Va. N.C. Ga. Ala. Miss. Ark. Mo. b7C

Specimens submitted for examination

Q1 Postcard card addressed to "ELVIS PRESLEY MEMPHIS, TENN" and bearing message beginning "If you don't..." and ending "...going to kill you." card, postmark "Niagara Falls, N.Y."

9-30861-5

BU 9-532

The above message on the postal card was written in pencil and is printed.

By letter dated September 20, 1956, the FBI Laboratory advised that the hand-printing on the postal card in question was searched through the anonymous letter file without identifying it with a prior submission.

On September 27, 1956, the facts of this case were discussed with Assistant United States Attorney RICHARD E. MOOT at Buffalo, New York, who advised that in the event the identity of the unsub was obtained, he would decline prosecution inasmuch as the card appears to be from a "crank." Mr. Moot further advised, however, that in the event additional threatening cards or letters are received by the victim, he should be advised and additional consideration would be given him to the prosecution of the person involved.

It is being pointed out that the complete text of the message on the postal card, including the obscene word, was furnished to Mr. MOOT.

FEDERAL BUREAU OF INVESTIGATION

Form No. 1
THIS CASE ORIGINATED AT BUFFALO

REPORT MADE AT	DATE WHEN MADE	PERIOD FOR WHICH MADE	REPORT MADE BY
BUFFALO, NEW YORK	9-28-56	9-27-56	[redacted]

TITLE	CHARACTER OF CASE
UNKNOWN SUBJECT; ELVIS PRESLEY - VICTIM	EXTORTION b7C

SYNOPSIS OF FACTS:

Anonymous post card addressed to ELVIS PRESLEY at Memphis, Tenn., postmarked 8 PM on 8-30-56, at Niagara Falls, NY, is obscene and contained threat to kill. FBI Lab searched postal card in question through anonymous letter file without identifying it with a prior submission. Facts of case discussed with USA, Buffalo, NY, who declined prosecution on grounds that card appeared to be from "crank" and states he would reconsider prosecution is the event victim received additional threatening communications.

DETAILS: By communication dated September 6, 1956, Postal Inspector in Charge at Chattanooga, Tennessee, furnished an anonymous postal card addressed to ELVIS PRESLEY at Memphis, Tenn., postmarked 8:00 PM on August 30, 1956, at Niagara Falls, New York, to FBI Office at New York City who, in turn, furnished this postal card to the Buffalo Office. This postal card reads as follows:

"If you don't stop this (obscene word) we're going to kill you."

9-30861-4

APPROVED AND FORWARDED: TARjtc | SPECIAL AGENT IN CHARGE | DO NOT WRITE IN THESE SPACES

RECORDED - 91

COPIES OF THIS REPORT
3 - Bureau (9-30361)
1 - USA, Buffalo
1 - Memphis (Info)
1 - Buffalo

OCT 8 1956

MEMPHIS BUFFALO	9-19-56	9-18-56
UNKNOWN SUBJECT ELVIS PRESLEY—VICTIM	########	
	character of case EXTORTION	

Superintendent of Mails, Memphis, Tennessee, advised post card taken from mail prior to delivery of addressee. Unable to furnish any information of value concerning origins of post card.

DETAILS: On September 18, 1956 Mr. ###### Superintendent of Mails, US Post Office, Memphis,
Tennessee advised that the instant post card in this case was received by him in his inter-office mail one morning with the notation that it was taken from the incoming mail of the previous night. He stated that all incoming mail is received at the Main Post Office and assorted by some 150 employees in that Post Office. He stated that one of them, whom he could not identify, had obviously run across this post card while assorting mail the night it was received at the Post Office. This employee then dropped the post card into the inter-office mail, directing it to ####### He stated that when he received it he forwarded it to the Postal Inspector in Charge at Chattanooga, Tennessee, which was his usual method of handling such matters.

RE # 9-792

b7C

[redacted] stated it might be possible to ascertain which employee had extracted the card; however, it would mean canvassing all of the employees. [redacted] stated that this employee would not be able to furnish any information in addition to the above as all of the mail was received in bulk in large mail bags and there would be no way of ascertaining any pertinent information as to the origin of the post card. He could furnish no further information of value concerning the post card.

9-30861-3

A16–17:

Interoffice memo from Louisville FBI to headquarters concerning the riots that seem to follow in the wake of Elvis appearances by frenzied youths.

Hoover's response is to warn police chief in cities where Presley is to appear.

DECODED COPY

XXX Radio ☐ Teletype

FROM LOUISVILLE 11-7-56 NR 071428

TO DIRECTOR URGENT

ELVIS PRESLEY; BILL HALEY AND HIS COMETS, INFORMATION CONCERNING, POLICE COOPERATION MATTER. COLONEL CARL E. HEUSTIS, CHIEF OF POLICE, LOUISVILLE, KENTUCKY, THIS DAY ADVISED THAT ELVIS PRESLEY AND BILL HALEY AND HIS COMETS, RIVALS FOR THE ATTENTION OF QUOTE ROCK AND ROLL UNQUOTE FANS, ARE SIMULTANEOUSLY BOOKED FOR APPEARANCES AT THE JEFFERSON COUNTY ARMORY AND THE KENTUCKY STATE FAIRGROUND EXPOSITION CENTER NOVEMBER 25 NEXT. COLONEL HEUSTIS ADVISED HE HAS RECEIVED INFORMATION THAT THERE HAVE BEEN RIOTS AT JERSEY CITY, NEW JERSEY, ASBURY PARK, NEW JERSEY, SANTA CRUZ, SANTA JOSE, CALIFORNIA, HARTFORD, CONNECTICUT, AND JACKSONVILLE, FLORIDA AS RESULT OF SUCH SIMULTANEOUS APPEARANCES. RIOTS REPORTEDLY RESULTED IN MANY THOUSANDS OF DOLLARS PROPERTY DAMAGE. COLONEL HEUSTIS REQUESTED INFORMATION FROM THIS BUREAU REGARDING ANY SUCH RIOTS IN AN EFFORT TO PREVENT SUCH RECURRENCES HERE. IN VIEW OF THE EXCELLENT COOPERATION BETWEEN LOUISVILLE PD AND THIS OFFICE IT IS REQUESTED THAT THE BUREAU FURNISH AN AIRTEL SUMMARY OF ANY INFORMATION APPEARING IN FILES SUITABLE FOR DISSEMINATION TO COLONEL HEUSTIS.

RECEIVED: 11:05 AM RADIO

11:22 AM CODING UNIT MJM

RECORDED . 118

63-3064

Mr. Rosen

NOV 9 1956

If the intelligence contained in the above message is to be disseminated outside the Bureau, it is suggested that it be suitably paraphrased in order to protect the Bureau's cryptographic systems.

11-7-56

AIRTEL

RECORDED - 118

SAC, Louisville

ELVIS PRESLEY;
BILL HALEY AND HIS COMETS
INFORMATION CONCERNING
POLICE COOPERATION MATTER

Reurradiogram 11-7-56, in which you request information in Bureau files concerning disturbances which occurred following appearances of above subjects. While the Bureau is aware that newspaper articles reported riots and disturbances following appearances of the above individuals no inquires have been made and the Bureau has no specific information regarding these disturbances. Since Colonel Heustis is aware of the places where riots allegedly occurred you may desire to tactfully suggest that he consult with the chiefs of police in those localities for any information in this regard.

Hoover

RFS:jdn
(4)

NOTE: Louisville was contacted by Colonel Heustis, Chief of Police, Louisville, Kentucky, who advised of the coming appearances of above subjects and his fear of the riots as occurred in several other cities. As a matter of cooperation Colonel Heustis requested information from this Bureau · regarding these riots. Louisville is being advise that while the Bureau is aware that such riots have occurred no inquiries were made and we have no specific information concerning these riots. It is being suggested to the SAC, Louisville, that he may desire to suggest to Colonel Heustis that he consult with chiefs of police in the cities where the riots occurred.

COMM - FBI
NOV 7 - 1956
MAILED TO

67 NOV 16 1956

A18–A20

Newspaper clippings on Elvis controversy.

etition Circulated
o Bar Elvis on TV

SYRACUSE, N. Y., Nov. 8 (P).
Syracuse housewives toured
y offices yesterday and ob-
ined signatures to a petition to
e Columbia Broadcasting Sys-
m demanding that Singer Elvis
esley be barred from television
ows.
A spokesman for the group,
ho asked that her name not be
ed, said she had obtained 48
gnatures to the petition yester-
y, and added that she and
5 to 30 others" expect to "get
ndreds more—including top
ty officials—before sending it
CBS the end of this week."
The petition terms Mr. Pres-
y's "physical contortions . . .
algar, suggestive and disgust-
g."
The spokesman said TV Per-
rmer Steve Allen would be
alled the petition too because
e had announced he had invited
lvis to appear on a program in
e near future.

ELVIS FACES WIGGLE BAN

LOUISVILLE, Ky., Nov. 15 (AP) A no-wiggle restriction has been place on Elvis Presley's appearance here Nov. 25.

Police chief Carl Heustis said yesterday he won't permit "any lewd, lascivious contortions that would excite a crowd" when the long-sideburned, guitar-strumming singer comes to town.

"As you can surmise," the Chief said, "I just don't happen to be one of his admirers."

"New York Journal-American"
New York, N.Y.
November 15, 1956
page 4

63 3064

NOT RECORDED
44 JUN 11 1958

he Evening Star"
shington, D.C.
vember 8, 1956

59 JUN 12 1958

Irate Teeners Demand Elvis

Most of the 1800 bobbysoxers lined up today for the opening of Elvis Presley's first movie. "Love Me Tender" were furious when they discovered their idol wouldn't appear personally at the Paramount Theatre.

"We want Elvis we want Elvis," the teenagers chanted, shivering from their night-long vigil behind police barricades at the theatre at Broadway and 43d st.

Although the theatre didn't open until 8 a.m., many had been in line since 9:30 last night in the hope of seeing the real-live Elvis.

"It'll be a miracle," said brunet Carol Olsen, 15, of 815 43d st., Brooklyn. "If this theatre is in one piece when we get out."

She and other bobbysoxers said they had been led to believe Elvis would hand out gifts to the first 2,000 in line for the him.

"New York Journal-American"
New York, N.Y.
November 15, 1956
page 1

L-A

A21–22

Files pertaining to Elvis' alleged racist remark concerning Mexican women and his refusal to kiss one.

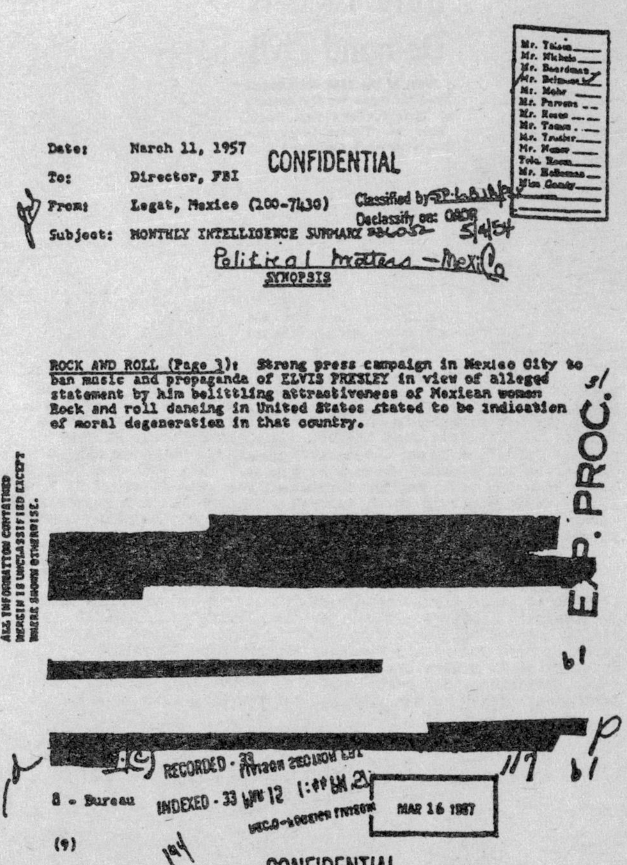

CONFIDENTIAL

Date: March 11, 1957

To: Director, FBI

From: Legat, Mexico (100-7430)

Subject: MONTHLY INTELLIGENCE SUMMARY

Political Matters—Mexico

SYNOPSIS

ROCK AND ROLL (Page 3): Strong press campaign in Mexico City to ban music and propaganda of ELVIS PRESLEY in view of alleged statement by him belittling attractiveness of Mexican women Rock and roll dancing in United States stated to be indication of moral degeneration in that country.

ALL INFORMATION CONTAINED HEREIN IS UNCLASSIFIED EXCEPT WHERE SHOWN OTHERWISE.

EX. PROC.

RECORDED - 33

INDEXED - 33

8 - Bureau

(9)

MAR 16 1957

CONFIDENTIAL

MC 100-7430

CONFIDENTIAL

ROCK AND ROLL

Mexican magazines and newspapers have for months pointed out that the vogue for rock and roll dancing among the youth in the United States was a sign of moral degeneration perfectly explainable in the United States, but not present in Mexico. It was said that the new dance rhythm would find no popular reception among the Mexican youth due to their strict upbringing and serious views toward life. Then rock and roll began to catch on. Considerable money was even invested in a locally made movie in which certain prominent Mexican entertainers danced and otherwise approved of the craze. At that time a news report reached Mexico City that during a radio interview in Los Angeles ELVIS PRESLEY had made a statement that he would rather kiss three Negresses rather than one Mexican girl. This reported statement has received tremendous publicity, so much so that it would almost appear contrived. A campaign has been successfully initiated to prevent the playing of any ELVIS PRESLEY recording over any Mexico City radio station, and on March 14 next university students are planning a protest celebration in a downtown Mexico City park where ELVIS PRESLEY music, magazines, and recordings will be publicly burned. The Communists, quick to ban rock and roll dancing from Mexican

-3-

CONFIDENTIAL

MC 100-743G

CONFIDENTIAL

Communist youth social functions, may try to spark the bonfire meeting in the plaza, but even The Communists may not stop rock and roll in Mexico. The new ads for the aforementioned movie point out that Mexican rock and roll is an independent dance of local origin. The ad reads: "Death to ELVIS PRESLEY! Burn his records, his pompadour, his photographs, his guitar, burn anything you want, but give yourself a treat with the true kings of happiness and of rock and roll!" At last reports the movie was receiving extremely good attendance.

ACTION TAKEN: None. Public source material.

-4-

CONFIDENTIAL

A23

Newspaper column on Presley's appeal to youth.

GIR

Bowdemas
Belmont
Mohr
Parsons
Rosen
Tamm
Trotter
Nease
Tele. Room
Holloman
Gandy

THESE DAYS:

She Believes Elvis Is 'The Greatest'

By GEORGE E. SOKOLSKY

I RECEIVED a most instructive letter from Miss Charlotte Jones of Dallas, Texas, which I am herewith reproducing in full as a contribution to Americana. Here is the letter:

"Dear Mr. Sokolsky:

"There are too many people saying that Elvis is going to die out. When Elvis dies out is when the sun quits burnin.

"You say everybody is forgotten that is once great: George Washington has never been forgotten and nobody can ever be as great a president or as long remembered as he. Nobody can ever take his place or do what he did. Well, it's the same with Elvis. He'll always be remembered and nobody has ever or ever will do the same thing as Elvis has. Elvis is the king of popularity and we (teens of America) love him and we'll see he lives forever. Not his body but his name. Adults won't admit he's so great, because they're jealous! They know that their top singers weren't as great as Elvis. They're mad because their taste isn't quite as good as ours.

"Look at James Dean, been dead for a year and he's bigger now than he ever was.

"God gifted Elvis to us and you oughta thank him, not tear down, the greatest thing the world has ever known: Elvis Presley!!!!!!

Sceerinuly yours,
Charlotte Jones

"P.S.: And if you're over 30, you're old. You're certainly not young."

* * *

It shows the advantage of an education, that Miss Jones compares Elvis Presley's accomplishments with those of George Washington. Of course, as history goes, Washington has not been so long remembered; he only died in 1799 which is not long ago compared with Alexander the Great, or Julius Caesar or, on the peaceful side, with Hammurabi, Moses or Solon. Nevertheless, it must be admitted that Miss Jones has a point and that George Washington is today better remembered than many another president and plenty of kings.

I find it hard quite to realize what is meant by "the king of popularity." Does Miss Jones really believe that Elvis is more popular than President Eisenhower or General Douglas MacArthur or the Queen of England or Dr. Albert Schweitzer? If that is so, then why should men devote themselves to noble deeds and great accomplishments? Why not just warble an old Civil War song and twang a banjo and achieve the accolade that way?

EX-116

INDEXED-93

NOT RECORDED
BY MAR 14 1957

Wash. Post and Times Herald
Wash. News
Wash. Star
N. Y. Herald Tribune
N. Y. Journal-American 18
N. Y. Mirror
N. Y. Daily News
N. Y. Times
Daily Worker
The Worker
New Leader

Date MAR 11 1957

53 MAR 13 1957

Apparently all adults are jealous of this Elvis, otherwise they would acknowledge that his voice is superior to Caruso's; his profile to John Barrymore's; his acting to E. H. Sothern's. Miss Jones's knowledge must be like Teddy Nadler's who said something the other day about having a tremendous knowledge of classical music. But what has he done with that knowledge? That is always the question.

She Likes What She Likes

I have no idea how old Charlotte Jones is. She does not introduce herself with vital statistics. But she does believe that she and her "teens" have better taste than her elders, by which she means that she likes what she likes and that anyone who disagrees is a square, a jerk or a dope. Could be.

Yet, I wonder what would happen to such a hero worshipper if she spent six weeks next summer at Tanglewood listening to Bach, Mozart, Beethoven, Brahms and Tschaikovsky. All long-hair, it is true. But music is music and is supposed to thrill the heart of civilized and savage. It would be an interesting experiment, like bringing Tarzan to the Colony Restaurant or Pavillon, to eat food as designed by Escoffier.

The real point of this letter is that it displays no cultural background. I heard Elvis sing and I believe that perhaps in five years or so, he might be able to carry a tune as well as Bing Crosby. But in 50 years, he could not make the chorus of the Metropolitan Opera.

The fault undoubtedly is in a school system which gives the child so little cultural background, so little basis for taste and so little understanding of beauty. Rock-N-Roll, which is a musical reversion to the tom-tom of the jungle, can stir so many of our young to ecstasy only because they know no better. It is curious that in a Western country a child could write "the greatest thing the world has even known: Elvis Presley." I used to hear them say that that title went to Jesus. How times do change!

A24–26

Files examining Presley's relationship with two beauty queens, then Miss Ohio, Kathy Gabriel and then Miss Austria, Hannah Melcher.

SECRET

ELVIS GETS A DRAFT REPRIEVE

Wash. Post and Times Herald
Wash. News
Wash. Star
N. Y. Herald Tribune
N. Y. Journal-American
N. Y. Mirror
N. Y. Daily News
N. Y. Times
Daily Worker
The Worker
New Leader

SECRET

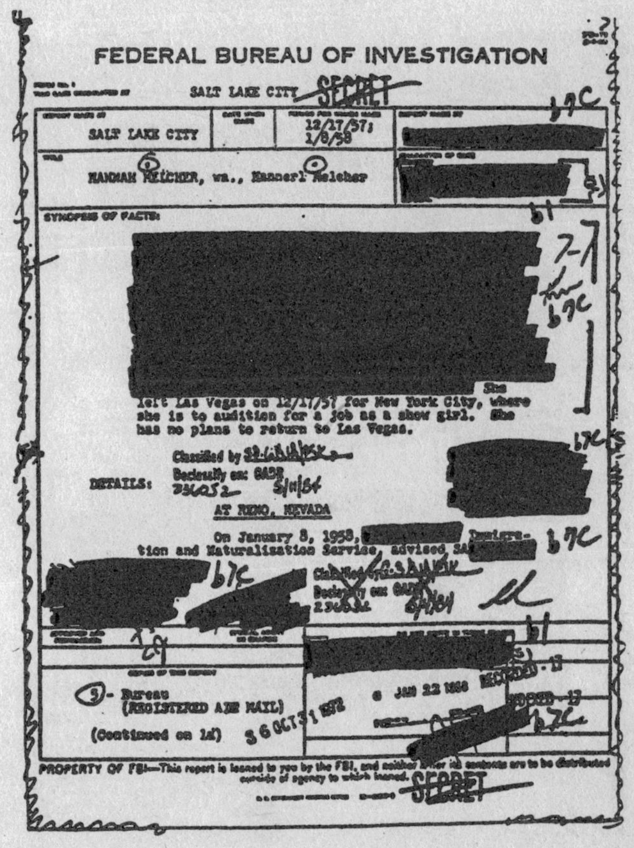

FEDERAL BUREAU OF INVESTIGATION

SALT LAKE CITY SECRET

REPORT MADE AT	DATE WHEN MADE	PERIOD FOR WHICH MADE	REPORT MADE BY
SALT LAKE CITY		12/27/57; 1/8/58	[redacted]

TITLE: HANNAH MELCHER, wa., Hannerl Melcher

SYNOPSIS OF FACTS:

[redacted] She left Las Vegas on 12/17/57 for New York City, where she is to audition for a job as a show girl. She has no plans to return to Las Vegas.

DETAILS:

AT RENO, NEVADA

On January 8, 1958, [redacted] Immigration and Naturalization Service, advised SA [redacted]

COPIES OF THIS REPORT

(3)- Bureau (REGISTERED AIR MAIL)

(Continued on 1a)

JAN 22 1958

PROPERTY OF FBI—This report is loaned to you by the FBI, and neither it nor its contents are to be distributed outside of agency to which loaned.

SECRET

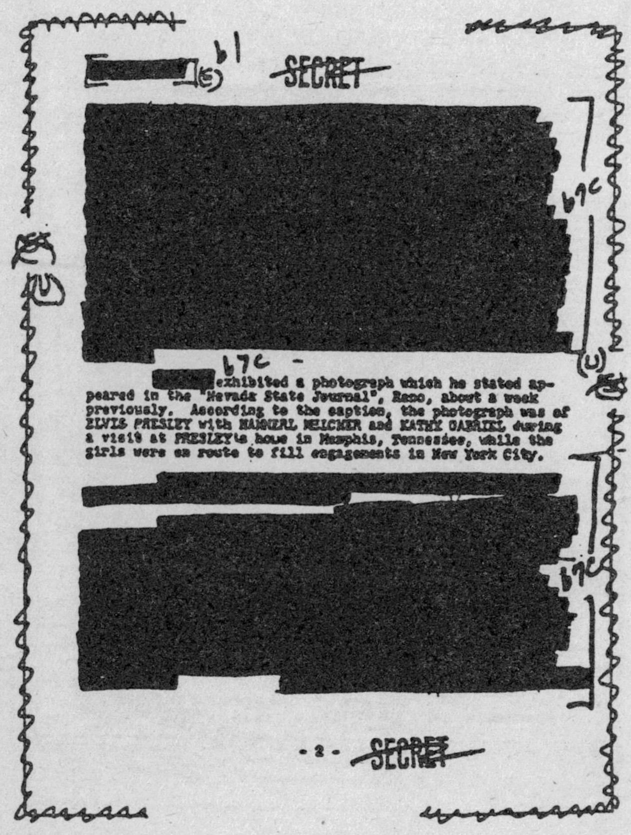

SECRET

exhibited a photograph which he stated appeared in the "Nevada State Journal", Reno, about a week previously. According to the caption, the photograph was of ELVIS PRESLEY with NANCIEL WELCHER and KATHY GABRIEL during a visit at PRESLEY's house in Memphis, Tennessee, while the girls were en route to fill engagements in New York City.

- 2 - SECRET

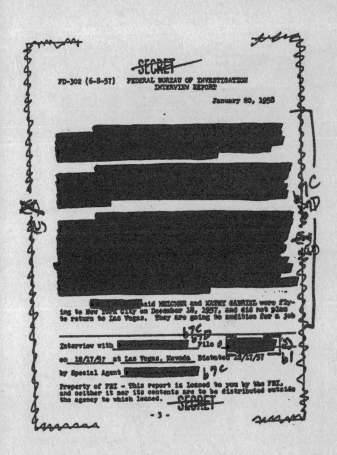

SECRET

FD-302 (6-8-57) FEDERAL BUREAU OF INVESTIGATION
INTERVIEW REPORT

January 20, 1958

said MELCHER and KATHY GABRIEL were flying to New York City on December 18, 1957, and did not plan to return to Las Vegas. They are going to auditioo for a job

Interview with ______ File # ______

on 12/27/57 at Las Vegas, Nevada Dictated 12/27/57

by Special Agent ______

Property of FBI - This report is loaned to you by the FBI, and neither it nor its contents are to be distributed outside the agency to which loaned.

SECRET

- 3 -

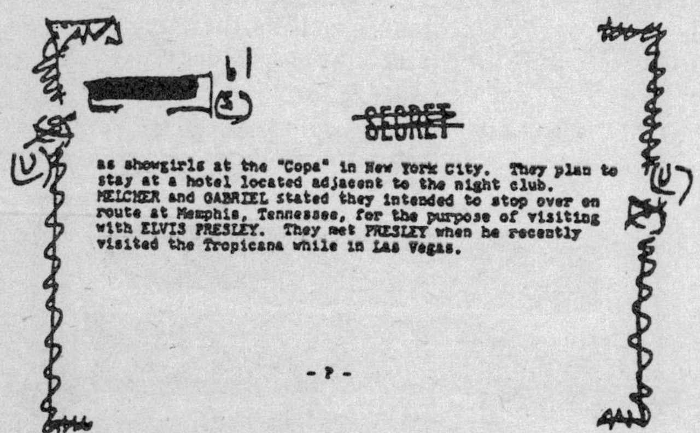
b1
(S)

~~SECRET~~

as showgirls at the "Copa" in New York City. They plan to stay at a hotel located adjacent to the night club. MELCHER and GABRIEL stated they intended to stop over en route at Memphis, Tennessee, for the purpose of visiting with ELVIS PRESLEY. They met PRESLEY when he recently visited the Tropicana while in Las Vegas.

(U)

- 3 -

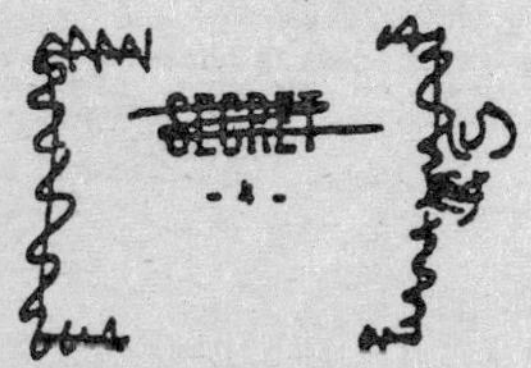
~~SECRET~~

(S)

- 4 -

A27–34

Extensive file on the blackmail attempt by "Hans Schmidt" on Elvis while Presley was in the Army stationed in Germany. Included are handwritten letters from the doctor as well as the Army's own investigation into the attempted extortion.

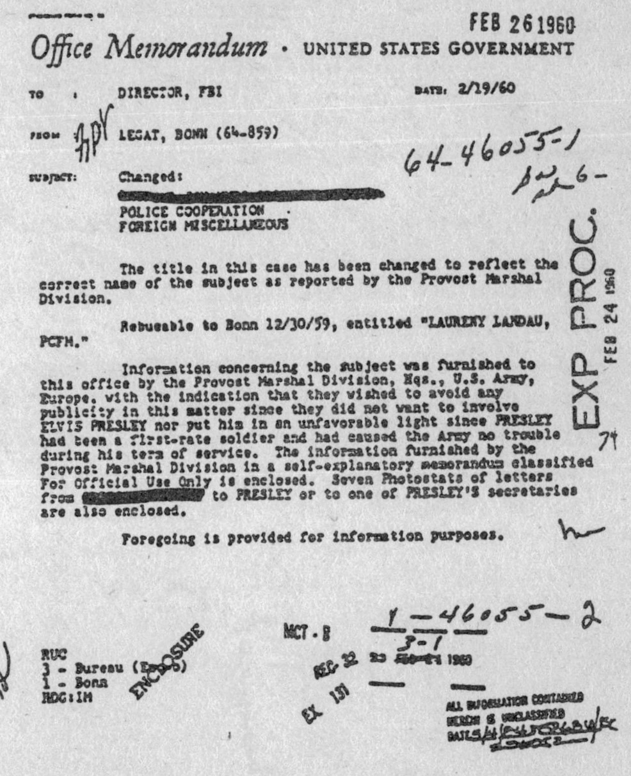

FEB 26 1960

Office Memorandum • UNITED STATES GOVERNMENT

TO : DIRECTOR, FBI DATE: 2/29/60

FROM : LEGAT, BONN (64-859)

64-46055-1

SUBJECT: Changed:
[redacted]
POLICE COOPERATION
FOREIGN MISCELLANEOUS

The title in this case has been changed to reflect the correct name of the subject as reported by the Provost Marshal Division.

Rebueable to Bonn 12/30/59, entitled "LAURENY LANDAU, PCFM."

Information concerning the subject was furnished to this office by the Provost Marshal Division, Hqs., U.S. Army, Europe, with the indication that they wished to avoid any publicity in this matter since they did not want to involve ELVIS PRESLEY nor put him in an unfavorable light since PRESLEY had been a first-rate soldier and had caused the Army no trouble during his term of service. The information furnished by the Provost Marshal Division in a self-explanatory memorandum classified For Official Use Only is enclosed. Seven Photostats of letters from [redacted] to PRESLEY or to one of PRESLEY'S secretaries are also enclosed.

Foregoing is provided for information purposes.

EXP. PROC. FEB 24 1960

RUC
3 - Bureau (Enc. 5)
1 - Bonn
RDC:IM

ENCLOSURE

MCT-8 64-46055-2
3-1

REC 32

EX 131

ALL INFORMATION CONTAINED HEREIN IS UNCLASSIFIED

62 MAR 3 1960

Salon de Fleur,
603/4/5 Clinical Centre.
c/o Plein & Wanderers Streets
Johannesburg.
South Africa.
9th/10/59.

Dear Miss Stefaniak,

In reply to your letter of the 5th October, I would like to give you the following information regarding my treatment. There are several substances used in my Aromatherapy treatments for the sake of their Remedial Therapeutic and Rejuvenating properties. I have recently received the World Patent Rights of this formula and the Treatments may be given advantageously to people of any Skin type and I would say it is very acceptable to

I

Salon de Fleur
603/4/5 Clinical Centre
c/o Plain & Wanderers Streets
Johannesburg
South Africa,
9th/10/59

Dear Miss Stefaniak,

In reply to your letter of the 5th October, I would like to give you the following information regarding my treatment. There are several substances used in my Aroma Therapy treatments for the sake of their remedial Therapeutic and Rejuvenating properties. I have recently received the World Patent Rights of this formula, and the treatments may be given advantageously to people of any Skin type and I would say it is Very acceptable to

II

people Suffeing from oily Skins, Enlarged pores, Acne Scars and Wrinkles—crowsfeet etc; and I expect Mr Elvis Presley to benefit from This Scientific Method and to receive Great Satisfaction as others have received. It has given me Great Pleasure to receive Your Enlightening and Most Welcome Letter and from the innermost recesses of my heart I would Welcome the opportunity to Treat Mr Presley. Mr. Elvis Presley's treatments will be exactly the Same as Those Based on the Aromatherapy technique practised in My Salon—through the odorous part of Flowers, aromatic plants and resins, and that of Roses, Carnations Orange blossoms, Mimosa, Camomile, Cinnamon, rosewood Sandalwood etc; the Treatments helps to revitalize the Skin Cells and Structure

II

people Suffering from oily Skins, Enlarged pores, acne scars and wrinkles—crowsfeet, etc; and I expect Mr Elvis Presley to benefit from this Scientific Method and to receive Great Satisfaction as others have received. It has given me Great Pleasure to receive Your Enlightening and Most Welcome Letter and from the innermost recesses of my heart I would Welcome the opportunity to treat Mr Presley. Mr. Elvis Presley's treatments will be exactly the Same as Those Based on the Aroma Therapy technique practised in My Salon—through the odorous part of Flowers, aromatic plants and resins, and that of Roses, Carnations Orange blossoms, Mimosa, Camomile, Cinnamon, rosewood Sandalwood etc. The Treatments helps to revitalize the Skin Cells and Structure

III

Beneath the Epidarmis - which is Continualy being discarded. The Method Employed requires the penetration in the Epidermis of the odoriferous Substances by a Method which are officious but not violent. Before the actual treatment starts a short preliminary Neuromuscular Massage will leave the Skin more receptive. This is accomplished with the aid of a Special Cream of most essential oils and finest ingrediants - which accomplishes a deep cleansing as it Contains Special Emulsifiers. By using Special Methods in Massage and Warmth - I aid the Skin so that the essential oils are readily assimilated by the Tissues. The Skin Tissues become activated and infused with new Life and the texture of the Skin is improved, the Complexion more alive,

III

Beneath the Epidermis—which is Continualy being discarded. The Method Employed requires the penetration in the Epidermis of the odoriferous Substances by a Method which are officious but not Violent. Before the actual treatment starts a short preliminary Neuramuscular Message will leave the Skin more receptive. This is accomplished with the aid of a Special Cream of most essential oils and finest ingredients—which accomplishes a deep cleansing as it contains Special Emulsifiers. By using Special Methods in Massage and Warmth—I aid the Skin so that the essential oils are readily assimilated By the Tissues. The Skin Tissues become activated and infused with new Life and the texture of the Skin is improved, the Complexion more alive,

4

the Epidermis more elastic The Muscles of the Face and features assume their youthful positions this is to be Understood because from a Scientific point of View it Can be proved that in These essential oils and ingredients Combined exist a great Number of free Electrons:- (and Nature Provides for this) these Electrons which are responsible for the odor of Certain perfectly organized Moleculas can penetrate the Epidermis and by infusing the epidermis with odoriferous Moleculas one injects Biological Energy - ie or in other "words New Life." Mr. Elvis Presley can Thus rest assured that his Treatments will be individualized - that is to Say;- adapted to Suit his Skin Type or Epidermis. I am now busy preparing his treatment and Composing

4

the Epidermis more elastic The Muscles of the Face and features assume their Youthful positions. This is to be Understood because from a Scientific point of View it can be proved that in These essential oils and ingredients combined exist a Great Number of Free Electrons.—(and Nature Provides for this)

These Electrons which are responsible for the odor of Certain perfectly organized Molecules can penetrate the Epidermis and by infusing the epidermis with odoriferous Molecules one injects Biological Energy—ie or in the other "words New Life." Mr. Elvis Presley can thus rest assured that his Treatments will be individualized—That is to Say,—adapted to Suit his Skin Type or Epidermis. I am now busy preparing His treatment and Composing

5.

mixtures of the essential oils and extracts that will Suit His particular Skin, the Treatments will be most efficacious for Enlarged pores-oily Skin and any Scars which will become less Visible as the weeks move on into Months.

Then too, there can be no possible bad affect to the Skin in the future years but: instead if Mr. Elvis Presley decides to follow a certain Routine or rather Make use of My Special Aromatherapy Mixture Elixir Home Method, He will not age but instead become as Handsome as I would Like him to be, "so, Mr. Presley please don't worry about the Small Wrinkles on your forehead;- You will Not age". One or two Cures per Year will Keep the Skin in perfect Condition. A Cure Consists of a Series of 10, 18 or 20 Treatments once or Twice

5

mixtures of the essential oils and extracts that will Suit His particular Skin, the Treatments will be most efficacious for Enlarged pores-oily Skin and any Scars which will become Less Visible as the weeks move on into Months.

Then too, there can be no possible bad effect to the Skin in the future years but instead if Mr. Elvis Presley decides to follow a certain Routine or rather Make use of My Special Aroma Therapy Mixture Elixir Home Method, He will not age but instead become as Handsome as I would Like him to be, "so, Mr. Presley please don't worry about The Small Wrinkles on Your Forehead—You will Not age." One or two Cures per Year will Keep the Skin in perfect Condition. A Cure Consists of a Series of 10, 18 or 20 treatments once or Twice

6.

a Week according to the demands of the particular case. The revitalized skin permits perfect Make-up. a great asset to actresses and actors whose faces. exposed to powerful flood lights must always be in perfect Condition in order to Retain a smooth Make up. The Treatments will therefore be a boon & a blessing for Mr. Presley and as you have stated.-I quote, "He feels that there can possibly be an improvement in his skin when he returns to the States" Well Miss Stefaniak, Why Not. I Can only suggest that Mr. Elvis Presley should start these treatments as quickly as possible. & you Can Convey my message of appreciation to Mr. Presley in the interest he has shown. and He has my Boy Scouts

6
a Week according to the demands of the particular Case. The revitalized Skin permits perfect Make-up. A Great *asset* to actresses and actors whose faces exposed to powerful Flood Lights Must always be in perfect condition in order to Retain a Smooth Make up. The Treatments will therefore be a Boon & a blessing for Mr. Presley and as you have stated.—I quote, "He feels that there can possibly be an improvement in his Skin when he returns to the States" Well Miss Stefaniak, Why Not. I Can only Suggest That Mr. Elvis Presley Should start these Treatments as quickly as possible. & You Can Convey my message of appreciation to Mr. Presley in the interest he has shown. and He has my Boy Scouts

2

Honour that I will not misplace
His Trust in me to Keep this very
Confidential.
You have asked me to
send You a prompt reply and how
I would like to arrange the matter.
Well, Miss Stefaniak I am due
to go back to our Farm within
The next 2 weeks and as my Cosmetics
are going on the Market, I intend on
having a short rest. So, I am free
to treat Mr. Elvis Presley and Can
Leave by air for Bad Nauheim
Germany as soon as it is Convenient.
and if Mr. Presley is quite Satisfied
I'll Come almost immediately! He
Deserves it. I shall await Your
reply to this letter and if Mr.
Presley desires it I'll Send You
an overseas telegram before I Leave

7
Honour that I will not misplace His Trust in me to Keep This Very Confidential.

You have asked me to send You a prompt reply and how I would Like to arrange The matter. Well, Miss Stefaniak I am due to go back to our Farm within The next 2 Weeks and as my Cosmetics are going on the Market, I intend on having a Short rest. So, I am free to treat Mr. Elvis Presley and can Leave by air for Bad Nauheim Germany as soon as it is Convenient. and if Mr. Presley is quite Satisfied I'll Come almost immediately. He Deserves it. I shall await Your reply to this Letter and if Mr. Presley desires it I'll Send You an overseas telegram before I Leave

8.

but: on the otherhand a Telegram is not a very Secretive thing as the telagraph administrations and Postoffice workers follow up the particulars. and to Learn to Know thing. I Could however address a Telegram to you in order to inform you When I'm due to Leave. would that be in Order?

Furthermore Miss Stefaniak. I dont intend charging Mr. Presley for the treatments Until it is Successful. But. I would expect my air passage Return to be paid or rather that I be reimbursed Subsequently. before my Return to South Africa if it So pLeases Mr. Presley. then too. as my treatment takes about two Months and two weeks duration. I would also expect my accommodation to be provided for during that time. In

FOR OFFICIAL USE ONLY

8

but; on the otherhand a Telegram is not a Very Secretive Thing as the telegraph administrations and Postoffice workers follow up the particulars, and to Learn to Know Thing. I could however address a telegram to you in order to inform you when I'm due to leave. Would that be in order?

Furthermore Miss Stefaniak, I dont intend charging Mr. Presley for the treatments until it is successful. But, I would expect My air passage Return to be paid or rather that I be reimbursed Subsequently, before my return to South Africa if it so pleases Mr. Presley. Then, too, as my treatment takes about two Months and two weeks duration, I would also expect my accommodation to be provided for during that time. In

9

this respect I am not expecting Lavish treatment. Mr Elvis Presley's treatments Could be carried out in the Privacy of his abode or in a Suitable Hotel Room allowing for strict Privacy. In this respect I should best leave all the arrange-ments to You after we have discussed the Matter. The amount of treatments I'm going to give Mr Presley also-depends on the Reaction I will get after each treatment. depending too on the equal Balance between the Acid and oil Content of the Skin and alternatively on the equal Balance between the alkaline & Moisture Content. I will work towards that end and in order to achieve and to Create a New healthy Skin - Time & patience is required and I do realize that

9

This respect I am not expecting Lavish treatment. Mr. Elvis Presley's treatments Could be carried out in the Privacy of his abode as in a Suitable Hotel Room allowing for strict Privacy. In this respect I should best Leave all the arrangements to you after we have discussed the Matter. The amount of treatments I'm going to give Mr Presley also—depends on the Reaction I will get after each treatment, depending too on the equal Balance between the acid and oil content of the Skin and alternatively on the equal Balance between the Alkaline & Moisture Content. I will work towards that end and in order to achieve and to Create a New healthy skin—Time & patience is required and I do realize that

10.

Mr. Presley owns the admirable qualities of tolerance and patience and I would add. Endurance; else how could he have achieved. While these Suitable arrangements will have to be made and I'm sure you will be able to make Suitable appointments at the Right time. The treatments last from about One to two and a half Hours depending once again on the Reaction I get. It will Surprise You to hear that the Better the reaction the Longer the treatment last.

Concludingly, Please Convey my heartfelt appreciation to Mr. Elvis Presley.

I shall also be very appreciative if you will again forward me a reply at Your earliest Convenience.

Thanking You. Yours Sincerely,

FOR OFFICIAL USE ONLY

10

Mr. Presley owns the admirable qualities of tolerance and patience and I would add Endurance; else how could he have achieved. While these Suitable arrangements will have to be made and Im sure You will be able to Make Suitable appointments at the Right time. The treatments last from about One to Two and a half Hours depending once again on the Reaction I get. It will Surprise You to hear that the Better the reaction the Longer the treatment Last.

Concludingly, Please Convey My heartfelt appreciation to Mr. Elvis Presley.

I shall also be very appreciative if you will again forword me a reply at Your earliest Convenience.

Thanking you.

Yours Sincerely,

I

Post Script.

Dear Miss Stefaniak,

On
Second Thought I'll let You
and Mr Presley know what
my Bank's address is In case
Mr Presley Cares to Send the
Bank a Sum of Money for my
Journey. My Bank is Barclays
Bank D.C.O. registerd Commercial
Bank with which is amalgamated
The National Bank of South Africa
Limited, there are Several Branches
within Johannesburg. I am Banking
with the "Bree street East Branch
Johannesburg, Transvaal, South Africa.
Furthermore, Mr. Presley could
get in touch with My Solicitor
Mr. D.I. Gordon who is a Lawyer

I

Post Script

Dear Miss Stefaniak,

On Second Thought I'll Let You and Mr Presley Know what my Bank's address is In case Mr Presley Cares to Send the Bank a Sum of Money for my Journey My Bank is Barclays Bank with which is amalgamated The National Bank of South Africa Limited, There are Several Branches within Johannesburg. I am Banking with the *"Bree Street East* Branch Johannesburg, Transvaal, South Africa.

Furthermore, Mr. Presley could get in touch with My Solicitor Mr. D.I. Jordon who is a Lawyer

II

of Repute. address:- Mr D.T. Gordon 98 Security Buildings Commissioner Street. Johannesburg.
Nevertheless I made certain Enquiries by "Trek-Airways" Pty Ltd Aircraft operators passengers etc, address, "Yorkshire House." c/o Rissik and Marshall Streets. Box 2758. Johannesburg, and they informed me that my air-passage to Germany ie to Dusseldorf will cost me £200 Return and £105 Single. From Dusseldorf arrangements well be made to take me to "Bad Nauheim". Better still However would be if you people arrange it and send my ticket from the Trek airways Office in Dusseldorf. and at

II

of Repute. Address:—Mr. D.I. Jordon 98 Security Buildings Commissioner Street, Johannesburg.

Nevertheless I made certain Enquirres by "Trek-Airways" Ltd aircraft Operators passengers etc, address, "Yorkshire House, c/o Rissik and Mooshad Streets, Box 2758, Johannesburg, and they informed me that my air passage to Germany ie to Dusseldorf will cost me £200 Return and £105 Single. From Dusseldorf arrangements will be made to take me to "Bad Nauheim". Better still However would be if you people arrange it and Send my ticket from the trek airways office in Dusseldorf, and at

III

one and the same time Request the "trek" office to inform their Johannesburg Branch about the ticket and arrangements. In that case please send the Ticket by Registered Post. There is a 10 % reduction on a Return ticket but; if Mr. Elvis Presley deems it fit a single ticket could be forwarded at the start. I mention this to You as I'm a little bit out of funds having paid for recent Song Recordings as I'm bringing some of my Songs to Mr Elvis Presley which I've Composed. then too I've had to buy farm equipment. Car tires and things in general. also Repaying of Income Tax. etc. therefore please explain the Matter

FOR OFFICIAL USE ONLY

III

one and the Same time Request the "trek" office to inform their Johannesburg Branch about the ticket arrangements. In that case please Send the Ticket by Registered Post. There is a 10% reduction on a Return ticket but, if Mr. Elvis Presley deems it fit a Single ticket Could be forwarded at the start. I mention this to you as I'm a Little bit out of funds having paid for recent Song Recordings as I'm bringing Some of My Songs to Mr Elvis Presley which I've Composed. Then too I've had to Buy farm equipment, Car tires and things in General, also the paying of Income Tax, etc. Therefore please explain The Matter

4

to Mr Elvis Presley who will
understand Reason
Thanking You. & hoping
for a early favaurable Reply.
Yours Truly,

4

to Mr Elvis Preseley who will understand Reason.

Thanking you, and hoping for a early favourable Reply.

Yours Truly,

Post Script

Dear Elvis,

An International Passport has been issued to me and all arrangements have been made & awaiting your further Instructions.

with best wishes
Thanking you.

Yrs Truly,

FOR OFFICIAL USE ONLY

Post Script
Dear Elvis,

An International Passport has been issued to Me and all arrangements have been made & awaiting Your further Instructions.

With Best Wishes
Thanking You,
Ys Truly,

NB Please not New address.

I [redacted]

"Elandskraal Farm",
P. O. Mooiwooi
Via-Pretoria.
Transvaal.
South Africa.
26/10/59.

To Mr Elvis Presley,

Dear Elvis,
Trusting that this note reaches You in good health and in fine Spirits. May I inform You that I have Cancelled many New bookings. and that I have Completed all arrangements for my departure to Germany

FOR OFFICIAL USE ONLY

NB Please note new Address

I

"Elandskaal Farm,"
P.O. Mooinooi
Via-Pretoria
Transvaal.
South Africa
26/10/59

To Mr Elvis Presley,

Dear Elvis,
Trusting that this note reaches you in good health and in fine Spirits. May I inform you that I have cancelled many new bookings and that I have completed all arrangements for my departure to Germany

II

and I shall meet You upon Your return from wildflicken so that you will be able to start with Your treatments almost immediately.

Also I feel honored and very privileged in having been chosen for this important task. In fact I am greatly enthused in my mission and assure You as You are soon to see, that I am going to work Wonders with Your skin. It is Certainly my cherished ambition to give You a Complete New Skin and I swear to achieve this within the quickest possible

II

and I shall meet you upon your return from wildflicken so that you will be able to start with your treatments almost immediately.

Also I feel honored and very privileged in having been chosen for this important task. In fact I am greatly enthused in my mission and assure you as you are soon to see, that I am going to work wonders with your skin. It is certainly my cherished ambition to give you a complete new skin and I swear to achieve this within the quickest possible

3.

Time. I shall spare myself no efforts in this direction.

Please convey to your very good and charming secretary my sincerest thanks for all her kind attentions. As you would say with your sense of Humour "Miss Postage Stamp" must be over-worked what with all the Mail:- Bless Her.

Enclosed find Latest clipping from our Weekend Local paper.

Au Révoir & best wishes.

Yrs, Truly.

FOR OFFICIAL USE ONLY

3.
time.
I shall spare myself no efforts in this direction.
Please convey to your very good and charming secretary my sincerest thanks for all her kind attentions. As you would say with your sense of humour "Miss Postage Stamp" must be over-worked what with all the mail.—
—Bless Her.
Enclosed find latest clipping from our Weekend Local paper.
Au Revoir & best wishes.
Yrs, Truly,

I [redacted]

"Elandskraal Farm,"
P. O. Mooinooi
Via-Pretoria.
Transvaal.
South Africa.
6/11/1959

Dear Miss Stefaniak,

not having had a reply to my last letter I thought I would write and let you know that I have now made all the arrangements to proceed to Germany. I have in the meantime provided for my fare from this end - so that if you have allready arranged for same from Germany you should let me know immediately.

Should I not hear from you within the next few days - to say that it is to early to leave in view of what you say in your letter, - then I shall proceed to Germany & cable you when

FOR OFFICIAL USE ONLY

I

"Elandskaal Farm,"
P.O. Mooinooi
Via-Pretoria
Transvaal
South Africa
/ /1959

Dear Miss Stefaniak,
Not having had a reply to my last letter I thought I would write and let you know that I have now made all the arrangements to proceed to Germany. I have in the meantime provided for my fare from this end—so that if you have allready arranged for same from Germany you should let me know immediately.
Should I not hear from you within the next few days—to say, that it is to early to leave in view of what you say in your letter—then I shall proceed to Germany and Cable you when

II

to expect Me. I'm Looking forward to being of Service to Mr Presley and have no doubt that I shall Surprise him with the Results.

Enclosed is a Photo of our Elvis out of an Italian Periodical Then too I'm Sending you "Show Biz" in which you'll see my advertisement, I'm also Enclosing 4 References from Ladies I have Treated & will post you more in future. if Required.

Thanking You in anticipation

I am - Miss-Stefaniak,

Yours Sincerely,

FOR OFFICIAL USE ONLY

II

to expect me. Im looking forward to being of Service to Mr. Presley and have no doubt that I shall surprise him with the results.

Enclosed is a photo of our Elvis out of an Italian Periodical. Then too, I'm sending you "Show Biz" in which you'll see my advertisement, I'm also enclosing 4 references from Ladies I have treated & will post you more in future if required.

Thanking you in anticipation.

I am—Miss Stefaniak,

yours Sincerely,

Post Script.

Miss Stefaniak,
Attached please find a few Nice pages all about Elvis—"the STAR OF THE CENTYRY." I would not like to See him grow older and who would.
(Page 7) I clearly noticed the wrinkles on Mr Presley's forehead & made a Note of it to You.
With Every best Wish.
Yrs; Truly,

FOR OFFICIAL USE ONLY

Post Script

Miss Stefaniak,
Attached please find a few nice pages all about Elvis—"The STAR OF THE CENTURY." I would not like to see him grow older and who would. (Page 7) I clearly noticed the wrinkles on Mr Presley's forehead & made a note of it to you.
With every best wish.
Yrs, Truly,

To. Mr Elvis Presley
c/o Miss E. Stefaniak
Bad Nauheim,

Dear Elvis,
I Sincerely Trust that this Epistle finds you in the Pink of Health and in high Spirits hoping too. That you are shaping up nicely in the army We are all Looking forward to your return to Civilian Life
I forwarded some recently References to your Private

FOR OFFICIAL USE ONLY

To: Mr. Elvis Presley
c/o Miss Stefaniak
Bad Nauheim

Dear Elvis,

I sincerely trust that this epistle finds you in the pink of health and in high spirits. Hoping too, that you are shaping up nicely in the army. We are all looking forward to your return to civilian life. I forwarded some recent references to your private

II

Secretary Miss Stefaniak & I Trust that You will peruse them and kindly take Notice of what some of my clients have to say. As You can see by the Attached advertisement in "Film World". "A Bevy of Ladies have received Satisfaction" and I might as well add I always give Satisfaction. Elvis. Once again I beg You to allow me to be of Great Service to You and Let me Know when to come.

Enclosed Please find two More recent References from two Satisfied Ladies,

Concludingly. I wish to Let You Know that I have given up my business and Cancelled many new Bookings in order to do You. So Elvis. Please Dont disappoint me. as I wont be able to get over it easily.

thank You & God Bless You:

Yrs. Sincerely Laurens.

II

secretary Miss Stefaniak & I trust that you will peruse them and kindly take notice of what some of my clients have to say. As you can see by the attached advertisement in "Film Worlds" "A bevy of ladies have received satisfaction" and I might as well add I always give satisfaction. Elvis, once again I beg you to allow me to be of great service to you and let me know when to come . . . Enclosed please find two more recent references from two satisfied ladies.

Concludingly, I wish to let you know that I have given up my business and cancelled many new bookings in order to do you. So Elvis, Please don't disappoint me, as I won't be able to get over it easily.

Thank you & God bless you.

Yrs, Sincerely,

Hotel Roc
Bad Nauheim.

Dear Mr Elvis Presley
I wrote the attached letter on a Solicitors instructions here in Bad Nauheim
But; I have decided since this Morning Sunday the 27/12/59 Not to Take Action against you.
I am deeply sorry for you and know & feel that you Miss something Big in Life, then too, it's Unchristian to take anyone to court & I will just have to make up the loss and make

Hotel Rex
Bad Nauheim

Dear Mr. Elvis Presley
I wrote the attached letter on a Solicitor's instructions here in Bad Nauheim.
But; I have decided since this Morning Sunday the 27/12/59 Not to take action against you.
I am deeply sorry for you and know I feel that you miss something big in life, then too, it's unchristian to take anyone to court & I will just have to make up the loss and make

II

The Very most of a Bad Situation
and start all over again with a New Salon.
One Must also have consideration
for those who suffered a Bereavement
as the attached article Marked (X)
states. You have Lost a Mother
and Since this is Your Second
Year in the Army & Since
You have had to go through
So Much in Life I Sympathise
with You & forgive You. I'm only sorry
You had no time for my treatments of longer duration.
Yes. We Must be forgiving one
to another—thats how it Goes. Regards
to Elizabeth and wish you all happiness.
I am Leaving Bad Nauheim for
a Better clime and wish You every
Success & happiness in the future. try & keep
up the Dist. [illegible] / Bless You Yours truly,

II

the very most of a bad situation and start all over again with a new salon.

One must also have consideration for those who suffered a bereavement as the attached article marked states. You have lost a mother and since this is your second year in the army & since you have had to go through so much in life I sympathize with you & I forgive you. I'm only sorry you had no time for my treatments of longer duration. Yes, we must be forgiving one to another—that's how it goes. Regards to Elizabeth and wish you all happiness.

I am leaving Bad Nauheim for a better clime and wish you every success & happiness in the future. Try & keep up the diet.

Bless you. Yours truly,

28/12/59

Dear Elvis,

Dont worry about this letter
Now I have been very hurt
Because things did not turn out
the way I expected. and as you had
more time for the other things which
interest you Most.- I could not carry on.
& get Results Well, as I've Said there
is No ill feeling anymore and I
wish you Well. and that Goes
for Elizabeth, Lamar, Rex, Cliff, Vee
Dee, your Dad-Vernon, Grandma & your
friends. Good Luck Elvis.

FOR OFFICIAL USE ONLY

28/12/59
Dear Elvis,

Don't worry about this Letter Now I have been very hurt Because things did not turn out the way I expected, and as you had more time for the other things which interest you Most—I Could not Carry on. I get Results Well, as I've Said There is no ill feeling anymore and I wish You Well, and that Goes for Elizabeth, Lamarr, Rex, Cliff, Vee Dee, Your Dad-Vernon,, Grandma & Your Friends.

Good Luck Elvis.

FOR OFFICIAL USE ONLY

MEMORANDUM 5 February 1960

1. Elvis Presley was interviewed on 28 December 1959 concerning his complaint that he was the victim of blackmail by a [redacted], of Johannesburg, South Africa. [redacted] represents himself to be a doctor specialist in the field of dermatology. [redacted] is not a medical doctor.

2. Copies of letters from [redacted] to Presley and Presley's private secretary were obtained on loan basis so that they could be photographed.

3. On or about 27 November 1959, [redacted] appeared at the residence of Elvis Presley in Bad Nauheim, Germany and began his treatments. These treatments took place in Presley's quarters in the presence of two female secretaries (both U. S.). The treatment involved Presley's shoulders and face.

4. Presley reports that [redacted] made several homosexual advances to some of his enlisted friends. [redacted] also is alleged to have admitted to Presley that he is bi-sexual. His first homosexual experiences took place early in his life in the orphanage in which he was brought up.

5. On 24 December 1959 Presley decided to discontinue the skin treatments. At the time that he told [redacted] of this decision he also thoroughly censured [redacted] for embarrassing him as a result of the improper advances that he [redacted] made to his (Presley's) enlisted friends. [redacted] immediately went into a fit of rage, tore up a photo album of Presley's, and threatened to ruin his singing career and to involve Presley's American girl friend (a 16 year old daughter of an Air Force captain). [redacted] further threatened to expose Presley by photographs and tape recordings which are alleged to present Presley in compromising situations. Presley assures us that this is impossible since he never was in any compromising situations. Presley contends that [redacted] is mentally disturbed. This is based upon the fits [redacted] has had and on his statements concerning the shock treatments he has been taking..

6. By negotiation, Presley agreed to pay [redacted] $200.00 for treatments received and also to furnish him with a $315.00 plane fare to London, England. [redacted] agreed to depart to England on 25 December 1959 at 1930 hours from Frankfurt, Germany. [redacted] did not leave as agreed, rather returned and demanded an additional $250.00, which Presley paid. A day later [redacted] made a telephonic demand for 2,000 £ for the loss of his practice which he closed in Johannesburg, South Africa prior to his departure for Bad Nauheim to treat Presley.

FOR OFFICIAL USE ONLY

FOR OFFICIAL USE ONLY

MEMORANDUM (Contd) 3 February 1960

7. [redacted] finally departed Rhein-Main Air Field, Frankfurt, Germany at 1600 hours, 6 January 1960 on Flight 491, British European Airway for London, England under the name of [redacted] He is alleged to be seeking entry into the United States. No contact between Presley and [redacted] has been reported since 5 January.

WARREN H. METZNER
Major, MPC
Chief, Investigations Branch

2

FOR OFFICIAL USE ONLY

A35–42

Letter to Elvis warning him of an East German plot to kill him and files of subsequent FBI investigation.

Recorded
3/27/59
dan

FEDERAL BUREAU OF INVESTIGATION
UNITED STATES DEPARTMENT OF JUSTICE

Laboratory Work Sheet NO LAB FILE

Re: ELVIS PRESLEY
INFORMATION CONCERNING

File # 63-3064
Lab. # D-303175 DG-

Examination requested by: FBI, New York (62-12152) 3/24/59

Examination requested: Document

Date received: 3/25/59 b7C

Result of Examination:

Examination by:

Specimens submitted for examination

Q1 Envelope postmarked "CANTON OHIO MAR 12 1959 2 30 PM," addressed to "R. C. A. Victor Records 155 E. 24th st New York 10 New York," and accompanying four-page letter dated 3/11/59, beginning "Dear Sir I have just..." and ending "....Thank You."

please note.
important
from
R.C.A. Victor Records.
155 E. 24th st
new york 10 new york

1

Canton O.
3-11-59

Dear sir
I have just read a letter
from a relative in
west germany.
Plans have been made &
already in the Hands of
a red soldier in east germany
to Kill Elvis Presley.
the mans own sister sliped
a note in to west germany
she read the Plans - & is
not in favor of what her
brother is being Paid to
do. this red soldier will be

1
Canton O.
3-11-59

Dear Sir

I have just read a letter from a relative in West Germany.
Plans have been made & already in the Hands of a red soldier in East Germany to Kill Elvis Presley. the mans own sister sliped a note in to West Germany she read the Plans-& is not in favor of what her brother is being Paid to do. this red soldier will be

2/
wearing an american
uniform - he is to leave
East germany slip in to
west Germany some Time
between mar 14 + 22-nd
he has been given orders
to Kill him even if he
has to blow up the
Hotel or home where he +
his Father live.
Please Please dont take
this as a crank letter
because as god is my
witness this every word
is true. i can not give

2

wearing an american uniform—he is to leave East Germany slip in to West Germany some Time between mar 14 & 22-nd he has been given orders to Kill him even if he has to blow up the Hotel or home where he & his Father lives—Please Please don't take this as a crank letter because as god is my witness this every word is true. i can not give

3/

my name or the relatives
name in Germany the
People in west Germany
would be in danger
and of course the sister
would be Killed
I had Thought of writing
to the President or some
Goverment offical - but I
felt they would just
consider it a letter from
crank + forget it.
as you have a contact
with Presley + know his
manager so well maybe

3

my name or the relatives name in Germany the People in Wets Germany would be in danger. and of course the sister would be Killed I had Thought of writing to the President or some Government Official, but I felt they would Just consider it a letter from crank & forget it. as you have a contract with Presley & Know his manager so well maybe

4/
god can get some
action. I am not a
teenager I am a mother
& Grandmother.
Please try to Protect
This young american soldier
in what every way you
can.

Thank you

4
god can get some action. i am not a teenager I am a mother & grandmother.
Please try to Protect This young american soldier in what every way you can.

Thank you.

FBI

Date: 3/24/59

Transmit the following in ______________ (Type in plain text or code)

Via AIRTEL (Priority or Method of Mailing)

Griffith

TO: DIRECTOR, FBI
ATT: FBI LABORATORY

303175

FROM: SAC, NEW YORK (62-12152)

SUBJECT: ELVIS PRESLEY
INFORMATION CONCERNING

Enclosed herewith are the original and a Photostat of a letter dated 3/11/59, and the envelope postmarked 3/12/59, addressed to RCA VICTOR RECORDS, 155 East 24th Street, NY 10, NY, which contains information from an anonymous writer that plans had been made for a Red Army soldier to kill ELVIS PRESLEY, well-known entertainer, who is presently stationed in US Army in Germany.

[redacted] Legal Department, RCA, who made letter available on 3/19/59, advised that it had been received 3/16/59, and was handled by numerous people on the staff. [redacted] stated that PRESLEY's manager, Col. THOMAS PARKER, Box 417, Madison, Tenn., phone # Nashville 8-2868, was informed of contents of letter and he advised that letter appeared identical to letters received in past from a woman in Ohio and that FBI had already looked into matter. PARKER stated woman was "nuts." Letter contained no personal threats from writer.

b7D

Two Photostats are being forwarded for assistance of Memphis Office and it is requested that Memphis instruct Laboratory as to what action desired.

RUC

3

REC-8

3 - Bureau (Encls 2)
(1 - FBI Laboratory)
2 - Memphis (Encls 2)
1 - NY (62-12152)

JMB:NIM
8

ENCLOSURE

SEVEN

Approved: ______________ Special Agent in Charge Sent ________ M Per ________

Recorded
3/27/59
dan

FEDERAL BUREAU OF INVESTIGATION
UNITED STATES DEPARTMENT OF JUSTICE

Laboratory Work Sheet NO LAB FILE

Re: ELVIS PRESLEY
INFORMATION CONCERNING

File # 63-9064-3
Lab. # D-303175 DG-

Examination requested by: FBI, New York (62-12152) 3/24/59

Examination requested: Document

Date received: 3/25/59 b7C

Result of Examination:

Examination by: [redacted] 1626

Specimens submitted for examination

Q1 Envelope postmarked "CANTON OHIO MAR 12 1959 2 30 PM," addressed to "R. C. A. Victor Records 155 E. 24th st New York 10 New York," and accompanying four-page letter dated 3/11/59, beginning "Dear Sir I have just..." and ending "....Thank You."

REPORT
of the
FBI
LABORATORY

FEDERAL BUREAU OF INVESTIGATION
WASHINGTON, D. C.

To: FBI, Memphis

Date: January 20, 1964
FBI File No.
Lab. No. D-440449 IK

Re: Unsub, aka [redacted]
ELVIS PRESLEY - VICTIM·
EXTORTION; POSSIBLE THREAT TO
PRESIDENT OF THE U. S.

b7C

Specimens received 1/17/64

Q1 Post card postmarked "HUNTSVILLE ALA. JAN 10 1964 5 30 PM" bearing handwritten address "Presdient Elvis Presly Memphis S, Tennessee" bearing on reverse side handwritten note beginning "You Will Be next on my list..."

Result of examination:

Specimen Q1 was searched through the appropriate sections of the Anonymous Letter File without identifying it with any of the writings therein. A representative copy will be added to the file for future reference.

Specimen Q1 contains no watermark, indented writing, or other feature which might assist in determining its immediate source.

Specimen Q1 is returned herewith. A photograph has been retained.

WSO:GFN (5)

MAIL ROOM ☐ TELETYPE UNIT ☐

Laboratory Transmittal Form
7-72

FBI
LABORATORY
WASHINGTON, D. C.

To: FBI, New York (62-12152)

Date: April 14, 1959

Re: ELVIS PRESLEY
INFORMATION CONCERNING

J. Edgar Hoover
John Edgar Hoover, Director

REC- 77
FBI File No. 63-3064
Lab. No. D-303175 DG

Examination requested by: FBI, New York

Reference: Airtel 3/24/59

Examination requested: Document

Remarks:

The case entitled [redacted] ELVIS PRESLEY, VICTIM, EXTORTION, has Bureau file 9-33135.

b7C

Enclosures (3) (3 Lab report)
1 - Memphis - Enclosure (Lab report) (62-New)
1 - Bureau file 9-33135

SFM:vb (7)

MAIL ROOM ☑ TELETYPE UNIT ☐

Date: April 22, 1959

To: Assistant Chief of Staff for Intelligence
Department of the Army
The Pentagon
Washington 25, D. C.

From: John Edgar Hoover, Director
Federal Bureau of Investigation

Subject: ELVIS PRESLEY
INFORMATION CONCERNING

Attached is a Photostat of an anonymous letter dated March 11, 1959, postmarked Canton, Ohio, and addressed to RCA Victor Records, 155 East 24th Street, New York 10, New York, which contains information to the effect that a Red Army soldier in East Germany is planning to kill Elvis Presley, a well-known entertainer, presently attached to the U. S. Army in Germany.

[redacted] Legal Department, RCA, has advised that the contents of this letter have been made available to Presley's manager, Colonel Thomas Parker, Box 417 Madison, Tennessee. For your information, during 1957 and 1958, one [redacted] wrote several threatening letters to Presley. [redacted] voluntarily entered the [redacted] Hospital an institution for mental patients, at [redacted] on Feb[redacted]. The Assistant U. S. Attorney at Cleveland, Ohio, declined prosecution of [redacted] for violation of the Extortion Statute in view of her mental condition.

The handwriting on the enclosed Letter was examined by the FBI Laboratory and it was concluded that the handwriting was not identical with that of known specimens by [redacted]

The above is being forwarded you for your information and no further investigation will be conducted by this Bureau.

Enclosure

MAS:spc
(4)

50 APR 27 1959

rg

ogh 8-1

b7D

b7C

b7C

3064-4

REC-1

EX-101

A43–48

Exhibits and reports on an apparent extortion/death threat to Elvis and other prominent personalities.

Q1

New York Dear Sir
I have just 5 Hands of
Cant Kill Elvis Presley
the favor of what do
will be

K of [redacted] K3 - 9-33135 b7C

Elvis Presley Estate is
Tennessee I kill now
and Gand

HUNTSVILLE
JAN 10
5 AM
1964
ALA.

President Elvis presley
Memphis S, Tennessee

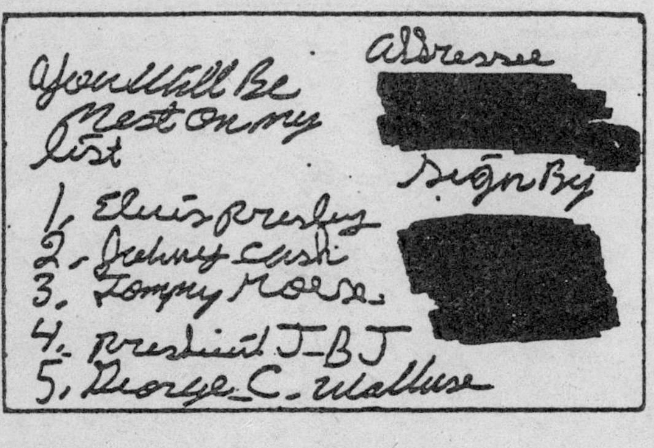

You Will Be
Next On my
list

Addressee
[redacted] b7C

Sign By
[redacted] b7C

1. Elvis presley
2. Johnny cash
3. Tommy Moore
4. president J-BJ
5. George C. Wallace

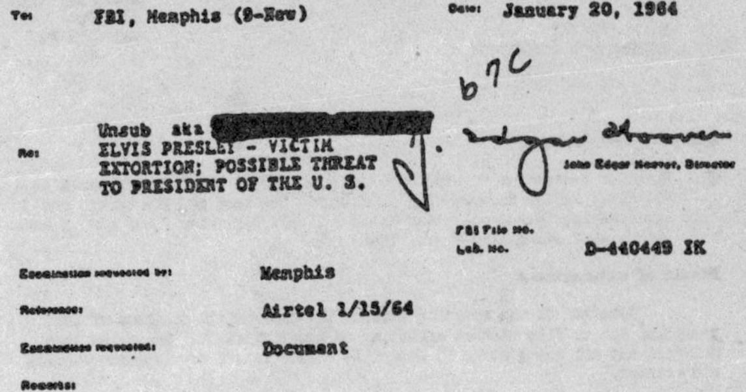
Laboratory Transmittal Form

FBI LABORATORY

FEDERAL BUREAU OF INVESTIGATION
WASHINGTON, D. C.

To: FBI, Memphis (9-New)

Date: January 20, 1964

b7C

Re: Unsub aka [redacted]
ELVIS PRESLEY - VICTIM
EXTORTION; POSSIBLE THREAT
TO PRESIDENT OF THE U. S.

J. Edgar Hoover
John Edgar Hoover, Director

FBI File No.
Lab. No. D-440449 IK

Examination requested by: Memphis

Reference: Airtel 1/15/64

Examination requested: Document

Remarks:

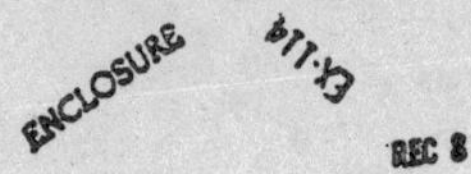
ENCLOSURE

EX-114

REC 8

Enclosures (3) (Q1, 2 Lab rpt.)

1 - Birmingham Enclosure (Lab rpt.)

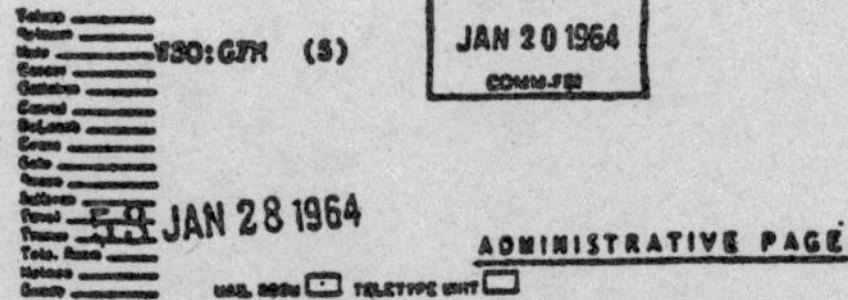
MAILED 8
JAN 20 1964
COMM-FBI

WSO:GFM (5)

JAN 28 1964

ADMINISTRATIVE PAGE

MAIL ROOM TELETYPE UNIT

7-1b

REPORT
of the

WASHINGTON, D. C.

To: FBI, New York

Re: ELVIS PRESLEY
INFORMATION CONCERNING

Date: April 14, 1959
FBI File No. 63-3064
Lab. No. D-303175 DG

Specimens received 3/25/59

Q1 Envelope postmarked "CANTON OHIO MAR 12 1959 2 30 PM," addressed to "R. C. A. Victor Records 155 E. 24th st New York 10 New York," and accompanying four-page letter dated 3/11/59, beginning "Dear Sir I have just .... " and ending " .... Thank You."

Result of examination:

Specimen Q1 was searched through the appropriate sections of the Anonymous Letter File without effecting an identification. Copies of this material are not being added to this file unless future developments warrant such action.

It was concluded that specimen Q1 was not prepared by [redacted] whose known handwriting has been designated as specimen K3 in the case entitled [redacted] ELVIS PRESLEY, VICTIM, EXTORTION.

b7C

Specimen Q1 is being retained in the files of the Bureau.

SWM:vb (8)

MAIL ROOM ☐ TELETYPE UNIT ☐

Recorded
1/20/64
gfm

FEDERAL BUREAU OF INVESTIGATION
UNITED STATES DEPARTMENT OF JUSTICE

No Lab File

Laboratory Work Sheet

Re: Unsub, aka [redacted] b7C
[redacted] ELVIS PREZZLEY PRESLEY -
Victim
EXTORTION: POSSIBLE THREAT TO
PRESIDENT OF THE UNITED STATES

File #
Lab. # D-440449 IK

Examination requested by: Memphis (9-New) 1/15/64

Examination requested: Document

Date received: 1/17/64

Result of Examination:

Examination by: [redacted] b7

PHOTOGRAPHED
JAN 20 1964

Specimens submitted for examination

Q1 Post card postmarked "HUNTSVILLE ALA. JAN 10 1964 5 30 PM" bearing handwritten address "Presdient Elvis Presly Menphis S, Tenneesee" bearing on reversé side handwritten note beginning "You Will Be next on my list..."

FBI

Date: 1/15/64

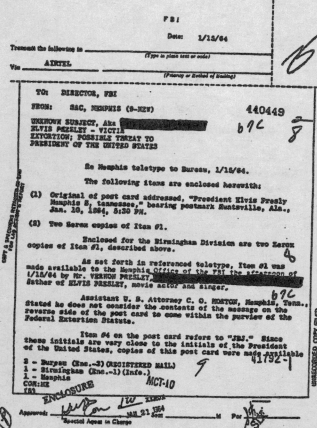

Transmit the following in ____________________
(Type in plain text or code)

Via AIRTEL ____________________
(Priority or Method of Mailing)

TO: DIRECTOR, FBI

FROM: SAC, MEMPHIS (9-NEW)

440449

UNKNOWN SUBJECT, Aka [redacted] b7C
ELVIS PRESLEY - VICTIM
EXTORTION; POSSIBLE THREAT TO
PRESIDENT OF THE UNITED STATES

Re Memphis teletype to Bureau, 1/15/64.

The following items are enclosed herewith:

(1) Original of post card addressed, "President Elvis Presly Memphis 5, tennessee," bearing postmark Huntsville, Ala., Jan. 10, 1964, 5:30 PM.

(2) Two Xerox copies of Item #1.

Enclosed for the Birmingham Division are two Xerox copies of Item #1, described above.

As set forth in referenced teletype, Item #1 was made available to the Memphis Office of the FBI the afternoon of 1/15/64 by Mr. VERNON PRESLEY, [redacted] father of ELVIS PRESLEY, movie actor and singer.

b7C

Assistant U. S. Attorney C. O. NORTON, Memphis, Tenn., stated he does not consider the contents of the message on the reverse side of the post card to come within the purview of the Federal Extortion Statute.

Item #4 on the post card refers to "JBJ." Since these initials are very close to the initials of the President of the United States, copies of this post card were made available

41792-1

3 - Bureau (Enc.-3) (REGISTERED MAIL)
1 - Birmingham (Enc.-1) (Info.)
1 - Memphis
COM:ME
(5)

MCT-10

ENCLOSURE

COPY & SPECIMENS RETAINED FOR LAB REPORT

UNRECORDED COPY FILED

JAN 21 1964

Approved: ____________ Special Agent in Charge   Sent ____________ M   Per ____________

FBI

Date:

Transmit the following in ______________________
(Type in plain text or code)

Via ______________ ______________________
(Priority or Method of Mailing)

ME# 8-New

b7C

immediately on 1/15/64 to [redacted] Special Agent in Charge, U. S. Secret Service, Federal Office Building, 167 N. Main St., Memphis, Tennessee.

As set forth in referenced teletype, UACB, this case is being closed in the Memphis Office with the submission of a confirmatory letter to the U. S. Attorney, Memphis.

- LEADS -

THE BIRMINGHAM DIVISION (INFORMATION)

A copy of this communication is being made available to Birmingham inasmuch as the post card was placed in the U. S. Mails at Huntsville, Ala. and subsequent developments might require investigation in the Birmingham Division.

-2-

Approved: ______________ Sent ________M Per ________
Special Agent in Charge

February 19, 1964

Airtel

To: SAC, Memphis

From: Director, FBI

b7C

UNSUB, AKA. [redacted]
ELVIS PRESLEY - VICTIM;
EXTORTION; POSSIBLE THREAT TO PRESIDENT
OF UNITED STATES.

ReMEtel dated 1/15/64.

Advise caption and date of communication forwarding threatening post card to Bureau for referral to U. S. Secret Service, Washington, D. C.

HAS/kst
(4)

REC- 20

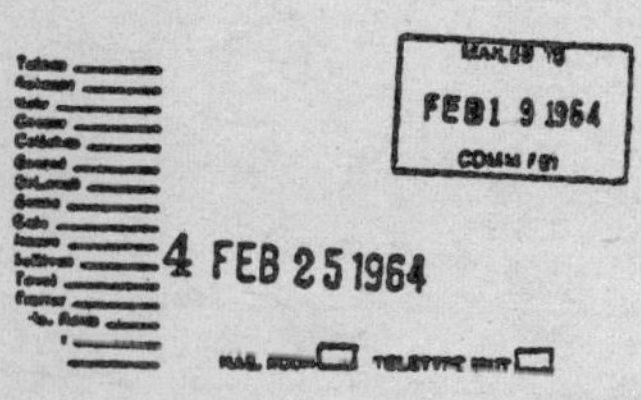
FEB 19 1964
COMM-FBI
4 FEB 25 1964

FD-36 (Rev. 12-13-56)

FBI

Date: 2/20/64

Transmit the following in ____________________
(Type in plain text or code)

Via AIRTEL ____________________
(Priority or Method of Mailing)

TO: DIRECTOR, FBI

FROM: SAC, MEMPHIS (9-1231) (C)

UNSUB, AKA [redacted] b7c
ELVIS PRESLEY - VICTIM
EXTORTION; POSSIBLE THREAT TO PRESIDENT
OF UNITED STATES

Re Bureau Airtel to Memphis, 2/19/64.

There is enclosed original of post card postmarked Huntsville, Ala., Jan. 10, 1964, 5:30 PM, bearing handwritten address, "Presdient Elvis Presly Memphis 8, tennessee," and bearing on the reverse side handwritten note, "You will be next on my list...."

The enclosed post card was forwarded to the Bureau with Memphis Airtel 1/13/64, captioned as above, and was returned to Memphis by the FBI Laboratory by Laboratory Report dated 1/20/64. The enclosure is for referral to U. S. Secret Service, Washington, D. C.

2 - Bureau (Enc.-1)(RM)
1 - Memphis
COH:ME
(4)

REC-123 9

FEB 21 1964

Approved: ____________________ Sent ____________ M Per ____________
Special Agent in Charge

A49–52

Investigation of harassing and crank phone calls to Presley relatives concerning an "Elvis is dead" hoax.

UNKNOWN SUBJECT;
HARASSING PHONE CALL
FROM LOUISVILLE, KENTUCKY
TO PHONE OF MRS. [redacted]
MEMPHIS, TENNESSEE
SEPTEMBER 7, 1968

b7C

The Plant Department of the phone company had not seized the line. The call was not completed to Memphis, Tennessee, as there was no answer by the telephone at Memphis.

[redacted] switchman, Plant Department, was able to seize the line from which the second call from Louisville to Memphis, Tennessee, was made, and it was traced to Louisville telephone [redacted] This was determined to be a non-published telephone with subscriber [redacted] Street, Louisville, Kentucky. This was a residence phone. b7C

A telephone call by the Louisville telephone operator to [redacted] shortly after the phone calls to Memphis, Tennessee, transpired, resulted in a woman answering who indicated that she had just returned to her residence address and that she had tried to make a phone call, however, her telephone line appeared to be open and the telephone was possibly inoperative. This individual denied use on her part or any other individual at her residence of her telephone in connection with any phone calls to Memphis, Tennessee. b7C

Louisville telephone 778-9341 was determined to be a pay telephone booth situated outside of a Convenient Food Market in the West End of Louisville.

Memphis, Tennessee telephone [redacted] was established as being a non-published telephone with subscriber Elvis Presley, 3764 Highway 51 South, Memphis, Tennessee. Memphis, Tennessee telephone [redacted] was determined to be a non-published telephone with subscriber Mrs. [redacted], [redacted] Memphis, Tennessee. b7C

Subsequently, the telephone company received a complaint from the Manning-Dunn Funeral Home at 518 North 26th Street, Louisville, Kentucky, phone 775-6414, relating that the funeral home had received a long distance telephone call from an individual who was purportedly the aunt of nationally prominent singer Elvis Presley, who noted that the uncle of Elvis Presley, had received a long distance telephone call wherein an unidentified male caller announced that Elvis Presley was killed in an airplane crash at Louisville, Kentucky, and that his body was at the Manning-Dunn Funeral Home.

- 2 -

UNKNOWN SUBJECT;
HARASSING PHONE CALL
FROM LOUISVILLE, KENTUCKY
TO PHONE OF MRS. ████
MEMPHIS, TENNESSEE
SEPTEMBER 7, 1968

This was a complete hoax and the aunt of Elvis Presley appeared to be extremely distraught over the matter.

████ pointed out that the Manning-Dunn Funeral Home, which is a prominent establishment in the Louisville, Kentucky area, with various branches in the city of Louisville, and Jefferson County, Kentucky, in the recent past had been subject of numerous local harassing telephone calls by an unidentified individual who by voice was possibly a male, who represented himself as ████ ████, and requested that the funeral home pick up bodies of deceased persons at specific locations in Louisville. These calls were hoaxes and harassing in nature as the funeral home dispatched its personnel to locations given without finding any substantiation to the presence of any deceased persons.

The matter relating to the Manning-Dunn Funeral Home had been handled jointly by the South Central Bell Telephone Company, as well as the Louisville Police Department, which has been conducting intensive investigation in connection with this matter. The telephone company has developed as suspect in connection with the harassing calls to the Manning- Dunn Funeral Home, the son of the owner of the establishment who has a radio telephone in one of the company limousines. The telephone company is conducting an investigation into the matter of the call to Memphis, Tennessee, as a telephone fraud.

Sergeant ████, Detective, Louisville Police Department, advised on September 9, 1968, that his agency had investigated the matter relating to the harassing phone call to Memphis, Tennessee, by an unknown individual from what was purported to be Louisville telephone ████ on September 7, 1968. He advised that ████ a white female, age 51, who operates a trucking business out of her residence at ████ Louisville, Kentucky, related that Louisville telephone ████ is the telephone at that address and that she had been absent from her residence

UNKNOWN SUBJECT;
HARASSING PHONE CALL
FROM LOUISVILLE, KENTUCKY
TO PHONE OF MRS. [redacted]
MEMPHIS, TENNESSEE
SEPTEMBER 7, 1968

b7C

on a job and upon returning to her home in mid-afternoon of September 7, 1968, found that her telephone was inoperative. She declared that she had been living in a common-law relationship with [redacted] who, at that time, was working on a farm out of the State of Kentucky. She denied any knowledge of any phone calls from her telephone by any party to Memphis, Tennessee, on that date. Investigation by the Louisville Police Department Detective Bureau determined that a window in the back door of the residence of [redacted] was broken and anyone could have readily entered this residence and utilized telephone therein, in the absence of [redacted]

b7C

Sergeant [redacted] further commented that his agency staked out the [redacted] residence for several days without noting anyone entering the premises during the absence of [redacted] A neighborhood inquiry established that [redacted] was away from her residence at approximately 1:30 PM on September 7, 1968, and that her boy friend had been away for approximately one month. No individuals were observed entering the residence at [redacted] at the time the calls to Memphis, Tennessee transpired.

b7D
b7C

Sergeant [redacted] advised that his agency will continue to pursue the matter relating to the phone call from the phone at [redacted], in connection with an intensive investigation that it has been conducting relative to a series of harassing telephone calls being made to the Manning-Dunn Funeral Home on 26th Street and other locations, in Jefferson County, Kentucky, in cooperation with the Jefferson County Police Department, as well as the South Central Bell Telephone Company in Louisville.

b7D
b7C

On September 10, 1968, Assistant United States Attorney Philip I. Huddleston, Western District of Kentucky, Louisville, Kentucky, advised that he was deferring prosecution in connection with this matter to local authorities, in view of of the local handling of the matter and the single interstate

-4-

UNKNOWN SUBJECT;
HARASSING PHONE CALL
FROM LOUISVILLE, KENTUCKY,
TO PHONE OF MRS. [redacted]
MEMPHIS, TENNESSEE
SEPTEMBER 7, 1966

b7C

call which appeared to be related to harassing calls received by the Manning-Dunn Funeral Home in Louisville.

FBI

Date: 9/10/68

Transmit the following in ______ (Type in plaintext or code)

AIRTEL ______ (Priority)

TO: DIRECTOR, FBI

FROM: SAC, LOUISVILLE (178-1) (P)

SUBJECT: UNKNOWN SUBJECT;
Harassing Phone Call
from Louisville, Kentucky
to Phone of Mrs. [redacted]
Memphis, Tennessee
9/7/68
INTERSTATE OBSCENE OR
HARASSING PHONE CALLS

OO:LOUISVILLE

South Central Bell Telephone Company operator, Louisville, Kentucky, in connection with a long distance call by an alleged man to Memphis, Tennessee, non-published telephone 901 - [redacted] had Louisville number traced as telephone number furnished by caller was a pay telephone station in Louisville, 778-8341, instead of a private number. Telephone company traced calling number as possibly [redacted] listed to [redacted] Louisville, Kentucky. Memphis telephone listed to Mrs. [redacted], reputed aunt of ELVIS PRESLEY.

Telephone company received complaint from Manning-Dunn Funeral Home, Louisville, that inquiry was received from aunt of ELVIS PRESLEY relative to long distance phone call by unknown male to the uncle of ELVIS PRESLEY, relating that ELVIS PRESLEY was killed in airplane crash at Louisville and his body was at Manning Funeral Home, Louisville. This was a hoax.

2 - Bureau
1 - Memphis (Info)
2 - Louisville
RHE/mfm
(5)

REC-15 178-0-23

6 SEP 12 1968

Approved: ______ Special Agent in Charge Sent ______ M Per ______

LS 178-1

Manning-Dunn Funeral Home subject of numerous recent local harassing telephone calls by individual representing himself as coroner and requesting funeral home pick up bodies of deceased persons. These calls were harassing in nature as no deceased persons located as reported by unknown caller.

Louisville Police Department conducting extensive investigation relative to hoax and harassing calls related to Manning-Dunn Funeral Home. Telephone company has as suspect [redacted] b7C

Telephone company investigating case as telephone fraud.

AUSA, WDKY, deferred prosecution to local authorities in view of local handling of matter and single interstate call which appears related to harassing calls received by Manning-Dunn Funeral Home.

No investigation conducted. Letterhead memorandum follows.

UNITED STATES GOVERNMENT

Memorandum

TO : DIRECTOR, FBI DATE: 9/12/68

FROM SAC, LOUISVILLE (178-1) (C)

SUBJECT: UNKNOWN SUBJECT;
Harassing Phone Call
From Louisville, Kentucky
To Phone of Mrs. [redacted] b7C
Memphis, Tennessee
9/7/68
INTERSTATE OBSCENE OR
HARASSING PHONE CALLS
OO: LOUISVILLE

Reference Louisville airtel to Director of 9/10/68.

Enclosed herewith for the Bureau are four copies of a letterhead memorandum relating to captioned matter, along with one copy for the Memphis Division for information.

A copy of this letterhead memorandum is being furnished the U. S. Attorney, Louisville.

2 - Bureau (Enc. 4)
1 - Memphis (Enc. 1) (Info)
1 - Louisville
[illegible]/ac
(4)

EX 110
REC-64 78-6-24

16 SEP 16 1968

59 SEP 24 1968

UNITED STATES DEPARTMENT OF JUSTICE

FEDERAL BUREAU OF INVESTIGATION

In Reply, Please Refer to
File No.

Post Office Box 1487
Louisville, Kentucky 40202

September 12, 1968

UNKNOWN SUBJECT;
HARASSING PHONE CALL
FROM LOUISVILLE, KENTUCKY,
TO PHONE OF MRS. [redacted] b7C
MEMPHIS, TENNESSEE
SEPTEMBER 7, 1968
INTERSTATE OBSCENE OR
HARASSING PHONE CALLS

On September 9, 1968, [redacted] b7C [redacted] South Central Bell Telephone Company, Louisville, Kentucky, advised that his office had received a report from Louisville Chief Telephone Operator, [redacted] b7C that on September 6, 1968, at 1:19 PM a telephone operator placed a call for an individual who appeared to be, by the sound of his voice, a male, to Memphis, Tennessee, 901-[redacted] b7C He gave the number from which he was calling in Louisville as 778-9341. Upon connecting the caller with the Memphis, Tennessee telephone number, she contacted [redacted] switchman b7C in the Plant Department of the telephone company, to seize the line or hold it open and trace the call to the Louisville telephone number, inasmuch as the phone number given by the caller related to a pay telephone booth, particularly as the last four digits of the Louisville telephone number were a series designated for commercial pay telephones. She felt that the caller was attempting to defraud the telephone company through his submission of a false telephone number as to the phone from which the call was originating.

Shortly thereafter, a second call was placed to Memphis, Tennessee, [redacted] by an unidentified male caller who furnished the telephone from which he was calling as Louisville telephone 778-9341, which was the same number furnished in connection with the phone call to Memphis [redacted] b7C

This document contains neither recommendations nor conclusions of the FBI. It is the property of the FBI and is loaned to your agency; it and its contents are not to be distributed outside your agency.

ENCLOSURE 94

A53

Another letter from the woman of A1, still upset over Elvis's continued popularity.

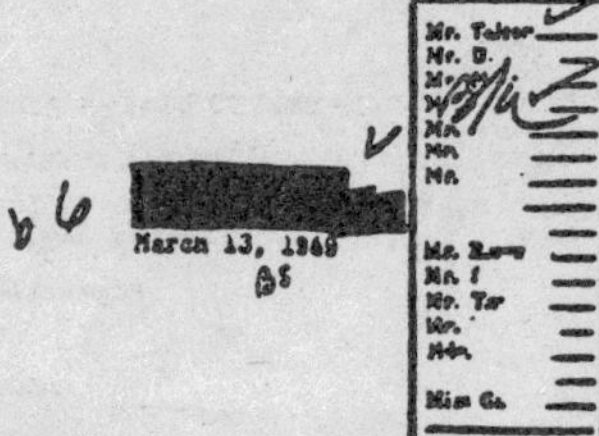

b6

March 13, 1969

Mr. J. Edgar Hoover
Washington, D. C.

Dear Honorable Sir,

Thank goodness you are still in Washington, still serving us all as no one else has or can. Congratulations!

Quite a few years ago I wrte to you about the repulsive antics of Elvis Presley. Look at the money he is making to-day! Still harming our youth! I believe he has done more harm in his style of dancing, to our young people than any one element in our society. It put the suggestive ideas into more young people because he was before them on television so much! This sort of thing had not been seen by many, many of our young people; before this time, it could only be seen at side-shows, so this was something new, something very thrilling to our boys and girls. It spread like wild-fire. It opened up something very daring and catching.

So much for Elvis. You were very kind, understanding and really did all you could about this guy. That's why I am coming to you now.

I am a mother of five daughters, seventeen grandchildren so my keen interest in young people, my own and others, is intensely keen.

b6

94-50519-551

EXP PROC.

31 MAR 17 1969

Now! Praise the Good Lord, they are beginning to wonder --out loud-- if these killer movies, war movies, obscene movies are having an effect on our young people! I wish I had time, I'd write a book!

MAR 17 1969

Let me say right here. I do believe you are very much in accord with the fact that these movies and pictures certainly have and make a sad impression on some of our youngsters. Let me tell you just what a four year old grandDAUGHTER said to her mother one day after they had been in a store in the city. Her mother said, "[redacted], why didn't you speak to Mrs. [redacted] when she spoke to you?" "You told me not to speak to strangers mommy and I was afraid she might kidnap me like that little girl on TV.". A four year old little girl! Impression!

b6

3-21-69

Another mother told of her little boy not wanting to speak to a man (an acquaintance of the father) because he was afraid he might kidnap him and take him away and turn him into a tiger. Impression!

I will say this--my daughter selects, very carefully the pictures or programs her children shall watch. Sometimes this is a problem because--maybe the child wants to watch after school, right after supper etc.. and nothing to look at but KILLING!

Oh, yes, indeed these programs affect our young people. AND adults are giving it to them!

Let's take music. College presidents have said it is"the greatest mind-trainer on the list".

A large part of a child's education is affected by music. Let's think that thru together, Mr. Hoover.

Let's take someone who says I am all wrong on this theory. Alright. A marching band goes by. They stop and play to a group of school children. While that band is in their midst, are they not watching the drummer, the trumpeter, whoever happens to be nearest,--and wishing they could play like that. Are they not keeping time with their feet, perhaps clapping their hands in time with the music? Are their thoughts not of the highest educational and emothical order? An impression!

Now let's take Elvis Presley and some of the other singers whom he has influenced. Compare impressions.

We can never say that music does not have an effect on the mind.

If it did not--we could play a ·edding march at a funeral, we could have jazz music in our churches, chants and hymns in our dance halls. There is no chance for argument.

All this leads me to this: if our country would come forth and realize the importance of musical training for EVERY child I do believe the crime in our country would be greatly erased!

You and many others may say that every child is not musical, does not care for music. That's where our trained teachers can MAKE it enjoyable and appealing. It can be done with very rewarding results.SO MANY WAYS TO MAKE GOOD MUSIC!

Our beloved Madame Nordica, the world's greatest Wagnerian singer began when she was a very little girl sitting beside a brook on their farm and listening to the birds, the water as it flowed over the rocks and she tried to imitate them. She did!

I do hope you will use your influence to ban, discard, throw out these horrible, destructive programs they are showing on TV, every day!

Thanks if you have stayed with me and We are so thankful for

YOU!

A friend,  b6

 b6

A54–58

FBI files of the death threat Elvis received while in Las Vegas.

FEDERAL BUREAU OF INVESTIGATION
COMMUNICATIONS SECTION
AUG 23 1970
TELETYPE

NR002 LA PLAIN
247 PM URGENT 8/28/70 DAB
TO DIRECTOR
LAS VEGAS
FROM LOS ANGELES (9-NEW)

Unknown Subject
UNSUB; ELVIS PRESLEY DASH VICTIM, EXTORTION.

VICTIM ELVIS PRESLEY, ENTERTAINER, IS CURRENTLY APPEARING AT THE INTERNATIONAL HOTEL, LAS VEGAS, NEVADA. E. GREGORY HOOKSTRATTEN, ATTORNEY FOR VICTIM, BEVERLY HILLS, CALIFORNIA, ADVISED TODAY AS FOLLOWS:

AT TWO FIFTY FIVE PM, AUGUST TWENTYSEVEN LAST, ANONYMOUS MALE CALLER CALLED OFFICE OF COL. PARKER, BUSINESS MANAGER OF VICTIM, AT LAS VEGAS. CALLER SAID ELVIS WAS GOING TO BE KIDNAPED THIS WEEKEND. CALL WAS TERMINATED. CALLER HAD SOUTHERN ACCENT.

REC-6 9-51 L59-3

SEP 1 1970

AT SIX FIFTEEN AM, AUGUST TWENTYEIGHT INSTANT, ___ ___ ___ TELEPHONE CALL WAS RECEIVED AT LOS ANGELES RESIDENCE OF [redacted] [redacted] [redacted] IS WIFE OF [redacted] CLOSE CONFIDANTE OF VICTIM WHO IS WITH VICTIM IN LAS VEGAS. CALLER

67C

END PAGE ONE

56 SEP 4 1970

MR. SULLIVAN FOR THE DIRECTOR

COPY SENT TO MR. TOLSON

PAGE TWO

LA 9-NEW

STATED WORDS TO EFFECT HE HAD TO GET IN TOUCH WITH HER HUSBAND. [redacted] HE DID NOT IDENTIFY HIMSELF AND SAID ELVIS IS GOING TO GET IT TOMORROW NIGHT. HE WANTED [redacted] TELEPHONE IN LAS VEGAS. [redacted] SAID HER HUSBAND WAS OUT OF TOWN AND DID NOT INDICATE HIS LOCATION OR FURNISH A TELEPHONE NUMBER.

THE CALL WAS TERMINATED LATER AT SEVEN AM THE SAME CALLER CALLED AGAIN AND TOLD [redacted] THAT A PARTICULAR PERSON IS GOING TO SHOOT ELVIS AND HE HAS A GUN WITH A SILENCER ON IT. CALLER SAID KILLER IS A MADMAN AND VICTIM QUOTE DONE HIM (KILLER) WRONG ABOUT A YEAR AGO UNQUOTE. CALLER SAID HE KNEW WHO AND WHERE THE KILLER WAS AND REQUESTED FIFTY THOUSAND DOLLARS IN SMALL BILLS FOR INFORMATION REGARDING IDENTITY OF KILLER. CALLER INDICATED HE WAS DOING VICTIM A FAVOR BY FURNISHING THIS INFORMATION. CALLER HAD CONVERSATION WITH [redacted] INDICATING HE WAS FAMILIAR WITH HER HUSBAND. [redacted] HE SAID HE WANTED TO GET PAID AND WOULD CALL BACK AT TWELVE NOON, AUGUST TWENTYEIGHT INSTANT, FOR FURTHER INSTRUCTIONS REGARDING PAYMENT. CALLER SPOKE WITH SOUTHERN ACCENT.

A PATERNITY SUIT IS IN THE PROCESS OF BEING FILED AGAINST VICTIM BY [redacted] AT LOS ANGELES. [redacted] RESIDES IN LOS ANGELES AND IS ATTEMPTING TO OBTAIN

END PAGE TWO

LA 9-NEW

PAGE THREE

ONE THOUSAND DOLLARS A MONTH SUPPORT. VICTIM'S ATTORNEY AT BEVERLY HILLS FEELS THERE IS POSSIBILITY [redacted] MAY BE INVOLVED; HOWEVER, THERE ARE NO FACTS TO SUBSTANTIATE THIS. 67C

LAS VEGAS WILL CONTACT COL. TOM PARKER, TELEPHONE SEVEN THREE FOUR ZERO SEVEN SIX EIGHT, FOR FURTHER FACTS REGARDING TELEPHONE CALL RECEIVED AT HIS OFFICE AUGUST TWENTYSEVEN LAST. INSURE LOCAL AUTHORITIES ARE AWARE OF THIS MATTER.

LOS ANGELES IS MAINTAINING CONTACT WITH [redacted] FOR ADDITIONAL DEVELOPMENTS IN THIS MATTER. VICTIM'S WIFE, PRISCILLA, AND THEIR THREE-YEAR OLD GIRL, RESIDE IN BEVERLY HILLS. LOCAL AUTHORITIES AT BEVERLY HILLS HAVE BEEN ADVISED OF THIS MATTER AND THEY ARE PROVIDING PROTECTION FOR PRISCILLA AND DAUGHTER.

END

LRC FBI WASH DC

CLR

CC-MR. ROSEN

FEDERAL BUREAU OF INVESTIGATION
COMMUNICATIONS SECTION
AUG 29 1970
TELETYPE

NR 023 LA PLAIN

1116 PM NITEL 8-28-70 VLB

TO DIRECTOR

LAS VEGAS

FROM LOS ANGELES (9-NEW)(P) 1P

Unknown Subject
UNSUB; ELVIS PRESLEY - VICTIM, EXTORTION.

RE LA TEL TODAY.

[redacted] RECEIVED TELCALL FROM SAME INDIVIDUAL WHO CALLED HER EARLY IN THE MORNING THIS DATE. CALL WAS RECEIVED AT TWELVE NOON AND CALLER STATED HE HAS THE CAR LICENSE NUMBER AND NAME OF INDIVIDUAL WHO IS GOING TO KILL ELVIS PRESLEY. THIS INDIVIDUAL HAS DEPARTED FROM LA AND HAS A RESERVATION FOR SAT. EVENING PERFORMANCE OF PRESLEY. CALLER REQUESTED "FIFTY THOUSAND GRAND BONUS" FOR INFO RE IDENTITY AND LICENSE NUMBER OF KILLER. IDENTIFIED THIS INDIVIDUAL AS PERSON WHO IS CRAZY AND ONE WHO COULD BE ON LSD. CALLER TERMINATED PHONE CALL ABRUPTLY STATING HE WOULD CALL BACK WITH FURTHER DETAILS. HE MADE NO INSTRUCTIONS RE PAYOFF. AS OF NINE PM, PDT. LA TIME, CALLER HAS NOT RECONTACTED [redacted]

LV INSURE ABOVE INFO IS FURNISHED TO LOCAL AUTHORITIES AND PERSONNEL ASSOCIATED WITH THE PRESLEY GROUP. LA IS MAINTAINING CONTACT WITH [redacted]

PENDING.

END

VLB FBI WASH DC CLR

CC MR. ROSEN

ST-112 REC 12 51659-2

SEP 10 1970

MR. SULLIVAN FOR THE DIRECTOR

NR 006 PLAIN LV

1046 PM 8-28-70 URGENT ALL

TO DIRECTOR

LOS ANGELES

FROM LAS VEGAS (9-368)

FEDERAL BUREAU OF INVESTIGATION
COMMUNICATIONS SECTION
AUG 29 1970
TELETYPE

UNSUB; ELVIS PRESLEY - VICTIM EXTORTION. OO: LA

RE LA TEL TO DIRECTOR AND LAS VEGAS AUGUST TWENTY EIGHT.

INTERVIEWS OF ELVIS PRESLEY AND PERSONNEL AFFILIATED WITH HIM AT LAS VEGAS, NEVADA, HAVE DEVELOPED NO INFORMATION INDICATING IDENTITY OF UNSUB.

ON AUGUST TWENTY SIX LAST SECURITY OFFICER, INTERNATIONAL HOTEL, LAS VEGAS, RECEIVED CALL FROM INDIVIDUAL IDENTIFYING SELF AS JIM REEDS (PH) WHO SAID HE HAD INFORMATION THAT VICTIM WAS TO BE KIDNAPPED THAT NIGHT. CALLER INDICATED HE HAD MET TWO MEN WHO CLAIMED TO HAVE ATTENDED PARTY FOR PRESLEY PRIOR TO HIS TRIP TO LAS VEGAS. THESE TWO MEN WHO WERE NOT FURTHER IDENTIFIED WERE ACCORDING TO CALLER SETTING UP PLANS TO KIDNAP PRESLEY AND WANTED HIM TO PLAY A PART IN IT. CALLER INDICATED HE WANTED TO ALERT SECURITY PERSONNEL AND ALSO TO ADVISE THEM THAT HE HAD NO INTENTION OF PARTICIPATING IN KIDNAPING. CALL BELIEVED TO HAVE BEEN A LONG DISTANCE CALL BUT POINT OF ORIGIN UNKNOWN.

END PAGE ONE

60SEP 10 1970

MR. SULLIVAN FOR THE DIRECTOR

LV 9-388

PAGE TWO

SECURITY PERSONNEL OF INTERNATIONAL HOTEL, LAS VEGAS, PROVIDING BEST AVAILABLE SECURITY FOR VICTIM DURING PERFORMANCES OF VICTIM AND CLARK COUNTY S. O. LAS VEGAS NEVADA, HAS BEEN PROVIDED WITH INFORMATION RELATING TO THIS MATTER. CCSO IN CONTACT WITH HOTEL SECURITY PERSONNEL.

LIAISON BEING MAINTAINED WITH [redacted] AND COL. PARKER, MANAGER OF VICTIM. b7C

END

SLB FBI AWASH DC CLR

CC-MR. ROSEN

August 29, 1970

GENERAL INVESTIGATIVE DIVISION

This is a new matter involving victim, Elvis Presley, well-known entertainer currently appearing at the International Hotel, Las Vegas, Nevada. Anonymous call received by victim's manager at Las Vegas 2:55 P.M., 8/27/70 stating Elvis was going to be kidnapped this weekend. At 6:15 A.M., 8/28/70 wife of a confidante of victim who is with him in Las Vegas, received anonymous call attempting to contact her husband and stated Elvis was going to get it tomorrow night; 45 minutes later same caller again called and stated a killer, who is a madman, was going to shoot Elvis, that he had a gun with a silencer. Caller said victim had "done him (killer) wrong about a year ago." Caller requested $50,000 in small bills for information regarding identity of killer whom he knew. Victim involved in paternity suit and victim's attorney believes there may be connection but no facts to substantiate this. Bureau is investigating. Local authorities providing protection to victim's wife and daughter at Los Angeles. Security personnel, International Hotel, Las Vegas, providing protection to victim. Local authorities, Las Vegas, have been furnished full details.

JCK:mfd

No further contact or callsmade concerning this.

FD-36 (Rev. 5-22-64)

FBI

Date: 8/31/70

Transmit the following in ____________________
(Type in plaintext or code)

Via AIRTEL AIR MAIL
(Priority)

TO: DIRECTOR, FBI

FROM: SAC, LOS ANGELES (9-4410) (P)

SUBJECT: UNSUB
ELVIS PRESLEY -
VICTIM
EXTORTION

Re Los Angeles teletype to the Bureau dated 8/28/70.

On 8/28/70, E. GREGORY HOOKSTRATTEN, attorney for victim, ELVIS PRESLEY, advised that Los Angeles Police Officer [redacted] has been hired to act as bodyguard for victim in Las Vegas, Nevada. [redacted] is on leave from the Los Angeles Police Department (LAPD) and he assumed duties as victim's bodyguard effective during the evening of 8/28/70. Mr. HOOKSTRATTEN said it is anticipated that [redacted] will provide his services for victim during victim's entire stay at Las Vegas. Victim is scheduled to terminate his entertainment at the International Hotel on Labor Day, 9/7/70.

Mr. HOOKSTRATTEN advised that the LAPD is also aware of this matter as the residence of [redacted] is located at [redacted] Los Angeles, California.

b7C

2 - Bureau
2 - Las Vegas
2 - Los Angeles

JPM/lke
(6)

ST-105

REC-23 9-51659-4

SEP 8 1970

66 SEP 14 1970

Approved: ____________ Special Agent in Charge Sent ________ M Per ________

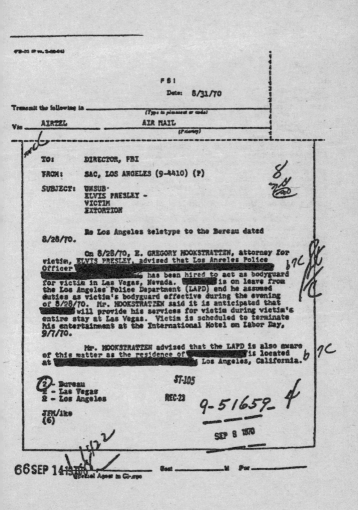

LA 9-4410

Contact was maintained with [redacted] during the weekend of 8/28-31/70. She advised she has received no other telephone calls threatening the life of victim and coupled with demand for information concerning identity of the alleged killer. b7C

On 8/31/70, Assistant United States Attorney ERIC A. NOBLES, Chief of the Complaint Unit, United States Attorney's Office, Los Angeles, advised facts of this matter at this time would not substantiate successful prosecution of anyone, if identified, in Federal Court for violation of the Federal Extortion Statute as there is lack of evidence that threatening telephone calls were made interstate and information concerning threat against life of victim did not take place over the weekend of 8/28-31/70.

On the same date, Mr. HOOKSTRATTEN was advised of the opinion of Mr. NOBLES. Las Vegas is requested to insure that appropriate personnel associated with victim are advised of Mr. NOBLES' opinion. No other investigation is requested. Los Angeles will confirm Mr. NOBLES' opinion by separate communication.

At 3:00 P.M. on 8/31/70, [redacted] advised that she and PRISCILLA PRESLEY, together with their children, were departing Los Angeles for Las Vegas, Nevada, whereupon they intend to stay with their husbands until the termination of victim's entertainment date at the International Hotel. b7C

A59–63

Interoffice memos detailing Elvis's offer to go undercover for the Bureau—and the FBI's upper-echelon opinion of the offer.

UNITED STATES GOVERNMENT

Memorandum

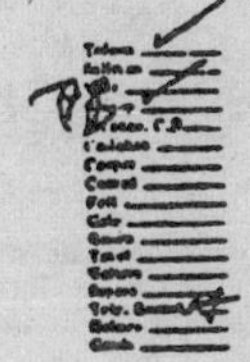

TO Mr. Bishop DATE: 12-22-70

FROM : M. A. Jones

SUBJECT: ELVIS PRESLEY

Senator George Murphy (R-California) telephoned your office late yesterday to advise that captioned individual who is, of course, the prominent entertainer and motion picture personality, had accompanied him to Washington on a flight from Los Angeles and expressed interest in meeting the Director during his stay in Washington.

According to Senator Murphy, Presley, whom he described as being a very sincere young man, is deeply concerned over the narcotics problem in this country and is interested in becoming active in the drive against the use of narcotics, particularly by young people.

According to Senator Murphy in response to Presley's request, he Murphy, has arranged an appointment for Presley with John Ingersoll, Director of the Bureau of Narcotics and Dangerous Drugs. Senator Murphy advised that he was aware that the FBI has no jurisdiction in narcotics matters but wished to pass Presley's request to see Mr. Hoover along to the Director.

Senator Murphy was advised that the Director was out of the City and not expected to return until around the first of the year. Thereupon Senator Murphy requested that someone from the Bureau get in touch with Presley and express the Director's regrets.

REC 63 MCT-51

This has been done and Presley expressed appreciation for the call noting that as he had advised Senator Murphy, he was becoming increasingly concerned with the dissident activities and use of narcotics by young people in this country and was desirous of doing whatever he could to be of service in alleviating this problem. Presley noted that his rise to prominence in the entertainment field is evidence of what can be accomplished in this country by the poor and the deprived. He said that his relative youth and his background in the entertainment industry has helped him establish rapport with the younger generation and that in gratitude for all this country has done for him he would like to be of service. In this regard he indicated that should the Bureau

1 - Mr. Sullivan
1 - Mr. Bishop
1 - Miss Gandy
1 - Miss Holmes

5 JAN 14 1971

SENT DIRECTOR

EX DEC 31 1970

GTQ:ksf
(6)

CONTINUED - OVER

M. A. Jones to Bishop Memo
RE: ELVIS PRESLEY

ever have need of his services he can be reached under the pseudonym of Colonel Jon Burrows, 3764 Highway 51, South, Memphis, Tennessee, telephone number EX7-4427.

INFORMATION IN BUFILES:

Bufiles reflect that Presley has been the victim in a number of extortion attempts which have been referred to the Bureau. Our files also reflect that he is presently involved in a paternity suit pending in Los Angeles, California, and that during the height of his popularity during the latter part of the 1950's and early 1960's his gyrations while performing were the subject of considerable criticism by the public and comment in the press.

RECOMMENDATION:

For information.

Ned

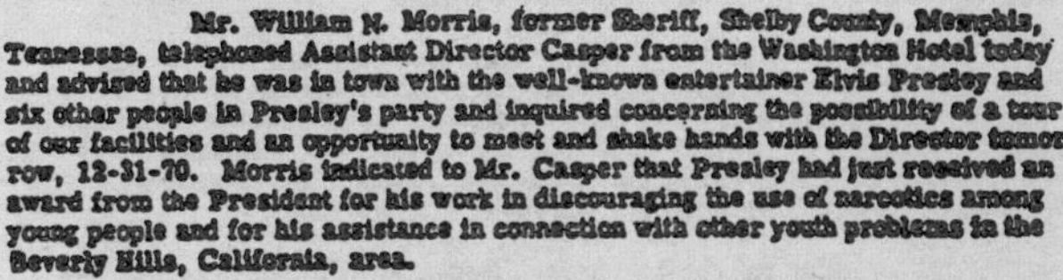

UNITED STATES GOVERNMENT

Memorandum

TO : Mr. Bishop DATE: 12-30-70

FROM : M. A. Jones

SUBJECT: WILLIAM N. MORRIS
FORMER SHERIFF, SHELBY COUNTY, TENNESSEE
ELVIS PRESLEY
REQUEST FOR BUREAU TOUR AND MEET WITH
THE DIRECTOR

Mr. William N. Morris, former Sheriff, Shelby County, Memphis, Tennessee, telephoned Assistant Director Casper from the Washington Hotel today and advised that he was in town with the well-known entertainer Elvis Presley and six other people in Presley's party and inquired concerning the possibility of a tour of our facilities and an opportunity to meet and shake hands with the Director tomorrow, 12-31-70. Morris indicated to Mr. Casper that Presley had just received an award from the President for his work in discouraging the use of narcotics among young people and for his assistance in connection with other youth problems in the Beverly Hills, California, area.

Mr. Casper advised Morris that the Director was out of the city, however, that he, Casper, would see what could be done to arrange a tour for Morris, Presley and party. Morris advised that he could be reached at Room 702, Washington Hotel, telephone number 638-5900.

BACKGROUND:

By memorandum dated 12-22-70, which is attached, you will recall that Senator George Murphy (Republican-California) telephoned your office on 12-21-70 and advised that Presley had accompanied him, Murphy, to Washington on a flight from Los Angeles and expressed interest in meeting the Director during his stay in Washington.

Murphy described Presley as a very sincere young man who was interested in becoming active in the drive against the use of narcotics, particularly by young people. Murphy indicated that he had arranged an appointment for Presley with John Ingersoll, Director of the Bureau of Narcotics and Dangerous Drugs.

Murphy was advised that the Director was out of the city and not expected to return until around the first of the year at which point he requested that someone from the Bureau get in touch with Presley and express the Director's regrets. This was done.

Enclosures (2)

1 - Mr. Sullivan
1 - Mr. Bishop
1 - Mr. Mohr
1 - Mr. Casper
1 - Miss Gandy
1 - Miss Holmes
1 - Mr. Malmfeldt
1 - Tour Room
1 - M.A.Jones

GTQ:el (10)

CONTINUED - OVER

M. A. Jones to Mr. Bishop Memo
RE: WILLIAM N. MORRIS AND ELVIS PRESLEY

INFORMATION IN BUFILES:

Bufiles reflect that Presley has been the victim in a number of extortion attempts which have been referred to the Bureau. Our files also reflect that he is presently involved in a paternity suit pending in Los Angeles California and that during the height of his popularity during the latter part of the 1950's and early 1960's his gyrations while performing were the subject of considerable criticism by the public and comment in the press. The files of the Identification Division fail to reflect any arrest record for Presley.

Our Memphis Office advised that relations with former Sheriff Morris were excellent during the period he was in office, and that several men from his department were accepted for attendance at the FBI National Academy while he was Sheriff. According to Memphis, Morris is now associated with a public relations firm in that city, but that he has political ambitions and it is Anticipated that he will eventually run for Mayor of Memphis.

Our files and the files of the Director's Office fail to reflect that the Director has ever met Presley or Morris.

OBSERVATIONS:

Presley's sincerity and good intentions notwithstanding he is certainly not the type of individual whom the Director would wish to meet. It is noted at the present time he is wearing his hair down to his shoulders and indulges in the wearing of all sorts of exotic dress. A photograph of Presley clipped from today's "Washington Post" is attached and indicates Presley's personal appearance and manner of dress.

RECOMMENDATION:

That the Director permit someone from your office to return former Sheriff Morris' call and advise him that while we will be pleased to afford him, Presley and their party a special tour of our facilities tomorrow, 12-31-70, that it will not be possible for the Director to see them.

- 2 -

PEOPLE

United Press International

Entertainer Elvis Presley leaves Trinity Baptist Church in Memphis after serving as best man in the wedding of his chief security officer. Presley wears a furry bell-bottomed suit. His fashion accessories include amber glasses, a medallion around his neck and a flashlight.

Tolson ____
Sullivan ____
Mohr ____
Bishop ____
Brennan, C.D. ____
Callahan ____
Casper ____
Conrad ____
Felt ____
Gale ____
Rosen ____
Tavel ____
Walters ____
Soyars ____
Tele. Room ____
Holmes ____
Gandy ____

The Washington Post
Times Herald B-2
The Washington Daily News ____
The Evening Star (Washington) ____
The Sunday Star (Washington) ____
Daily News (New York) ____
Sunday News (New York) ____
New York Post ____
The New York Times ____
The Daily World ____
The New Leader ____
The Wall Street Journal ____
The National Observer ____
People's World ____

Date DEC 30 1970

63-3-69-7

UNITED STATES GOVERNMENT

Memorandum

TO : Mr. Bishop

DATE: 1-4-71

FROM : M. A. Jones

SUBJECT: ELVIS PRESLEY
WILLIAM N. MORRIS
FORMER SHERIFF, SHELBY COUNTY, TENNESSEE
BUREAU TOUR 12-31-70

Presley and Morris and six individuals who provide security for Presley visited FBI Headquarters and were afforded a very special tour of our facilities in accordance with plans approved by the Director.

Regrets were expressed to Presley and his party in connection with their request to meet the Director. Presley indicated that he has long been an admirer of Mr. Hoover, and has read material prepared by the Director including "Masters of Deceit," "A Study of Communism" as well as "J. Edgar Hoover on Communism." Presley noted that in his opinion no one has ever done as much for his country as has Mr. Hoover, and that he, Presley, considers the Director the "greatest living American." He also spoke most favorably of the Bureau.

Despite his rather bizarre personal appearance, Presley seemed a sincere, serious minded individual who expressed concern over some of the problems confronting our country, particularly those involving young people. In this regard, in private comments made following his tour, he indicated that he, Presley, is the "living proof that America is the land of opportunity" since he rose from truck driver to prominent entertainer almost overnight. He said that he spends as much time as his schedule permits informally talking to young people and discussing what they consider to be their problems with them. Presley indicated his long hair and unusual apparel were merely tools of his trade and provided him access to and rapport with many people particularly on college campuses who considered themselves "anti-establishment." Presley said that while he has a limited education, he has been able to command a certain amount of respect and attention from this segment of the population and in an informal way point out the errors of their ways. He advised that he does not consider himself

Enclosure 1-4-71

REC-79

1 - Mr. Sullivan - Enclosure
1 - Mr. Bishop - Enclosure
1 - C. D. Brennan - Enclosure
GTQ:dkg (9)

1 - Miss Gandy - Enclosure
1 - Miss Holmes - Enclosure
1 - M. A. Jones - Enclosure
(CONTINUED - OVER)

M. A. Jones to Bishop Memo
RE: ELVIS PRESLEY

competent to address large groups but much rather prefers small gatherings in community centers and the like, where he makes himself accessible for talks and discussions regarding the evils of narcotics and other problems of concern to teenagers and other young people.

Following their tour, Presley privately advised that he has volunteered his services to the President in connection with the narcotics problem and that Mr. Nixon had responded by furnishing him an Agent's badge of the Bureau of Narcotics and Dangerous Drugs. Presley was carrying this badge in his pocket and displayed it.

Presley advised that he wished the Director to be aware that he, Presley, from time to time is approached by individuals and groups in and outside of the entertainment business whose motives and goals he is convinced are not in the best interests of this country and who seek to have him to lend his name to their questionable activities. In this regard, he volunteered to make such information available to the Bureau on a confidential basis whenever it came to his attention. He further indicated that he wanted the Director to know that should the Bureau ever have any need of his services in any way that he would be delighted to be of assistance.

Presley indicated that he is of the opinion that the Beatles laid the groundwork for many of the problems we are having with young people by their filthy unkempt appearances and suggestive music while entertaining in this country during the early and middle 1960's. He advised that the Smothers Brothers, Jane Fonda, and other persons in the entertainment industry of their ilk have a lot to answer for in the hereafter for the way they have poisoned young minds by disparaging the United States in their public statements and unsavory activities.

Presley advised that he resides at 3764 Highway 51, South, Memphis, Tennessee, but that he spends a substantial portion of his time in the Beverly Hills, California - Las Vegas, Nevada, areas fulfilling motion picture assignments and singing commitments.

He noted that he can be contacted anytime through his Memphis address and that because of problems he has had with people tampering with his mail, such correspondence should be addressed to him under the pseudonym, Colonel Jon Burrows

- 2 -

CONTINUED - OVER
↓ ↓ ↓

M. A. Jones to Bishop Memo
RE: ELVIS PRESLEY

It should be here noted following their tour and prior to their departure from the building, Mr. Morris indicated that Presley had been recently selected by the Junior Chamber of Commerce as one of the "ten outstanding men" in the United States and that of these ten in a ceremony to be held in Memphis sometime in January, 1971, Presley would be named as the "most outstanding" of the ten. According to Morris, similar recognition was afforded President Nixon some 25 years ago and the late President Kennedy was also a recipient of this award.

Morris observed that he has known Presley for many years, that despite his manner of dress, he is a sober, clean minded young man who is good to his family and his friends and who is very well regarded by all, including the law enforcement community in the Memphis, Tennessee, area where he was raised and still resides.

Presley, Morris, and their party expressed appreciation for the courtesies extended them.

OBSERVATION:

Presley did give the impression of being a sincere, young man who is conscious of the many problems confronting this country. In view of his unique position in the entertainment business, his favorable comments concerning the Director and the Bureau, and his offer to be of assistance as well as the fact that he has been recognized by the Junior Chamber of Commerce and the President, it is felt that a letter from the Director would be in order.

RECOMMENDATION:

That the attached letter to Presley be approved and sent.

ST 117

REC 85

January 4, 1971

Mr. Elvis Presley
3764 Highway 51, South
Memphis, Tennessee 38101

Dear Mr. Presley:

I regret that it was not possible for me to see you and your party during your visit to FBI Headquarters; however, I do hope you enjoyed your tour of our facilities.

Your generous comments concerning this Bureau and me are appreciated, and you may be sure we will keep in mind your offer to be of assistance.

Sincerely yours,
J. Edgar Hoover

1 - Memphis
1 - Las Vegas
1 - Los Angeles

PERSONAL ATTENTION SAC'S: For your information, Presley, accompanied by Mr. William N. Morris, former Sheriff of Shelby County, Tennessee, and a party of six other individuals visited FBI Headquarters on 12-31-70. Presley offered to be of assistance on a confidential basis should there ever be need of his services.

MAILED 3
JAN 4 1971
COMM-FBI

- Mr. Sullivan (detached)
- Mr. Bishop (detached)
- Mr. C. D. Brennan (detached)
1 - Miss Gandy (detached)
1 - Miss Holmes (detached)
1 - Mr. M. A. Jones (detached)

NOTE: See M. A. Jones to Mr. Bishop Memo dated 1-4-71, captioned "Elvis Presley, William N. Morris, Former Sheriff, Shelby County, Tennessee, Bureau Tour 12-31-70."

GTQ:dkg/el
(12)

WC

DS 9A

402

MAIL ROOM ☐ TELETYPE UNIT ☐

56 JAN 14 1971

A64

A handwritten letter from Elvis to the Bureau offering his services.

Dear Mr. President:

First I would like to introduce myself.
I am Elvis Presley and admire you
and Have Respect for your
office. I talked to Vice President
Agnew in Palm Springs 3 weeks ago and
expressed my concern for our country.
The Drug Culture, The Hippie Elements,
The SDS, Black Panthers, etc do *not*
consider me as their enemy or as they
call it The Establishment. *I call it America and*

(Written 12/70)

Dear Mr. President

First I would like to introduce myself I am Elvis Presley and admire you and Have Great Respect for your office. I talked to Vice President Agnew in Palm Springs 3 weeks ago and expressed my concern for our country. The Drug Culture, The Hippie Elements, The SDS, Black Panthers, etc do <u>not</u> consider me as their enemy or as they call it the Establishment. <u>I call it America and</u>

I Love it. Sir I can and Will be of any Service that I can to help the country out. I have no concern or Motives other than helping the country out. So I wish not to be given a title or an appointed position, I can and will do more good if I were made a Federal agent at Large, and I will help out by doing it my way through my communication with people of all ages. First and Foremost I am an entertainer but all I need is the Federal credentials. I am on this Plane with

Sen. George Murphy and We have been discussing the problems that our Country is faced with.

So I am Staying at the Washington hotel Room 505-506-507- I have 2 men who work with me by the

I Love it. Sir I can and Will be of any Service that I can to help the country out. I have no concern or Motives other than helping the country out. So I wish not to be given a title or an appointed position, I can and will do more good if I were made a Federal Agent At Large, and I will help best by doing it my way through my communication with people of all ages. First and Foremost I am an entertainer but all I need is the Federal Credentials. I am on the plane with Sen. George Murphy and we have been discussing the problems that our Country is faced with. So I am Staying at the Washington hotel room 505-506-507- I have 2 men who work with me by the

name of Jerry Schilling and Sonny
west. I am registered under the name
of Jon Burrows. I will be here
for as long as it takes to get
the credentials of a Federal Agent.
I have done an in depth study of
Drug Abuse and Communist Brainwashing
Techniques and I am right in the
middle of the whole thing, where
I can and will do the most good
I am Glad to help just so long
as it is kept very Private. You can
have your staff or whomever call
me anytime today tonight or Tomorrow
I was nominated the coming year
one of America's Ten most outstanding
young men. That will be in January
18 in my Home Town of Memphis Tenn.

name of Gerry Schilling and Sonny West. I am registered under the name of Jon Burrows. I will be here for as long as it takes to get the credentials of a Federal Agent. I have done an in depth study of drug abuse and Communist Brainwashing Techniques and I am right in the middle of the whole thing, where I can and will do the most good. I am Glad to help just so long as it is kept very Private. You can have your staff or whomever call me anytime today tonight or Tomorrow I was nominated the coming year one of America's Ten Most Outstanding young men. That will be in January 18 in My Home Town of Memphis Tenn.

I am sending you the short autobiography about myself so you can better understand this approach. I would love to meet you just to say hello if you're not to Busy.

Respectfully

Elvis Presley

P.S. I believe that you Sir were one of the Top Ten outstanding Men of America also.

I am sending you the short autobiography about myself so you can better understand this approach. I would love to meet you just to say hello if you're not too busy.
Respectfully,

Elvis Presley

P.S. I believe that you Sir were one of the Top Ten Outstanding Men of America also.

I have a personal gift for you also which I would like to present to you and you can accept it or I will keep it for you until you can take it.

Mr. President NUMBERS

These are all my PVT numbers

Beverly Hills	278-3496
	278-5935
Palm Spring's Pvt #	325-3241
Memphis	397-4427
	398-4882
	398-9722
Pvt. #	
Col. P.S. #	325-4781
Col. B.H. #	274-8498
Col. Off. M.P.M	870-0870

WASHINGTON HOTEL, PHONE ME 85900
RM 505-506-
UNDER THE NAME
OF JON BURROWS

PRIVATE
AND CONFIDENTIAL

Attn. President Nixon
via Sen George Murphy
from
Elvis Presley

I have a personal gift for you also which I would like to present to you and you can accept it or I will keep it for you until you can take it.

APPENDIX B: LAST WILL AND TESTAMENT OF ELVIS PRESLEY

State of Tennessee,
SHELBY COUNTY

I, B. J. DUNAVANT, Clerk of the Probate Court of this County, do hereby certify that the foregoing Thirteen (13) - - - - - - - - - - - - - pages contain a full, true and exact copy of the Last Will and Testament of Elvis A. Presley, Deceased: -

- - - -

- - - -

- - - -

as the same appears of record or on file in Will Book 209, Page 266 of this office.

IN TESTIMONY WHEREOF, I have hereunto set my hand and affixed the seal of said Court, at office, in the City of Memphis, this 24th day of August 1977

PROBATE COURT OF SHELBY COUNTY TENN

B. J. DUNAVANT, Clerk

By Margaret Hare D. C.

LAST WILL AND TESTAMENT
OF
ELVIS A. PRESLEY

I, ELVIS A. PRESLEY, a resident and citizen of Shelby County, Tennessee, being of sound mind and disposing memory, do hereby make, publish and declare this instrument to be my last will and testament, hereby revoking any and all wills and codicils by me at any time heretofore made.

ITEM I
Debts, Expenses and Taxes

I direct my Executor, hereinafter named, to pay all of my matured debts and my funeral expenses, as well as the costs and expenses of the administration of my estate, as soon after my death as practicable. I further direct that all estate, inheritance, transfer and succession taxes which are payable by reason of my death, whether or not with respect to property passing under this will, be paid out of my residuary estate; and I hereby waive on behalf of my estate any right to recover from any person any part of such taxes so paid. My Executor, in his sole discretion, may pay from my domiciliary estate all or any portion of the costs of ancillary administration and similar proceedings in other jurisdictions.

ITEM II
Instructions Concerning Personal Property: Enjoyment in Specie

I anticipate that included as a part of my property and estate at the time of my death will be tangible personal property of various kinds, characters and values, including trophies and other items accumulated by me during my professional career. I hereby specifically instruct all concerned that my Executor, herein appointed, shall have complete freedom and discretion as to disposal of any and all such property so long as he shall act in good faith and in the best interest of my estate and my beneficiaries, and his discretion so exercised shall not be subject to question by anyone whomsoever.

I hereby expressly authorize my Executor and my Trustee, respectively and successively, to permit any beneficiary of any and all trusts created hereunder to enjoy in specie the use or benefit of any household goods, chattels, or other tangible personal property (exclusive of choses in action, cash, stocks, bonds or other securities) which either my Executor or my Trustee may receive in kind, and my Executor and my Trustee shall not be liable for any consumption, damage, injury to or loss of any tangible property so used, nor shall the beneficiaries of any trusts hereunder or their executors or administrators be liable for any consumption, damage, injury to or loss of any tangible personal property so used.

ITEM III
Real Estate

If I am the owner of any real estate at the time of my death, I instruct and empower my Executor and my Trustee (as the case may be) to hold such real estate for investment, or to sell same, or any portion thereof, as my Executor or my Trustee (as the case may be) shall in his sole judgment determine to be for the best interest of my estate and the beneficiaries thereof.

ITEM IV
Residuary Trust

After payment of all debts, expenses and taxes as directed under ITEM I hereof, I give, devise, and bequeath all the rest, residue, and remainder of my estate, including all lapsed legacies and devises, and any property over which I have a power of appointment, to my Trustee, hereinafter named, in trust for the following purposes:

(a) The Trustee is directed to take, hold, manage, invest and reinvest the corpus of the trust and to collect the income therefrom in accordance with the rights, powers, duties, authority and discretion hereinafter set forth. The Trustee is directed to pay all the expenses, taxes and costs incurred in the management of the trust estate out of the income thereof.

(b) After payment of all expenses, taxes and costs incurred in the management of the trust estate, the Trustee is authorized to accumulate the net income or to pay or apply so much of the net income and such portion of the principal at any time and from time to time for the health, education, support, comfortable maintenance and welfare of: (1) my daughter, Lisa Marie Presley, and any other lawful issue I might have, (2) my grandmother, Minnie Mae Presley, (3) my father, Vernon E. Presley, and (4) such other relatives of mine living at the time of my death who in the absolute discretion of my Trustee are in need of emergency assistance for any of the above mentioned purposes and the Trustee is able to make such distribution without affecting the ability of the trust to meet the present needs of the first three numbered categories of beneficiaries herein mentioned or to meet the reasonably expected future needs of the first three classes of beneficiaries herein mentioned. Any decision of the Trustee as to whether or not distribution shall be made, and also as to the amount of such distribution, to any of the persons described hereunder shall be final and conclusive and not subject to question by any legatee or beneficiary hereunder.

(c) Upon the death of my father, Vernon E. Presley, the Trustee is instructed to make no further distributions to the fourth category of beneficiaries and such beneficiaries shall cease to have any interest whatsoever in this trust.

(d) Upon the death of both my said father and my said grandmother, the Trustee is directed to divide the Residuary Trust into separate and equal trusts, creating one such equal trust for each of my lawful children then surviving and one such equal trust for the living issue collectively, if any, of any deceased child of mine. The share, if any, for the issue of any such deceased child, shall immediately vest in such issue in equal shares but shall be subject to the provisions of ITEM V herein. Separate books and records shall be kept for each trust, but it shall not be necessary that a physical division of the assets be made as to each trust.

The Trustee may from time to time distribute the whole or any part of the net income or principal from each of the aforesaid trusts as the Trustee, in its uncontrolled discretion, considers necessary or desirable to provide for the comfortable support, education, maintenance, benefit and general welfare of each of my children. Such distributions may be made directly to such beneficiary or to any person standing in the place of a parent or to the guardian of the person of such beneficiary and without responsibility on my Trustee to see to the application of any such distributions and in making such distributions, the Trustee shall take into account all other sources of funds known by the Trustee to be available for each respective beneficiary for such purpose.

(e) As each of my respective children attains the age of twenty-five (25) years and provided that both my father and grandmother then be deceased, the trust created hereunder for such child shall terminate, and all the remainder of the assets then contained in said trust shall be distributed to such child so attaining the age of twenty-five (25) years outright and free of further trust.

(f) If any of my children for whose benefit a trust has been created hereunder should die before attaining the age of twenty-five (25) years, then the trust created for such child shall terminate on his death, and all remaining assets then contained in said trust shall be distributed outright and free of further trust and in equal shares to the surviving issue of such deceased child but subject to the provisions of ITEM V herein; but if there be no such surviving issue, then to the brothers and sisters of such deceased child in equal shares, the issue of any other deceased child being entitled collectively to their deceased parent's share. Nevertheless, if any distribution otherwise becomes payable outright and free of trust under the provisions of this paragraph (f) of this ITEM IV of my will to a beneficiary for whom the Trustee is then administering a trust for the benefit of such beneficiary under the provisions of this last will and testament, such distribution shall not be paid outright to such beneficiary but shall be added to and become a part of the trust so being administered for such beneficiary by the Trustee.

ITEM V
Distribution to Minor Children

If any share of corpus of any trust established under this will becomes distributable outright and free of trust to any beneficiary before said beneficiary has attained the age of eighteen (18) years, then said share shall immediately vest in said beneficiary, but the Trustee shall retain possession of such share during the period in which such beneficiary is under the age of eighteen (18) years, and, in the meantime, shall use and expend so much of the income and principal of each share as the Trustee deems necessary and desirable for the care, support and education of such beneficiary, and any income not so expended shall be added to the principal. The Trustee shall have with respect to each share so retained all the power and discretion had with respect to such trust generally.

ITEM VI

Alternate Distributees

In the event that all of my descendants should be deceased at any time prior to the time for the termination of the trusts provided for herein, then in such event all of my estate and all the assets of every trust to be created hereunder (as the case may be) shall then be distributed outright in equal shares to my heirs at law per stirpes.

ITEM VII

Unenforceable Provisions

If any provisions of this will are unenforceable, the remaining provisions shall, nevertheless, be carried into effect.

ITEM VIII

Life Insurance

If my estate is the beneficiary of any life insurance on my life at the time of my death, I direct that the proceeds therefrom will be used by my Executor in payment of the debts, expenses and taxes listed in ITEM I of this will, to the extent deemed advisable by the Executor. All such proceeds not so used are to be used by my Executor for the purpose of satisfying the devises and bequests contained in ITEM IV herein.

ITEM IX

Spendthrift Provision

I direct that the interest of any beneficiary in principal or income of any trust created hereunder shall not be subject to claims of creditors or others, nor to legal process, and may not be voluntarily or involuntarily alienated or encumbered except as herein provided. Any bequests contained herein for any female shall be for her sole and separate use, free from the debts, contracts and control of any husband she may ever have.

ITEM X

Proceeds From Personal Services

All sums paid after my death (either to my estate or to any of the trusts created hereunder) and resulting from personal services rendered by me during my lifetime, including, but not limited to, royalties of all nature, concerts, motion picture contracts, and personal appearances shall be considered to be income, notwithstanding the provisions of estate and trust law to the contrary.

ITEM XI

Executor and Trustee

I appoint as Executor of this, my last will and testament, and as Trustee of every trust required to be created hereunder, my said father.

I hereby direct that my said father shall be entitled by his last will and testament, duly probated, to appoint a successor Executor of my estate, as well as a successor Trustee or successor Trustees of all the trusts to be created under my last will and testament.

If, for any reason, my said father be unable to serve or to continue to serve as Executor and/or as Trustee, or if he be deceased and shall not have appointed a successor Executor or Trustee, by virtue of his last will and testament as stated above then I appoint National Bank of Commerce, Memphis, Tennessee, or its successor or the institution with which it may merge, as successor Executor and/or as successor Trustee of all trusts required to be established hereunder.

None of the appointees named hereunder, including any appointment made by virtue of the last will and testament of my said father, shall be required to furnish any bond or security for performance of the respective fiduciary duties required hereunder, notwithstanding any rule of law to the contrary.

ITEM XII

Powers, Duties, Privileges and

Immunities of the Trustee

Except as otherwise stated expressly to the contrary herein, I give and grant to the said Trustee (and to the duly appointed successor Trustee when acting as such) the power to do everything he deems advisable with respect to the administration of each trust required to be established under this, my last will and testament, even though such powers would not be authorized or appropriate for the Trustee under statutory or other rules of law. By way of illustration and not in limitation of the generality of the foregoing grant of power and authority of the Trustee, I give and grant to him plenary power as follows:

(a) To exercise all those powers authorized to fiduciaries under the provisions of the Tennessee Code Annotated, Sections 35-616 to 35-618, inclusive, including any amendments thereto in effect at the time of my death, and the same are expressly referred to and incorporated herein by reference;

(b) Plenary power is granted to the Trustee, not only to relieve him from seeking judicial instruction, but to the extent that the Trustee deems it to be prudent, to encourage determinations freely to be made in favor of persons who are the current income beneficiaries. In such instances the rights of all subsequent beneficiaries are subordinate, and the Trustee shall not be answerable to any subsequent beneficiary for anything done or omitted in favor of a current income beneficiary, but no current income beneficiary may compel any such favorable or preferential treatment. Without in anywise minimizing or impairing the scope of this declaration of intent, it includes investment policy, exercise of discretionary power to pay or apply principal and income, and determination of principal and income questions;

(c) It shall be lawful for the Trustee to apply any sum that is payable to or for the benefit of a minor (or any other person who in the judgment of the Trustee, is incapable of making proper disposition thereof) by payments in discharge of the costs and expenses of educating, maintaining and supporting said beneficiary, or to make payment to anyone with whom said beneficiary resides or who has the care or custody of the beneficiary, temporarily or permanently, all without intervention of any guardian or like fiduciary. The receipt of anyone to whom payment is so authorized to be made shall be a complete discharge of the Trustee without obligation on his part to see to the further application thereof, and without regard to other resources that the beneficiary may have, or the duty of any other person to support the beneficiary;

(d) In dealing with the Trustee, no grantee, pledgee, vendee, mortgagee, lessee or other transferee of the trust properties, or any part thereof, shall be bound to inquire with respect to the purpose or necessity of any such disposition or to see to the application of any consideration therefor paid to the Trustee.

ITEM XIII

Concerning the Trustee

And the Executor

(a) If at any time the Trustee shall have reasonable doubt as to his power, authority or duty in the administration of any trust herein created, it shall be lawful for the Trustee to obtain the advice and counsel of reputable legal counsel without resorting to the courts for instructions; and the Trustee shall be fully absolved from all liability and damage or detriment to the various trust estates or any beneficiary thereunder by reason of anything done, suffered or omitted pursuant to advice of said counsel given and obtained in good faith, provided that nothing contained herein shall be construed to prohibit or prevent the Trustee in all proper cases from applying to a court of competent jurisdiction for instructions in the administration of the trust assets in lieu of obtaining advice of counsel.

(b) In managing, investing, and controlling the various trust estates, the Trustee shall exercise the judgment and care under the circumstances then prevailing, which men of prudence, discretion and judgment exercise in the management of their own affairs, not in regard to speculation, but in regard to the permanent disposition of their funds, considering the probable income as well as the probable safety of their capital, and, in addition, the purchasing power of income distribution to beneficiaries.

(c) My Trustee (as well as my Executor) shall be entitled to reasonable and adequate compensation for the fiduciary services rendered by him.

(d) My Executor and his successor Executor shall have the same rights, privileges, powers and immunities herein granted to my Trustee wherever appropriate.

(e) In referring to any fiduciary hereunder, for purposes of construction, masculine pronouns may include a corporate fiduciary and neutral pronouns may include an individual fiduciary.

ITEM XIV
Law Against Perpetuities

(a) Having in mind the rule against perpetuities, I direct that (notwithstanding anything contained to the contrary in this last will and testament) each trust created under this will (except such trusts as have heretofore vested in compliance with such rule or law) shall end, unless sooner terminated under other provisions of this will, twenty-one (21) years after the death of the last survivor of such of the beneficiaries hereunder as are living at the time of my death; and thereupon that the property held in trust shall be distributed free of all trust to the persons then entitled to receive the income and/or principal therefrom, in the proportion in which they are then entitled to receive such income.

(b) Notwithstanding anything else contained in this will to the contrary, I direct that if any distribution under this will becomes payable to a person for whom the Trustee is then administering a trust created hereunder for the benefit of such person, such distribution shall be made to such trust and not to the beneficiary outright, and the funds so passing to such trust shall become a part thereof as corpus and be administered and distributed to the same extent and purpose as if such funds had been a part of such trust at its inception.

ITEM XV
Payment of Estate and
Inheritance Taxes

Notwithstanding the provisions of ITEM X herein, I authorize my Executor to use such sums received by my estate after my death and resulting from my personal services as identified in ITEM X as he deems necessary and advisable in order to pay the taxes referred to in ITEM I of my said will.

IN WITNESS WHEREOF, I, the said ELVIS A. PRESLEY, do hereunto set my hand and seal in the presence of two (2) competent witnesses, and in their presence do publish and declare this instrument to be my Last Will and Testament, this 3 day of MARCH, 1976.

ELVIS A. PRESLEY

The foregoing instrument, consisting of this and eleven (11) preceding typewritten pages, was signed, sealed, published and declared by ELVIS A. PRESLEY, the Testator, to be his Last Will and Testament, in our presence, and we, at his request and in his presence and in the presence of each other, have hereunto subscribed our names as witnesses, this 3 day of MARCH, 1976, at Memphis, Tennessee.

residing at 4152 Royal Crest Place

residing at 3764 Elvis Presley Blvd
2237 Court Avenue

STATE OF TENNESSEE)
COUNTY OF SHELBY)

GINGER ALDEN, CHARLES F. HODGE and ANN DEWEY SMITH after being first duly sworn, make oath or affirm that the foregoing Last Will and Testament was signed by ELVIS A. PRESLEY and for and at that time acknowledged, published and declared by him to be his Last Will and Testament, in the sight and presence of us, the undersigned, who at his request and in his sight and presence, and in the sight and presence of each other, have subscribed our names as attesting witnesses on the 3 day of MARCH, 1976, and we further make oath or affirm that the Testator was of sound mind and disposing memory and not acting under fraud, menace or undue influence of any person, and was more than eighteen (18) years of age; and that each of the attesting witnesses is more than eighteen (18) years of age.

SWORN TO AND SUBSCRIBED before me this 3 day of MARCH, 1976.

NOTARY PUBLIC

My commission expires:
Aug. 8, 1979

Admitted to Probate and Ordered Recorded August 22, 1977
JOSEPH W. EVANS, JUDGE

Recorded August 22, 1977
B. J. Dunavant, Clerk
By: Jan Scott, D. C.

LAST WILL AND TESTAMENT OF ELVIS A. PRESLEY

I, ELVIS A. PRESLEY, a resident and citizen of Shelby County, Tennessee, being of sound mind and disposing memory, do hereby make, publish and declare this instrument to be my last will and testament, hereby revoking any and all wills and codicils by me at any time heretofore made.

ITEM I
Debts, Expenses and Taxes

I direct my Executor, hereinafter named, to pay all of my matured debts and my funeral expenses, as well as the costs and expenses of the administration of my estate, as soon after my death as practicable. I further direct that all estate, inheritance, transfer and succession taxes which are payable by reason of my death, whether or not with respect to property passing under this will, be paid out of my residuary estate; and I hereby waive on behalf of my estate any right to recover from any person any part of such taxes so paid. My executor, in his sole discretion, may pay from my domiciliary estate all or any portion of the costs of ancillary administration and similar proceedings in other jurisdictions.

ITEM II
Instructions Concerning Personal Property: Enjoyment in Specie

I anticipate that included as a part of my property and estate at the time of my death will be tangible personal property of various kinds, characters and values, including trophies and other items accumulated by me during my professional career. I hereby specifically instruct all concerned that my Executor, herein appointed, shall have complete freedom and discretion as to disposal of any and all such property so long as he shall act in good faith and in the best interest of my estate and my beneficiaries, and his discretion so exercised shall not be subject to question by anyone whomsoever.

I hereby expressly authorize my Executor and my Trustee, respectively and successively, to permit any beneficiary of any and all trusts created hereunder to enjoy in specie the use or benefit of any household goods, chattels, or other tangible personal property (exclusive of choses in action, cash, stocks, bonds or other securities) which either my Executor or my Trustee may receive in kind, and my Executor and my Trustee shall not be liable for any consumption, damage, injury to or loss of any tangible property so used, nor shall the beneficiaries of any trusts hereunder or their executors or administrators be liable for any consumption, damage, injury to or loss of any tangible personal property so used.

ITEM III
Real Estate

If I am the owner of any real estate at the time of my death, I instruct and empower my Executor and my Trustee (as the case may be) to hold such real estate for investment, or to sell same, or any portion thereof, as my Executor or my Trustee (as the case may be) shall in his sole judgment determine to be for the best interest of my estate and the beneficiaries thereof.

ITEM IV
Residuary Trust

After payment of all debts, expenses and taxes as directed under ITEM I hereof, I give, devise, and bequeath all the rest, residue, and remainder of my estate, including all lapsed legacies and devises, and any property over which I have a power of appointment, to my Trustee, hereinafter named, in trust for the following purposes:

(a) The Trustee is directed to take, hold, manage, invest and reinvest the corpus of the trust and to collect the income therefrom in accordance with the rights, powers, duties, authority and discretion hereinafter set forth. The Trustee is directed to pay all the expenses, taxes and costs incurred in the management of the trust estate out of the income thereof.

(b) After payment of all expenses, taxes and costs incurred in the management of the trust estate, the Trustee is authorized to accumulate the net income or to pay or apply so much of the net income and such portion of the principal at any time and from time to time for the health, education, support, comfortable maintenance and welfare of: (1) my daughter, Lisa Marie Presley, and any other lawful issue I might have, (2) my grandmother, Minnie Mae Presley, (3) my father, Vernon E. Presley, and (4) such other relatives of mine living at the time of my death who in the absolute discretion of my Trustee are in need of emergency assistance for any of the above mentioned purposes and the Trustee is able to make such distribution without affecting the ability of the trust to meet the present needs of the first three numbered categories of beneficiaries herein mentioned or to meet the reasonably expected future needs of the first three classes of beneficiaries herein mentioned. Any decision of the Trustee as to whether or not distribution shall be made, and also as to the amount of such distribution, to any of the persons described hereunder shall be final and conclusive and not subject to question by any legatee or beneficiary hereunder.

(c) Upon the death of my father, Vernon E. Presley, the Trustee is instructed to make no further distributions to the fourth category of beneficiaries and such beneficiaries shall cease to have any interest whatsoever in this trust.

(d) Upon the death of both my said father and my said grandmother, the Trustee is directed to divide the Residuary Trust into separate and equal trusts, creating one such equal trust for each of my lawful children then surviving and one such equal trust for the living issue collectively, if any, of any deceased child of mine. The share, if any, for the issue of any such deceased child, shall immediately vest in such issue in equal shares but shall be subject to the provisions of ITEM V herein. Separate books and records shall be kept for each trust, but it shall not be necessary that a physical division of the assets be made as to each trust.

The Trustee may from time to time distribute the whole or any part of the net income or principal from each of the aforesaid trusts as the Trustee, in its uncontrolled discretion, considers necessary or desirable to provide for the comfortable support, education, maintenance, benefit and general welfare of each of my children. Such distributions may be made directly to such beneficiary or to any person standing in the place of a parent or to the guardian of the person of such beneficiary and without responsibility on my Trustee to see to the application of any such distributions and in making such distributions, the Trustee shall take into account all other sources of funds known by the Trustee to be available for each respective beneficiary for such purpose.

(e) As each of my respective children attains the age

of twenty-five (25) years and provided that both my father and grandmother then be deceased, the trust created hereunder for such child shall terminate, and all the remainder of the assets then contained in said trust shall be distributed to such child so attaining the age of twenty-five (25) years outright and free of further trust.

(f) If any of my children for whose benefit a trust has been created hereunder should die before attaining the age of twenty-five (25) years, then the trust created for such child shall terminate on his death, and all remaining assets then contained in said trust shall be distributed outright and free of further trust and in equal shares to the surviving issue of each deceased child but subject to the provisions of ITEM V herein; but if there be no such surviving issue, then to the brothers and sisters of such deceased child in equal shares, the issue of any other deceased child being entitled collectively to their deceased parent's share. Nevertheless, if any distribution otherwise becomes payable outright and free of trust under the provisions of this paragraph (f) of this ITEM IV of my will to a beneficiary for whom the Trustee is then administering a trust for the benefit of such beneficiary under the provisions of this last will and testament, such distribution shall not be paid outright to such beneficiary but shall be added to and become a part of the trust so being administered for such beneficiary by the Trustee.

ITEM V
Distribution to Minor Children

If any share of corpus of any trust established under this will becomes distributable outright and free of trust to any beneficiary before said beneficiary has attained the age of eighteen (18) years, then said share shall immediately vest in said beneficiary, but the Trustee shall retain possession of such share during the period in which such beneficiary is under the age of eighteen (18) years, and, in the meantime, shall use and expend so much of the income and principal of each share as the Trustee deems necessary and desirable for the care, support and education of such beneficiary, and any income not so expended shall be added to the principal. The Trustee shall have with respect to each share so retained all the power and discretion had with respect to such trust generally.

ITEM VI
Alternate Distributees

In the event that all of my descendants should be deceased at any time prior to the time for the termination of the trusts provided for herein, then in such event all of my estate and all the assets of every trust to be created hereunder (as the case may be) shall then be distributed outright in equal shares to my heirs at law per stirpes.

ITEM VII
Unenforceable Provisions

If any provisions of this will are unenforceable, the remaining provisions shall, nevertheless, be carried into effect.

ITEM VIII
Life Insurance

If my estate is the beneficiary of any life insurance on my life at the time of my death, I direct that the proceeds therefrom will be used by my Executor in payment of the debts, expenses and taxes listed in ITEM I of this will, to the extent deemed advisable by the Executor. All such proceeds not so used are to be used by my Executor for the purpose of satisfying the devises and bequests contained in ITEM IV herein.

ITEM IX
Spendthrift Provision

I direct that the interest of any beneficiary in principal or income of any trust created hereunder shall not be subject to claims of creditors or others, nor to legal process, and may not be voluntarily or involuntarily alienated or encumbered except as herein provided. Any bequests contained herein for any female shall be for her sole and separate use, free from the debts, contracts and control of any husband she may ever have.

ITEM X
Proceeds from Personal Services

All sums paid after my death (either to my estate or to any of the trusts created hereunder) and resulting from personal services rendered by me during my lifetime, including, but not limited to, royalties of all nature, concerts, motion picture contracts, and personal appearances shall be considered to be income, notwithstanding the provisions of estate and trust law to the contrary.

ITEM XI

Executor and Trustee

I appoint as Executor of this, my last will and testament, and as Trustee of every trust required to be created hereunder, my said father.

I hereby direct that my said father shall be entitled by his last will and testament, duly probated, to appoint a successor Executor of my estate, as well as a successor Trustee or successor Trustees of all the trusts to be created under my last will and testament.

If, for any reason, my said father be unable to serve or to continue to serve as Executor and/or as Trustee, or if he be deceased and shall not have appointed a successor Executor or Trustee, by virtue of his last will and testament as stated above then I appoint National Bank of Commerce, Memphis, Tennessee, or its successor or the institution with which it may merge, as successor Executor and/or as successor Trustee of all trusts required to be established hereunder.

None of the appointees named hereunder, including any appointment made by virtue of the last will and testament of my said father, shall be required to furnish any bond or security for performance of the respective fiduciary duties required hereunder, notwithstanding any rule of law to the contrary.

ITEM XII

Powers, Duties, Privileges and Immunities of the Trustee

Except as otherwise stated expressly to the contrary herein, I give and grant to the said Trustee (and to the duly appointed successor Trustee when acting as such) the power to do everything he deems advisable with respect to the administration of each trust required to be established under this, my last will and testament, even though such powers would not be authorized or appropriate for the Trustee under statutory or other rules of law. By way of illustration and not in limitation of the generality of the foregoing grant of power and authority of the Trustee, I give and grant to him plenary power as follows:

(a) To exercise all those powers authorized to fiduciaries under the provisions of the Tennessee Code Annotated, Sections 35–616 to 35–618, inclusive, including any amendments thereto in effect at the time of my death, and the same are expressly referred to and incorporated herein by reference;

(b) Plenary power is granted to the Trustee, not only to relieve him from seeking judicial instruction, but to the extent that the Trustee deems it to be prudent, to encourage determinations freely to be made in favor of persons who are the current income beneficiaries. In such instances the rights of all subsequent beneficiaries are subordinate, and the Trustee shall not be answerable to any subsequent beneficiary for anything done or omitted in favor of a current income beneficiary, but no current income beneficiary may compel any such favorable or preferential treatment. Without in anywise minimizing or impairing the scope of this declaration of intent, it includes investment policy, exercise of discretionary power to pay or apply principal and income, and determination of principal and income questions;

(c) It shall be lawful for the Trustee to apply any sum that is payable to or for the benefit of a minor (or any other person who, in the judgment of the Trustee, is incapable of making proper disposition thereof) by payments in discharge of the costs and expenses of educating, maintaining and supporting said beneficiary, or to make payment to anyone with whom said beneficiary resides or who has the care or custody of the beneficiary, temporarily or permanently, all without intervention of any guardian or like fiduciary. The receipt of anyone to whom payment is so authorized to be made shall be a complete discharge of the Trustee without obligation on his part to see to the further application thereof, and without regard to other resources that the beneficiary may have, or the duty of any other person to support the beneficiary;

(d) In dealing with the Trustee, no grantee, pledgee, vendee, mortgagee, lessee or other transferee of the trust properties, or any part thereof shall be bound to inquire with respect to the purpose or necessity of any such disposition or to see to the application of any consideration therefor paid to the Trustee.

ITEM XIII
Concerning the Trustee And the Executor

(a) If at any time the Trustee shall have reasonable doubt as to his power, authority or duty in the administration of any trust herein created, it shall be lawful for the Trustee to obtain the advice and counsel of reputable legal counsel without resorting to the courts for instructions; and the Trustee shall be fully absolved from all liability and damage or detriment to the various trust estates or any beneficiary thereunder by reason of anything done, suffered or omitted pursuant to advice of said counsel given and obtained in good faith, provided that nothing contained herein shall be construed to prohibit or prevent the Trustee in all proper cases from applying to a court of competent jurisdiction for instructions in the administration of the trust assets in lieu of obtaining advice of counsel.

(b) In managing, investing, and controlling the various trust estates, the Trustee shall exercise the judgment and care under the circumstances then prevailing, which men of prudence, discretion and judgment exercise in the management of their own affairs, not in regard to speculation, but in regard to the permanent disposition of their funds, considering the probable income as well as the probable safety of their capital, and, in addition, the purchasing power of income distribution to beneficiaries.

(c) My Trustee (as well as my Executor) shall be entitled to reasonable and adequate compensation for the fiduciary services rendered by him.

(d) My Executor and his successor Executor shall have the same rights, privileges, powers and immunities herein granted to my Trustee wherever appropriate.

(e) In referring to any fiduciary hereunder, for purposes of construction, masculine pronouns may include a corporate fidiuciary and neutral pronouns may include an individual fiduciary.

ITEM XIV
Law Against Perpetuities

(a) Having in mind the rule against perpetuities, I direct that (notwithstanding anything contained to the contrary in this last will and testament) each trust created under this will (except such trusts as have heretofore vested in compliance with such rule or law) shall end, unless sooner teminated under other provisions of this will, twenty-one (21) years after the death of the last survivor of such of the beneficiaries hereunder as are living at the time of my death; and thereupon that the property held in trust shall be distributed free of all trust to the persons then entitled to receive the income and/or principal therefrom, in the proportion in which they are then entitled to receive such income.

(b) Notwithstanding anything else contained in this will to the contrary, I direct that if any distribution under this will becomes payable to a person for whom the Trustee is then administering a trust created hereunder for the benefit of such person, such distribution shall be made to such trust and not to the beneficiary outright, and the funds so passing to such trust shall become a part thereof as corpus and be administered and distributed to the same extent and purpose as if such funds had been a part of such trust at its inception.

ITEM XV
Payment of Estate and Inheritance Taxes

Notwithstanding the provisions of ITEM X herein, I authorize my Executor to use such sums received by my estate after my death and resulting from my personal services as identified in ITEM X as he deems necessary and advisable in order to pay the taxes referred to in ITEM I of my said will.

IN WITNESS WHEREOF, I, the said ELVIS A. PRESLEY, do hereunto set my hand and seal in the presence of two (2) competent witnesses, and in their presence do publish and declare this instrument to be my Last Will and Testament, this 3 day of MARCH, 1976.

Elvis A Presley

ELVIS A. PRESLEY

The foregoing instrument, consisting of this and eleven (11) preceding typewritten pages, was signed, sealed, published and declared by ELVIS A. PRESLEY, the Testator, to be his Last Will and Testament, in our presence,

and we, at his request and in his presence and in the presence of each other, have hereunto subscribed our names as witnesses, this 3 day of MARCH, 1976, at Memphis, Tennessee.

Ginger Alden residing at 4152 Royal Crest Place

Charles F Hodge residing at 3764 Elvis Presley Blvd
Ann Dewey Smith 2237 Court Avenue

STATE OF TENNESSEE)
COUNTY OF SHELBY)

GINGER ALDEN, CHARLES F. HODGE and ANN DEWEY SMITH, after being first duly sworn, make oath or affirm that the foregoing Last Will and Testament was signed by ELVIS A. PRESLEY and for and at that time acknowledged, published and declared by him to be his Last Will and Testament, in the sight and presence of us, the undersigned, who at his request and in his sight and presence, and in the sight and presence of each other, have subscribed our names as attesting witnesses on the 3 day of MARCH, 1976, and we further make oath or affirm that the Testator was of sound mind and disposing memory and not acting under fraud, menace or undue influence of any person, and was more than eighteen (18) years of age; and that each of the attesting witnesses is more than eighteen (18) years of age.

Ginger Alden
Charles F. Hodge
Ann Dewey Smith

SWORN TO AND SUBSCRIBED before me this 3 day of MARCH, 1976.

Drayton Beecher Smith II
NOTARY PUBLIC

My commission expires:

Aug. 8, 1979

Admitted to Probate and Ordered Recorded August 22, 1977
JOSEPH W. EVANS, JUDGE

Recorded August 22, 1977
B. J. Dunavant, Clerk
By: Jan Scott, D. C.